Excel

ADVANCED SKILLS

MATHS

YEAR 3

AGES 8–9

STAR MATHS

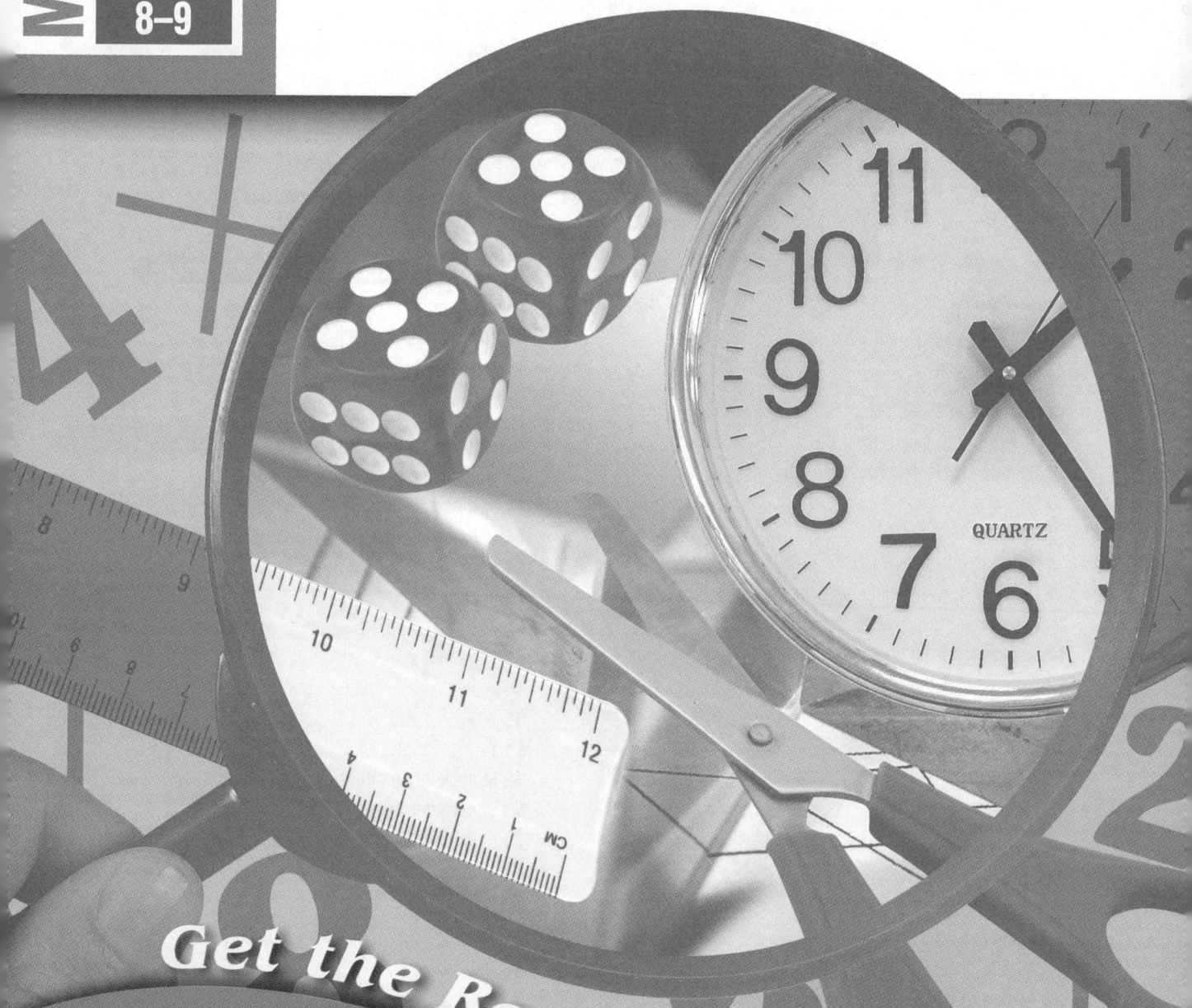

Get the Results You Want!

PASCAL PRESS

Damon James

Contents

iv

Unit 1 Numbers to 999 — page 13

1 **Base ten blocks** are read as short = 1 unit, long = 1 ten, flat = 1 hundred and cube = 1 thousand.
2 An **abacus** is read as the number of discs above each letter, where U = unit, T = tens, H = hundreds and Th = thousands.
3 – 4 A number can be written with **words** or **numerals** (digits) e.g. one hundred and fifty-two or 152.

Unit 2 Place value — page 13

1 See Unit 1 Nos 1 – 2
2 **The place of a digit** in a number gives the value. e.g. in 215, 5 = 5 units, 1 = 1 ten and 2 = 2 hundreds.
3 **Largest and smallest numbers** can be determined by first looking at digits in the hundreds column and comparing them. If they are the same, then look at the digits in the tens column and so on.
4 The **next number** is found by counting on by 1. Note: when 9 is reached, 1 is added to the units place making 0; therefore 1 is added to the tens place. The next number after 29 is 30.

Unit 3 Numbers to 9999 — page 14

1 See Unit 1 Nos 1 – 2. A **number expander** shows values of numbers. The digit is written next to each value, units, tens, etc.
2 The **number of digits** is found by counting each separate digit, e.g. 23 has two digits and 240 has three digits.
3 – 4 Compare the numbers then order them. See Unit 1 Nos 3 – 4

Unit 4 Ordering numbers (1) — page 14

1 See Unit 2 No. 2
2 Determine the **counting pattern** of units, tens or hundreds, by looking at the value of the units, tens or hundreds place, then count on or count back.
3 – 4 See Unit 2 No. 3, then order once compared.

Unit 5 Counting by tens (1) — page 15

1 To **count pencils**, the bundles = 1 ten and each stick = 1 unit.
2 – 3 **Counting by tens** means counting on or counting back by ten. Counting forwards by 10 from 100 is 110 and this can be completed by adding 1 to the tens place. Note: when 90 is reached, 1 is added to the tens place making 0, therefore 1 is added to the hundreds place, e.g. 10 after 190 is 200.
Counting backwards by 10 from 150 is 140 and this can be completed by subtracting 1 from the tens place. Note: when 100 is reached, 1 is subtracted from the tens place making 90, therefore 1 is also subtracted from the hundreds place. e.g. 490 is 10 less than 500.
4 See Unit 4 No. 2

Unit 6 Counting by tens (2) — page 15

1 – 4 See Unit 5 Nos 2 – 3

Unit 7 Counting by hundreds — page 16

1 – 4 **Counting by hundreds** means **counting on or counting back by 100**. **Counting forwards by 100** from 200 is 300 and this can be completed by adding 1 to the hundreds place. Note: when 900 is reached, 1 is added to the hundreds place making 0, therefore 1 is added to the thousands place. e.g. 6000 is 100 more than 5900.

Counting backwards by 100 from 500 is 400 and this can be completed by subtracting 1 from the hundreds place. Note: when 1000 is reached, 1 is subtracted from the hundreds place making 900, therefore 1 is also subtracted from the thousands place, e.g. 3900 is 100 less than 4000.

Unit 8 Ordering numbers (2) — page 16

1 See Unit 2 No. 3 and Unit 4 Nos 3 – 4
2 To **write the smallest number**, find the smallest digit and write it first, then the next smallest and write it second, and so on. e.g. Using all the digits 4, 2, 5 the smallest number is 245 and using the digits 0, 4, 3 the smallest number is 304.
3 To **write the largest number**, find the largest digit and write it first, then the next largest digit and write it second, and so on. e.g. Using the digits 1, 7, 9, 3 the largest number is 9731.
4 **< means less than** and **> means greater than.** So 141 > 120 reads: 141 is greater than 120.

Unit 9 Counting forwards and backwards — page 17

1, 3 and 4 **To count forwards** start at the specified number, such as 25, and count on by the said number.
2, 3 and 4 **To count backwards** start at the specified number, such as 51, and count back by the said number.

Unit 10 Patterns (1) — page 17

1 **Patterns** are sets of numbers or objects made by a rule, e.g. □, □□, □□□ is increasing by one block at a time.
2 See Unit 4 No. 2
3 – 4 **Words** can be used to describe a pattern. e.g. Start at 2 and make a pattern by adding 4. The pattern is: 2, 6, 10, 14.

Unit 11 Expanding 3-digit numbers — page 18

1 See Unit 3 No. 1
2 To **write the number**, take the first digit of each number, and put them in order of place. e.g. 300 + 70 + 6 = 376, so the number is 376.
3 To **expand a number**, break the number into its components of thousands, hundreds, tens and units. Write it as an addition equation. e.g. 425 = 400 + 20 + 5
4 See Unit 2 No. 2

Unit 12 Expanding 4-digit numbers — page 18

1 See Unit 1 No. 2
2 See Unit 11 No. 2
3 See Unit 11 No. 3
4 See Unit 2 No. 2

Unit 13 4-digit numbers — page 19

1 See Unit 11 No. 3
2 **Counting back by 1** gives the number before and **counting on by 1** gives the number after.
3 See Unit 2 No. 3 and Unit 4 Nos 3 – 4
4 See Unit 8 No. 3

Unit 14 Ordering numbers (3) — page 19

1 See Unit 2 No. 3 and Unit 4 Nos 3 – 4
2 See Units 8 No. 3
3 See Unit 8 No. 2
4 See Unit 2 No. 3

Unit 15 Odd and even numbers page 20

1 An **odd** number is a number that cannot be evenly divisible by 2.

2 An **even** number is a number that can be evenly divisible by 2.

3 To **count by twos**, start at the specified number, and keep adding 2 each time. For example: 10, 12, 14, 16, 18, 20.

4 To group the items into **groups of two**, circle 2 items together.

For example:

Unit 16 Looking for ten when adding page 20

1, 2 and 4 By **looking for combinations of 10**, this makes addition easier. e.g. For $4 + 9 + 6$

$$4 + 6 = 10 \text{ then } 10 + 9 = 19$$
$$\text{so } 4 + 9 + 6 = 19$$

3 Looking for tens can also be **extended to 20, 30** and so on.

e.g. For $17 + 8 + 3$

$$17 + 3 = 20 \text{ then } 20 + 8 = 28$$
$$\text{so } 17 + 8 + 3 = 28$$

Unit 17 Adding to 20 page 21

1 **Add** is to combine or join things together.

e.g.

is $4 + 11 = 15$

Note: a short = 1 unit, a long = 1 ten and a flat = 1 hundred

2 – 3 Addition is the combining of two or more numbers to make a larger one. This can be done with numerals or words.

Note: addition is the same as **add** or **sum** or **total** or **plus**. It can be completed by counting on.

4 **Addition grids** can be completed by adding each number to the number beside the +.

+	2
1	$1 + 2 = 3$
3	$3 + 2 = 5$
5	$5 + 2 = 7$

Unit 18 Adding to 50 page 21

1 See Unit 17 No. 1

2 – 3 See Unit 17 Nos 2 – 3

4 **Missing numbers** can be found by counting on.

e.g. $24 + \underline{\quad} = 31$

24, 25, 26, 27, 28, 29, 30, 31 is counting on by 7.

$$24 + 7 = 31$$

Alternatively, it is possible to say '24 + what = 31'? The 'what' is 7.

Unit 19 Adding to 99 (1) page 22

1 See Unit 17 No. 1

2 **Addition** can be completed horizontally or vertically. Remember to line up units and tens in the correct columns.

3 – 4 See Unit 17 Nos 2 – 3

Note: units are added first and then tens. e.g. for $12 + 56$ first add $2 + 6 = 8$ and then add $1 + 5 = 6$ and the answer is 68.

Unit 20 Adding to 99 (2) page 22

1 See Unit 17 Nos 2 – 3 and Unit 19 No. 2

2 See Unit 19 No. 2

3 – 4 See Unit 17 Nos 2 – 3 and Unit 19 Nos 3 – 4 and don't forget the units at the end of the number, e.g. apples.

Unit 21 Adding to 99 (3) page 23

1 See Unit 17 Nos 2 – 3 and Unit 19 Nos 3 – 4

2 See Unit 19 No. 2

3 See Unit 17 Nos 2 – 3. Note: this applies to money as well as to amounts such as kilograms and metres. Just don't forget to include the signs ($ or c) or the amounts (kg, m).

4 See Unit 19, No. 2. **Missing numbers** can be found by saying '2 plus what equals 6?', therefore the 'what' is 4.

Unit 22 Adding with trading to 99 (1) page 23

1 See Unit 17 No. 1

2 To **estimate** means to make an approximation or rough calculation. To round to the **nearest ten**, numbers 5 and greater are rounded up; numbers less than 5 are rounded down.

e.g. $18 + 21$ could be estimated as $20 + 20 = 40$ by rounding to the nearest ten, then adding. Or $3.05 + 2.95$ is $3.00 + 3.00 = 6.00$ to the nearest dollar.

3 – 4 The **jump strategy** is jumping along a number line by tens then units to find the answer.

e.g. $45 + 24$

$45 + 20 + 4 = 69$

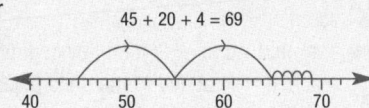

Note: jumps are forwards for addition and backwards for subtraction.

Unit 23 Adding with trading to 99 (2) page 24

1 See Unit 17 No. 1 and Unit 22 Nos 3 – 4

3 – 4 If a column in an addition sum adds up to more than ten, then a **ten will need to be traded to the next column**.

e.g.
$$\begin{array}{r} 4\,{}^1\!6\,{}^1\!5 \\ +\ 2\,8\,9 \\ \hline 7\,5\,4 \end{array}$$

Note: always start in the right hand (units) column and move to the left. This also applies to numbers in the hundreds and thousands columns.

2 See Unit 22 Nos 3 – 4

Unit 24 Adding with trading to 99 (3) page 24

1 See Unit 23 No. 1 and 3 – 4

2 The process of **adding with trading** applies for money, just don't forget to include the $ and c signs.

e.g.
$$\begin{array}{r} \$\,4\,{}^1\!6 \\ +\ \$\,3\,5 \\ \hline \$\,8\,1 \end{array} \qquad \begin{array}{r} \$\,3.25 \\ +\ \$\,1.30 \\ \hline \$\,4.55 \end{array}$$

3 See Unit 23 Nos 3 – 4

4 To complete **addition wheels**, add the number in the centre to each number in the wheel. The answers are in the outer layer.

Note: it may be necessary to add with trading (See Unit 23 Nos 3 – 4).

$24 + 14 = 38$ $36 + 14 = 50$ $49 + 14 = 63$ $25 + 14 = 39$ centre $+14$

Unit 25 Adding three or more numbers page 25

1 – 3 The process of **adding three or more numbers** is the same as with two numbers. It may be necessary to complete with trading (See Unit 23 Nos 3 – 4)

4 In a **magic square**, numbers are arranged in the square so that they add up to the same total vertically, horizontally and diagonally.

e.g. The magic number is 15:

6		2
	5	
		4

with solution:

6	7	2
1	5	9
8	3	4

Unit 26 Adding 3-digit numbers   page 25
1 – 3 See Unit 23 Nos 3 – 4
4 See Unit 24 No. 2

Unit 27 Mental strategies for adding   page 26
1 The **hundreds numbers can be added first** then zeros added afterwards.
e.g. $300 + 600$, first $3 + 6 = 9$ then add the zeros giving 900.
2 See Unit 16 Nos 1 – 2
3 Addition can be completed **by counting on**.
e.g. For $18 + 3$, counting on gives 18, 19, 20, 21 and the answer is 21.
4 See Unit 17 Nos 2–3 and Unit 19 Nos 3 – 4

Unit 28 Rounding numbers (1)   page 26
1 and 3 **Rounding** is giving an approximate answer. For rounding to the **nearest ten**, numbers ending in the digits 0, 1, 2, 3, 4 are rounded down, and numbers ending in the digits 5, 6, 7, 8, 9 are rounded up. e.g. To the nearest ten, 742 is rounded down to 740 and 746 is rounded up to 750.
2 and 4 **Rounding to the nearest hundred**: if the numerals being considered are from 0 to 49, then the number is rounded down. If the numerals being considered are from 50 to 99 the number is rounded up.
e.g. To the nearest hundred, 235 is rounded down to 200 and 275 is rounded up to 300.

Unit 29 Subtraction   page 27
1 **Subtraction** is the process of taking one quantity away from another. Subtract means **take away** or **minus** or **difference**.
2 – 4 The **subtraction answer** can be found by counting back.
e.g. For $10 - 4$, counting back gives 10, 9, 8, 7, 6. The answer is 6. This can be completed with a number line, with pictures or with numbers.

Unit 30 Subtraction patterns   page 27
1 **Patterns in subtraction** are useful.
e.g. $4 - 2 = 2$
$40 - 20 = 20$
$400 - 200 = 200$
In this example, just including the same number of zeros each time.

$15 - 5 = 10$
$25 - 5 = 20$
In this example, adding 10 each time to the original number and the answer.

2 – 4 **Addition is reversible** but subtraction is not.
e.g. $2 + 5 = 7$ and $5 + 2 = 7$
$7 - 5 = 2$ but $5 - 7$ does not give 2.
3 See Unit 29 Nos 2 – 4

Unit 31 2-digit subtraction to 50   page 28
1 See Unit 29 Nos 2 – 4
2 – 3 See Unit 22 Nos 3 – 4

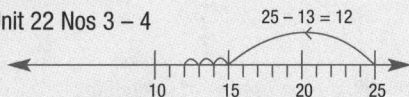

$25 - 13 = 12$

10   15   20   25

4 **Subtraction** can be completed horizontally $26 - 13 = 13$ or vertically (remember to keep units and tens and so on lined up).

T	U
2	6
– 1	5
1	1

Unit 32 2-digit subtraction to 99   page 28
1 – 2 See Unit 31 No. 4
3 – 4 See Unit 22 Nos 3 – 4 and Unit 31 Nos 2 – 3

Unit 33 Subtraction with trading (1)   page 29
1 – 4 **Subtraction with trading** is when a subtraction such as $5 - 9$ cannot be completed, so a ten needs to be traded.

e.g.
$$\begin{array}{r} {}^{5}\!\!\not6\,{}^{1}5 \\ -\ 2\ 9 \\ \hline 3\ 6 \end{array}$$
$5 - 9$ can't do, so trade from 6, making $15 - 9$.

The answer can be checked by adding the answer and the subtracted number.

26   →   12
−14   +14
12   26

Unit 34 Subtraction with trading (2)   page 29
1 – 3 See Unit 33 Nos 1 – 4
4 **Missing boxes** can be found by either working out the missing subtracted numbers:
e.g.

$$\begin{array}{r} 5\ 3 \\ -1\ \square \\ \hline 4\ 1 \end{array}$$
$3 - \boxed{2} = 1$ so
$$\begin{array}{r} 5\ 3 \\ -1\ \boxed{2} \\ \hline 4\ 1 \end{array}$$

or by working backwards and adding:
e.g.

$$\begin{array}{r} 2\ \square \\ -1\ 4 \\ \hline 1\ 3 \end{array}$$
$4 + 3 = 7$ so
$$\begin{array}{r} 2\ 7 \\ -1\ \boxed{4} \\ \hline 1\ 3 \end{array}$$

Unit 35 Subtraction with trading (3)   page 30
1 – 2 See Unit 33, Nos 1 – 4.
3 Subtraction with trading applies as normal for **money**, just don't forget to include the $ and c signs.
e.g.
$$\begin{array}{r} {}^{3} \\ \$\ 3.4\,{}^{1}2 \\ -\ \$\ 2.\not3\ 6 \\ \hline \$\ 1.0\ 6 \end{array}$$
4 See Unit 33 Nos 1 – 4

Unit 36 Subtraction with 3-digit numbers   page 30
1 See Unit 31 No. 4
2 See Unit 34 No. 4
3 – 4 See Unit 35 No. 3

Unit 37 Patterns with subtraction   page 31
1 – 3 See Unit 29 Nos 2 – 4
4 See Unit 30 No. 1

Unit 38 Checking subtraction by adding   page 31
1 – 4 Subtraction and addition are opposite (**inverse**) operations. That means subtraction can be checked with addition. So if $25 - 12 = 13$ it can be checked by adding the answer and the subtracted number. In this case $13 + 12 = 25$. Conversely **addition can be checked with subtraction**.
e.g. $19 + 10 = 29$ therefore $29 - 10 = 19$

Unit 39 Estimating
page 32

1 – 4 See Unit 22 No. 2

Unit 40 Rounding numbers (2)
page 32

1 – 2 See Unit 28 Nos 1, 2 and 4
3 – 4 See Unit 28 Nos 1 and 3

Unit 41 Rounding numbers (3)
page 33

1 See Unit 28 Nos 1 and 3
2 See Unit 28 Nos 1 and 3 and Unit 19 No. 2
3 See Unit 28 Nos 1, 3 and Unit 31 No. 4
4 See Unit 19 No. 2 and Unit 29 Nos 2 – 4

Unit 42 Multiplication with modelling
page 33

1 – 3 **Multiplication** is the total in the number groups or rows.

e.g. $\begin{array}{c}\times\times\times\times\\ \times\times\times\times\end{array}$ = 8 crosses or $\begin{array}{c}\circ\circ\\ \circ\circ\\ \circ\circ\end{array}$ = 6 circles

Note: **groups of** is the same as **times** or **multiply** or **product**.
4 **Multiplication equations are reversible**, so $2 \times 5 = 10$ and $5 \times 2 = 10$. Multiplication equations can also be expressed as addition equations, e.g. $3 \times 2 = 6 = 2 + 2 + 2$, or groups of 2 added together 3 times.

Unit 43 × 2 and × 4
page 34

1 – 4 See Unit 42 Nos 1 – 3

Unit 44 × 5 and × 10
page 34

1 – 3 See Unit 42 Nos 1 – 3
4 **Multiplication table grids** can be completed by multiplying each number by the number below the ×.

×	1	2	3
2	1×2 2	2×2 4	3×2 6

Unit 45 × 0, × 1, × 2 and × 4
page 35

1 – 2 See Unit 42 Nos 1 – 3
Note: **anything × 0 = 0** and **anything × 1 = itself**.
3 See Unit 44 No. 4
4 When there are two sums either side of an answer, the answer should be the same for both **equations**.
e.g. $2 \times 2 = 4 = 4 \times 1$ where both equations equal 4.

Unit 46 × 3 and × 6
page 35

1 See Unit 42 Nos 1 – 3
2 See Unit 45 No. 4
3 On a **triangle** there are **3 points**.
4 See Unit 42 Nos 1 – 3

Unit 47 × 9
page 36

1 – 3 See Unit 42 Nos 1 – 3
4 See Unit 45 No. 4

Unit 48 × 3, × 6 and × 9
page 36

1 – 2 See Unit 42 Nos 1 – 3
3 **Multiplication** can be completed vertically or horizontally.

e.g. $4 \times 3 = 12$ or $\begin{array}{r}4\\ \times 3\\ \hline 12\end{array}$ Note: units and tens columns need to line up vertically.

4 See Unit 45 No. 4

Unit 49 × 8
page 37

1 – 3 See Unit 42 Nos 1 – 3
4 See Unit 48 No. 3

Unit 50 × 2, × 4 and × 8
page 37

1 – 2 See Unit 42 Nos 1 – 3
3 See Unit 44 No. 4
4 See Unit 45 No. 4

Unit 51 × 7
page 38

1 There are **7 days in 1 week** (Monday to Sunday).
2 – 3 See Unit 42 Nos 1 – 3
4 See Unit 48 No. 3

Unit 52 Multiplication tables
page 38

1 – 2 See Unit 42 Nos 1 – 3
3 **Multiplication circles** are completed by multiplying the number in the circle by each number on the outside, and the answer is written in the outer layer.
e.g.

$$
\begin{array}{cc}
4 \times 1 = 4 & 4 \times 2 = 8 \\
4 \times 5 = 20 & 4 \times 3 = 12
\end{array}
$$

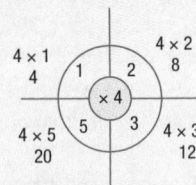

4 See Unit 48 No. 3

Unit 53 Square numbers
page 39

1 – 4 A **square number** is a number that can be represented in the shape of a square. e.g. $9 = 3 \times 3$ or $\begin{array}{ccc}\square&\square&\square\\ \square&\square&\square\\ \square&\square&\square\end{array}$

A number that is multiplied by itself results in an answer that is a square number.

Unit 54 Multiples
page 39

1 – 4 **Multiple** is the product of two or more **factors**.
e.g. $7 \times 5 = 35$; 35 is a multiple of 7 and a multiple of 5.

Unit 55 Sharing
page 40

1 – 4 **Sharing** is dividing into equal groups.

e.g. 6 shared by 3 is 2.

Note: sometimes there may be some left over.
e.g. 5 shared by 2 is 2 and 1 left over.

Unit 56 Division (1)
page 40

1 – 4 **Division** is the sharing or grouping of objects into equal groups.
e.g.

2 groups of 3
or $6 \div 2 = 3$

Division also means **groups of** or **dividing**.

Unit 57 Division as repeated subtraction
page 41

1 – 3 An **amount** can be subtracted from a number a certain **number of times** to find the number of groups.
e.g. $10 - 2 - 2 - 2 - 2 - 2 = 0$, $10 \div 2 = 5$
4 See Unit 56 Nos 1 – 4

Unit 58 Division (2) page 41
1 – 4 See Unit 56 Nos 1 – 4

Unit 59 Division with number lines page 42
1 – 4 The **jump strategy** can be used for division.
e.g. How many 2s are there in 8?

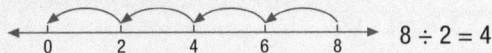

 $8 ÷ 2 = 4$

Unit 60 Division (3) page 42
1 **Division** can be expressed in the form $30 ÷ 6 = 5$

or $6\overline{)30}^{\,5}$ Note: units and tens line up above one another.

2 – 3 **Division in money** is the same as normal division but don't forget the $ and c signs. e.g. $20c ÷ 4 = 5c$
4 See Unit 56 Nos 1 – 4

Unit 61 Division with remainders (1) page 43
1 – 4 When a division or grouping is made, and there are some items or numbers left over, these are called **remainders**. The abbreviation for remainder is r.
e.g. $13 ÷ 5$ says how many groups of 5 in 13. There are 2 groups of 5 and 3 left over. This can be written as 2 r 3.

Unit 62 Division with remainders (2) page 43
1 – 4 See Unit 61 Nos 1 – 4

Unit 63 Division practice page 44
1 See Unit 60 No. 1
2 See Unit 56 Nos 1 – 4
3 – 4 See Unit 61 Nos 1 – 4

Unit 64 Multiplication and division page 44
1 See Unit 56 Nos 1 – 4
2 – 4 Multiplication and division are **inverse operations**.
e.g. $10 × 2 = 20$ and $20 ÷ 2 = 10$ and $20 ÷ 10 = 2$

Unit 65 Using number lines page 45
1 – 2 See Unit 22 Nos 3 – 4
3 The **jump strategy** can be used for multiplication, with counting by the multiple.
e.g. $4 × 2$ would have jumps to 2, 4, 6 ending on 8.
4 See Unit 59 Nos 1 – 4

Unit 66 Inverse operations page 45
1 – 2 See Unit 38 Nos 1 – 4
3 – 4 See Unit 64 Nos 2 – 4

Unit 67 Which order? page 46
1 See Unit 16 Nos 1 – 4
2 See Unit 17 Nos 2 – 3
3 See Unit 42 No. 4
4 Addition equations are reversible.
e.g. $2 + 3 = 5$ and $3 + 2 = 5$, and See Unit 42 No. 4

Unit 68 Bingo! page 46
1 **Bingo** is the game where the player is trying to cross out all of the numbers on the grid or a complete row. See Unit 17 Nos 2 – 3

2 See Unit 29 Nos 2 – 4
3 See Unit 42 Nos 1 – 3
4 See Unit 56 No. 1

Unit 69 Missing numbers page 47
1 See Unit 18 No. 4 and Unit 29 No. 1
2 See Unit 42 Nos 1 – 3
3 See Unit 56 Nos 1 – 4
4 By **trial and error,** the correct sign for an equation can be found. If the answer is smaller, the sign will be − or ÷. If the answer is larger, the sign will be + or ×.

Unit 70 Patterns (2) page 47
1 See Unit 10 Nos 1 – 2
2 See Unit 10 Nos 1 – 2. A **rule** is an instruction that applies to a sequence of numbers or a pattern.
e.g. For 2, 4, 8 the rule is doubling the number each time.
3 The **tenth number** can be found by examining the pattern and completing the counting sequence.
4 See Unit 5 Nos 2 – 3, Unit 10 Nos 1 – 2 and Unit 17 No. 4

Unit 71 Rules for patterns page 48
1 – 4 See Unit 10 Nos 1 – 4 and Unit 70 No. 2

Unit 72 Calculator – place value page 48
1 – 4 A **calculator sentence** is the information you would enter into a calculator to obtain the answer, e.g. the sentence you would use to change 49 to 9 is $49 – 40 = 9$.

Unit 73 Calculator – addition and subtraction page 49
1 – 3 A **calculator** can be used to find answers to equations or to check answers.
4 See Unit 72 Nos 1 – 4

Unit 74 Calculator – multiplication and division page 49
1 – 3 See Unit 73 Nos 1 – 3
4 See Unit 72 Nos 1 – 4

Unit 75 Fraction names page 50
1 The **numerator** is the top part of the fraction (over the line). It shows how many parts out of the whole.
The **denominator** is the bottom part of the fraction (the number under the line). It shows how many parts there are in the whole,
e.g. $\dfrac{2}{4}$ is 2 out of 4 equal parts.

2 – 3 Fractions can be represented with **words or numbers**,
e.g. one third and $\dfrac{1}{3}$.

4 Fractions can be represented with pictures or diagrams where the **fraction is the shaded part**.
e.g. $\dfrac{1}{2}$ = or or

Unit 76 Naming fractions (1) page 50
1 See Unit 75, No. 1.
2 – 3 See Unit 75, No. 4.
4 **Fractions of an object** and fractions of a group can be found,
e.g. $\dfrac{1}{4}$ or

Unit 77 Naming fractions (2)   page 51
1 – 4 See Unit 75 No. 4 and Unit 76 No. 4

Unit 78 Naming fractions (3)   page 51
1, 2 and 4 See Unit 75 No. 4

3 Equivalent fractions are fractions that have the same value,

e.g. All these fractions are equal to $\frac{1}{2}$.

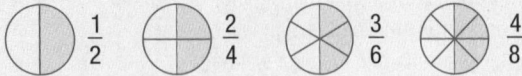

$\frac{1}{2}$ $\frac{2}{4}$ $\frac{3}{6}$ $\frac{4}{8}$

Unit 79 Comparing fractions   page 52
1 – 4 When **fractions** with the same denominator **are compared**, the fraction with the largest number as the numerator is the largest fraction.

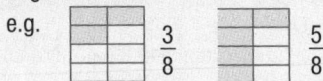

e.g. $\frac{3}{8}$ $\frac{5}{8}$

$\frac{5}{8}$ is larger than $\frac{3}{8}$ as more parts are shaded.

Also, $\frac{3}{8}$ is smaller than $\frac{5}{8}$.

If required, fractions can then be written in order.

Unit 80 Fractions of a collection   page 52
1 – 4 See Unit 76 No. 4

Unit 81 Equivalent fractions   page 53
1 See Unit 75 No. 4
2 See Unit 79 Nos 1 – 4
3 – 4 See Unit 78 No. 3

Unit 82 Hundredths (1)   page 53
1 – 4 A **hundredth** is one part of one whole which is divided into 100 parts.

As a decimal 1 hundredth = 0.01 and as a fraction = $\frac{1}{100}$.

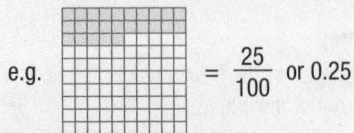

e.g. $= \frac{25}{100}$ or 0.25

Unit 83 Hundredths (2)   page 54
1 – 2 See Unit 82 Nos 1 – 4
3 To work out which is **larger,** look at the number on the top of the fraction (when the numbers on the bottom are the same) and the larger number is the larger fraction,

e.g. $\frac{4}{100}$ and $\frac{40}{100}$. As 40 is larger than 4, $\frac{40}{100}$ is the larger fraction.

4 It is possible to **count in hundredths** by looking at the top number of the fraction (if all the bottom numbers are the same) and working out the pattern.

Unit 84 Tenths (1)   page 54
1 – 3 A **tenth** is one part of one unit (which is divided into 10 equal parts).

As a decimal one tenth = 0.1 and as a fraction = $\frac{1}{10}$.

On a grid: $= \frac{1}{10}$

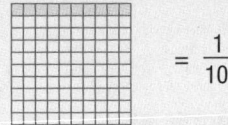

4 A **decimal** is a fraction written with a decimal point. e.g. 0.65 and 5.6. In words 0.6 = six tenths.

Unit 85 Tenths (2)   page 55
1 See Unit 84 No. 4
2 – 4 Decimals can be written as a **fraction** out of 10 or 100.

$\frac{1}{10}$ = 0.1 $\frac{32}{100}$ = 0.32 $1\frac{46}{100}$ = 1.46

The number of zeros in the denominator indicates the number of decimal places.

Unit 86 Counting forwards and backwards with decimals   page 55
1 – 4 Counting with decimals is the same as numbers, except there is a decimal point. Counting forwards is adding on and counting backwards is taking away.

e.g. 0.2, 0.4, 0.6, 0.8. Sometimes it is easier to draw a number line and use the jump strategy.

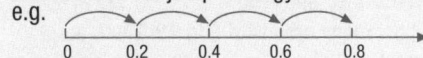

e.g.

| 0 | 0.2 | 0.4 | 0.6 | 0.8 |

Unit 87 Decimals   page 56
1 – 2 See Unit 82 Nos 1 – 4
3 Numeral expanders can apply to decimal numbers and include tenths and hundredths,

e.g. | 3 | tenths | 2 | hundredths | = 0.32

4 See Unit 85 Nos 2 – 4

Unit 88 Fractions to decimals   page 56
1 – 2 See Unit 85 Nos 2 – 4
3 See Unit 82 Nos 1 – 4 and Unit 84 Nos 1 – 3
4 See Unit 85 Nos 2 – 4

Unit 89 Decimals and fractions   page 57
1 See Unit 84 Nos 1 – 3
2 See Unit 82 Nos 1 – 4
3 See Unit 85 Nos 2 – 4
4 As with all **ordering**, start with the left digit, and compare them; if all are the same, move to the first digit after the decimal point and so on to the right.

Unit 90 Less than and greater than and rounding decimals   page 57
1 – 2 See Unit 8 No. 4 and Unit 79 Nos 1 – 4
3 To round decimals to the **nearest whole number**, look at the number to the right of the decimal point. If it is 5 or greater, round up. If it is less than 5, round down.

e.g. 2.5 rounds up to 3 and 8.25 rounds down to 8.

4 See Unit 8 No. 4

Unit 91 Decimal addition   page 58
1 – 4 Adding decimals is the same as normal addition. Units, tenths and hundredths all need to line up in the correct columns. The easiest way is to line up the decimal point first,

e.g.   1 . 5   which continues in the answer.
     + 0 . 3
     _____
       1 . 8

Unit 92 Decimal subtraction page 58

1 – 4 Subtracting decimals is the same as normal subtraction. Units, tenths and hundredths all need to line up in the correct columns. The easiest way is to line up the decimal point first, and this continues in the answer.

e.g.
$$\begin{array}{r} 2.5 \\ -1.3 \\ \hline 1.2 \end{array}$$

Unit 93 Decimal addition and subtraction with trading page 59

1 – 4 Addition and subtraction with decimals is the same as normal, but the columns (units, tenths, etc.) and the decimal point need to line up. The decimal point follows in the answer.

e.g.
$$\begin{array}{r} {}^{1} \\ 8.25 \\ +1.46 \\ \hline 9.71 \end{array} \qquad \begin{array}{r} {}^{2} \\ 5.3^{1}6 \\ -2.19 \\ \hline 3.17 \end{array}$$

Unit 94 Simple percentages page 59

1 – 4 Percentage means out of 100. It is represented by the percentage sign, %, e.g. 20% is 20 out of 100 or $\frac{20}{100}$ or 0.2.

As all percentages are out of 100, the larger the number, the larger the percentage, e.g. 50% is larger than 20%.

4 See Unit 8 No. 4

Unit 95 Money – coins page 60

1, 2 and 4 There are six different **coins** in Australia's money system: 5c, 10c, 20c, 50c, $1 and $2.

3 Change is the left over amount of money owed back to the person making the purchase, e.g. I spent $7.00 of $10.00 therefore the change is $3.00. It can be found by counting on. e.g. Change from $5 after spending $4.65 is: 5c makes $4.70, then 10c makes $4.80 and 20c makes $5.00. So the total change is 5c + 10c + 20c = 35c.

Unit 96 Money – notes page 60

1 – 2 There are five different **notes** in Australia's money system: $5, $10, $20, $50 and $100. See also Unit 95 Nos 1, 2 and 4

3 See Unit 95 No. 3

4 The **total** (or sum) of money is the same as normal addition, just don't forget the $ sign. See Unit 24 No. 2

Unit 97 Money – addition and subtraction page 61

1 and 3 See Unit 24, No. 2.

2 See Unit 35 No. 3

4 See Unit 95 No. 3

Unit 98 Money – multiplication and division page 61

1 and 3 The process of **multiplication with money** is the same as normal, just remember to include the $ and c signs, e.g. 20c × 3 = 60c

2 and 4 The process of **division with money** is the same as normal, just remember to include the $ and c signs, e.g. $20 ÷ 5 = $4

Unit 99 Money – rounding page 62

1 and 4 Rounding with money is the same as usual. See Unit 28 Nos 1 – 4. As there are 100 cents in one dollar,

50 cents and above round up to the nearest dollar, while amounts less than 50 cents round down to the nearest dollar.

2 See Unit 28 Nos 1 – 4

3 To **round to the nearest** 10c, if the amount ends in:
* a 1, 2, 3 or 4, it is rounded down 0
* a 5, 6, 7, 8 or 9, it is rounded up to 0.
e.g. $3.92 is rounded down to $3.90

4 See also Unit 91 Nos 1 – 4

Unit 100 Money – estimating page 62

1 – 4 See Unit 22 No. 2

Unit 101 Symmetry page 63

1 – 4 Symmetry is when one half of a shape is a reflection of the other, so when folded on the line (axis) of symmetry the two halves fit exactly.

Note: a shape may have more then one line of symmetry.

e.g.

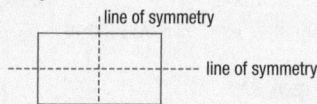

Unit 102 2D shapes (1) page 63

1 – 4 2D shapes have two dimensions, length and width. They do not have depth. See Geometry Unit (page 12)

Unit 103 2D shapes (2) page 64

1, 2 and 4 See Geometry Unit (page 12)

3 A **corner** is where lines meet (also called a vertex).

Unit 104 2D shapes (3) page 64

1 – 4 See Unit 102 Nos 1 – 4 and Geometry Unit (page 12)

Unit 105 Pentagons and octagons page 65

1 – 4 An **angle** is formed when two lines meet at a point.

A **pentagon** is a polygon with five straight sides.

An **octagon** is a polygon with eight straight sides.

See also Geometry Unit (page 12)

Unit 106 Trapeziums and parallelograms page 65

1 – 4 A **trapezium** is a special quadrilateral (4-sided shape) where one pair of opposite sides is parallel.

A **parallelogram** is a special quadrilateral where opposite sides are parallel and opposite angles are equal. See Geometry Unit (page 12)

Unit 107 Rigidity   page 66

1 See Geometry Unit (page 12)

2 – 4 A **rigid shape/object** is one that is firmly fixed and not easily moved or squashed. A triangle is a rigid shape at the vertices.

A **non-rigid shape** is one in which the shape/object is easily pushed out of shape or moved easily, e.g. a square. Shapes can be made more rigid with supports (like a picnic table).

Unit 108 Regular and irregular shapes   page 66

1 – 4 **Regular shapes** are shapes where all sides and all angles are equal, e.g. square.
Irregular shapes are shapes where all sides and angles are not equal, e.g. rectangle or rhombus.
See also Units 105, 106 and Geometry Unit (page 12)

Unit 109 Angles in real life   page 67

1 and 3 An **angle** is the amount of turn between two straight lines (arms) fixed at a point. Note: is larger than

2 A **right angle** is indicated by:

4 The **hands on a clock face** form angles.

Unit 110 Angles   page 67

1, 3 and 4 See Unit 109 Nos 1 and 3. There are 7 angles inside the figure.

2 See Unit 109 No. 2

Unit 111 Right angles   page 68

1 – 4 See Unit 109 No. 2

Unit 112 Parallel lines   page 68

1 – 4 **Parallel lines** are two or more lines that do not meet.

Note: they are indicated by the arrows on the lines.

Unit 113 Perpendicular lines   page 69

1 – 4 **Perpendicular lines** are lines that intersect at right angles.

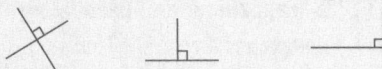

Note: they are indicated by the square representing a right angle.

Unit 114 3D objects (1)   page 69

1 and 3 A **3D** object has height, width and length.

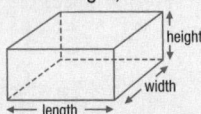

A **surface** is the top or outside layer of an object; it can be flat or curved. See Geometry Unit (page 12)

2 and 4 A **face** is a flat surface of a solid object. See Geometry Unit (page 12)

Unit 115 3D objects (2)   page 70

1 – 4 See Unit 114 Nos 1 – 3 and Geometry Unit (page 12)

Unit 116 Properties of 3D objects   page 70

1 and 4 See Unit 114 Nos 2 and 4

2 An **edge** is where two faces meet. See also Unit 114 Nos 1 and 3

3 A **cross-section** is what you see when a 3D object is cut through.

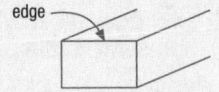

Unit 117 Prisms and cylinders   page 71

1 – 2 A **prism** is a 3D object which has two identical ends that give the prism its name. All other faces are rectangles.
triangular prism
A **cylinder is** a 3D object that has two circular ends and a curved surface joining them.

3 See Unit 114 Nos 2 and 4

4 See Unit 116 No. 2 and Geometry Unit (page 12)

Unit 118 Pyramids   page 71

1 A **pyramid is** a 3D object. It has one base which gives the pyramid its name and all of the other faces are triangles.
square pyramid

2 – 3 See Unit 114 Nos 2 and 4

4 See Unit 116 No. 2 and see Geometry Unit (page 12)

Unit 119 Nets and 3D objects   page 72

1 See Unit 114 Nos 2 and 4

2 A **cube** is a 3D object which has six identical square faces. A **net** is a flat pattern which can be folded to make a 3D object.

3 The **number of blocks** can be counted to find the number for the 3D shape.

4 See Geometry Unit (page 12)

Unit 120 Movement of shapes   page 72

1, 2 and 4 A **reflection** (flip) is a shape or object as seen in a mirror.
A **translation** (slide) is to move an object left/right or up/down without rotating it.
A **rotation** (turn) is to turn an object about a point.

3 A **tessellation** is a pattern of one or more identical shapes that fit together without any gaps.

Unit 121 Position – giving directions   page 73

1 – 4 **Position** is where something is placed in relation to the things around it. It can be defined by giving directions such as left/right or up/down and forwards/backwards, as well as compass directions.

Unit 122 Position   page 73

1 – 4 See Unit 121 Nos 1 – 4

Unit 123 Compass directions
page 74

1 – 4 A **compass** is an instrument that gives direction.
Its main points are north (N), south (S), east (E) and west (W).

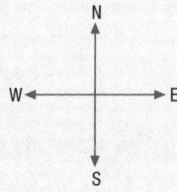

N
W ← → E
S

Unit 124 Maps
page 74

1 – 4 A **map** is a diagram of a place that shows its position in the area or world. See also Unit 121 Nos 1 – 4

Unit 125 Coordinates
page 75

1 – 2 See Unit 121 Nos 1 – 4
3 – 4 **Coordinates** are used to show position on a grid. They are represented by pairs of letters or numbers, e.g. A2 or (6, 3). Note: the first coordinate is the horizontal or x-value. The second coordinate is the vertical or y-value.

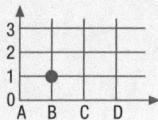

3
2
1
0
A B C D

e.g. The dot is at B1.

Unit 126 Analog time (1)
page 75

1 – 2 **Time** is the space between one event and the next. It is measured on a clock. An **analog clock** uses the numerals 1 to 12 and rotating hands to show the time. Time that is 'on the hour', or when the long hand is pointing to the 12, is stated as '**o'clock**'.

e.g. 1 o'clock

3 – 4 Time that is 'on the half-hour' or when the long hand is pointing to the 6, is stated as '**half past**'.

e.g. half past 6

Unit 127 Analog time (2)
page 76

1 – 4 Time that is 'on the quarter hour' or when the long hand is pointing to the 3, is stated as '**quarter past**' and when the long hand is pointing to the 9, is stated as '**quarter to**'.

e.g. quarter to 10   and quarter past 5

3 – 4 See also Unit 126 Nos 1 – 4

Unit 128 Analog time in minutes
page 76

1 – 4 A clock is marked with numerals 1 to 12 and when the long hand moves between each one, this is **5 minutes**.

e.g.   Five minutes has passed.

Unit 129 Digital time (1)
page 77

1 – 4 A **digital clock** uses only numerals to show the time. This can be expressed in words, e.g. seven forty-five is 7:45. The numerals after the dots mean minutes past, e.g. 1:23 means 23 minutes past 1.

Unit 130 Digital time (2)
page 77

1 – 3 See Unit 129 Nos 1 – 4
4 To find the time in **5 minutes,** count on by 5 until 59 and then move to the next hour.

Unit 131 Digital and analog time
page 78

1 See Unit 129 Nos 1 – 4
2 – 3 See Unit 128 Nos 1 – 4
4 See Unit 129 Nos 1 – 4

Unit 132 Calendars
page 78

1 – 4 A **calendar** is a table showing the year broken up into months, weeks and days. There are 12 months in a year and 52 weeks in a year. There are 365 days in a year, except a leap year which has 366 days. There are 7 days in a week and 14 days in a fortnight.

Unit 133 Timelines and timetables
page 79

1 and 3 A **timetable** is a table where times are organised for when different events happen. Timetables are used in schools, hospitals and by transport.
2 and 4 A **timeline** is a diagram used to show the length of time between events happening.

Unit 134 Length in centimetres
page 79

1 – 4 **Length** is the distance from one end to the other or how long something is.
A **centimetre** is equal to one hundredth of a metre. Its abbreviation is cm and it can be measured with a ruler. Remember: start measuring at 0, not 1.

Unit 135 Length (1)
page 80

1 – 2 See Unit 134 Nos 1 – 4
3 – 4 A **metre** is equal to 100 centimetres. Its abbreviation is m and it can be measured with items such as a metre ruler or a tape measure. Note: 1 m is longer than 1 cm.

Unit 136 Length (2)
page 80

1 – 2 1 metre = 100 centimetres
Thus 1 m 30 cm = 100 cm + 30 cm = 130 cm
and 150 cm = 100 cm + 50 cm = 1 m 50 cm
3 See Unit 135 Nos 3 – 4
4 See Unit 134 Nos 1 – 4

Unit 137 Length in millimetres
page 81

1 and 4 A **millimetre** is one tenth of a centimetre or one thousandth of a metre. Its abbreviation is mm. It can be measured with a ruler.
Note: 1 mm is shorter than 1 cm and 1 m.
2 and 3 1 cm = 10 mm
Therefore 1 cm 5 mm = 10 mm + 5 mm = 15 mm
and 49 mm = 40 mm + 9 mm = 4 cm 9 mm.

Unit 138 Length with decimals   page 81

1 See Unit 136 Nos 1 – 2

2 2 m 40 cm can be written as a **decimal** where 2 is the whole
   number and 40 is the decimal.
   e.g. 2.40 m or 2 m 40 cm = 240 cm
   As there are 100 cm in 1 metre, there are 2.40 m in 240 cm.

3 See Unit 137 Nos 2 – 3
   Note: 29 mm as a decimal is 2.9 cm.

4 See Unit 137 Nos 1 and 4

Unit 139 Perimeter (1)   page 82

1 – 4 **Perimeter** is the distance around the outside of a shape.
   Note: to estimate is to make a reasonable guess.
   e.g.

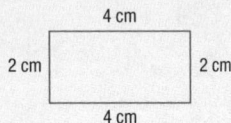

```
        4 cm
  ┌──────────────┐
2 cm│              │2 cm
  └──────────────┘
        4 cm
```

   Perimeter = 4 cm + 2 cm + 4 cm + 2 cm
             = 12 cm

Unit 140 Perimeter (2)   page 82

1 – 4 See Unit 139 Nos 1 – 4

Unit 141 Area (1)   page 83

1 – 4 The **area** is the size of a surface. It is measured in square
   units. It can be found by counting squares.
   e.g. Area = 8 square units

Unit 142 Area (2)   page 83

1 See Unit 141 Nos 1 – 4

2 and 4 One **square metre** is 1 m × 1 m.
   One **square centimetre** is 1 cm × 1 cm.

3 The **abbreviation** of square centimetre is cm^2 and for
   square metre is m^2.

Unit 143 Mass in kg (1)   page 84

1 – 4 A **kilogram** is the standard unit for measuring mass. Its
   abbreviation is kg. One kilogram equals 1000 grams,
   therefore 1 kilogram is heavier than 1 gram.

Unit 144 Mass in kg (2)   page 84

1 **Mass** is the amount of matter in an object. It is measured in
   kilograms.

2 See Unit 143 Nos 1 – 4

3 – 4 Masses can be **added** together like normal addition.
   e.g. 1 kg + 5 kg = 6 kg (don't forget the units!)

Unit 145 Mass in grams   page 85

1 One **gram** is one thousandth of a kilogram. The abbreviation for
   gram is g.

2 See Unit 143 Nos 1 – 4

3 See Unit 144 Nos 3 – 4

4 Ordering from **lightest to heaviest** is like smallest to largest.
   See Unit 2 No. 3 and Unit 4 Nos 3 – 4

Unit 146 Capacity – informal   page 85

1 – 4 **Capacity** is the amount a container can hold. It is measured
   in litres. Its abbreviation is L. 1 litre is equal to 1000 millilitres.
   Therefore 1 millilitre is less than 1 litre.

Unit 147 Capacity in litres   page 86

1 – 4 See Unit 146 Nos 1 – 4

Unit 148 Capacity in millilitres   page 86

1 – 4 Abbreviation of millilitres is **mL**.
   1000 millilitres equals 1 litre.

Unit 149 Cubic centimetres   page 87

1 – 4 A **cubic centimetre** is a standard unit for measuring
   volume. Its abbreviation is cm^3. The number of cubic centimetres
   in an object can be found by counting the number of cubes.

Unit 150 Volume   page 87

1 – 4 See Unit 149 Nos 1 – 4

Unit 151 Arrangements   page 88

1 and 4 The same set of objects can be **arranged** in different
   orders.
   e.g. The digits 1, 2, 3 can be arranged in the following different
   ways: 123, 132, 213, 231, 321, 312

2 – 3 **Chance** is the probability or likelihood of something
   happening. It can be described with words such as certain,
   likely, unlikely, impossible, rarely, never or equal chance.

Unit 152 Chance (1)   page 88

1 – 4 See Unit 151 Nos 2 – 3

Unit 153 Chance (2)   page 89

1 – 4 See Unit 151 Nos 2 – 3
   Note: a **spinner** is an object that is spun, landing on a result.
   e.g.

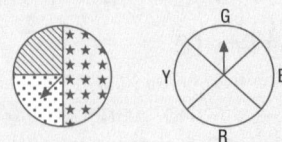

Unit 154 Picture graphs   page 89

1 – 4 A **picture graph** is a graph which uses pictures to represent
   quantities.

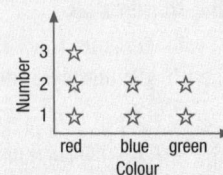

Unit 155 **Tally marks** page 90

1 – 4 A **tally** is the use of marks to record counting.

| = 1 || = 2 ||| = 3 |||| = 4 |##1 = 5

|##1 |##1 = 10

Information recorded as a tally in a table is often called a **tally sheet** or **tally table**.

R	|||
G	|##1	
B	|##1 |##1

Unit 156 **Reading tables** page 90

1 – 4 A **table** is mathematical information organised in rows and columns.

Heads	5
Tails	6

and

Colour	Number
red	3
green	6
blue	10

4 See also Unit 155 Nos 1 – 4

Unit 157 **Column graphs** page 91

1, 3 and 4 A **column graph** uses bars or columns to show the number of an object so they can be compared.

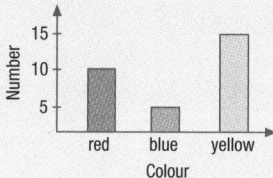

2 See Unit 155 Nos 1 – 4

Unit 158 **Two-way tables** page 91

1 – 4 **Two-way tables** have information in the vertical and horizontal directions. They usually consist of likes and dislikes or have and don't have.
e.g. 4 people don't like peas, but do like potatoes
6 people like potatoes
6 people don't like peas
7 people don't like potatoes
7 people like peas.

	Like potatoes	Don't like potatoes
Like peas	2	5
Don't like peas	4	2

Unit 159 **Guided problem solving** page 92

1 See Unit 17 No. 1
2 See Unit 33 Nos 1 – 4
3 See Unit 42 Nos 1 – 3
4 See Unit 56 Nos 1 – 4

Unit 160 **Problem solving** page 92

1 See Unit 18 No. 4, Unit 29 No. 1, Unit 42 Nos 1 – 3 and Unit 56 Nos 1 – 4
2 See Unit 17 No. 1 and Unit 33 Nos 1 – 4
3 See Unit 42 Nos 1–3 and Unit 56 Nos 1 – 4
4 See Unit 24 No. 2, Unit 35 Nos 3 and 4, Unit No. 3 and Unit 98 Nos 1 – 4

Unit 161 **Tables practice (1)** page 93

1 – 4 See Unit No. 42 Nos 1 – 3

Unit 162 **Tables practice (2)** page 93

1 See Unit 42 Nos 1 – 3
2 See Unit 48 No. 3
3 See Unit 45 No. 4
4 See Unit 44 No. 4

Unit 163 **Addition practice** page 94

1 See Unit 22 Nos 3 – 4
2 – 4 See Unit 22 No. 1 and Unit 25 Nos 1 – 3

Unit 164 **Subtraction practice** page 94

1 – 2 See Unit 29 No. 1
3 See Unit 31 No. 4
4 See Unit 33 Nos 1 – 4

Unit 165 **Multiplication practice** page 95

1 – 2 See Unit 42 Nos 1 – 3
3 See Unit 42 No. 4
4 See Unit 48 No. 3

Unit 166 **Division practice** page 95

1 See Unit 55 Nos 1 – 4
2 See Unit 56 Nos 1 – 4
3 See Unit 60 No. 1 and Unit 64 Nos 2 – 4
4 See Unit 61 Nos 1 – 4

Unit 167 **Fractions practice** page 96

1 See Unit 75 No. 1
2 – 3 See Unit 76 No. 4
4 See Unit 79 Nos 1 – 4

Unit 168 **Decimals practice** page 96

1 See Unit 84 No. 4
2 See Unit 85 Nos 2 – 4
3 See Unit 91 Nos 1 – 4 and Unit 93 Nos 1 – 4
4 See Unit 92 Nos 1 – 4 and Unit 93 Nos 1 – 4

Unit 169 **Money practice** page 97

1 See Unit 24 No. 2
2 See Unit 95 No. 3
3 See Unit 99 Nos 3 – 4
4 See Unit 22 No. 2

Unit 170 **Time practice** page 97

1 See Unit 129 Nos 1 – 4
2 See Unit 126 Nos 1 – 4 Unit 127 Nos 1 – 3 and Unit 128 Nos 1 – 4
3 See Unit 129 Nos 1 – 4
4 See Unit 128 Nos 1 – 4 and Unit 129 Nos 1 – 4

START UPS: Geometry

Geometry Unit

2-dimensional shapes

□ square

▭ rectangle

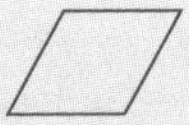

▱ rhombus

▱ parallelogram

▱ trapezium

Note: quadrilaterals have four sides

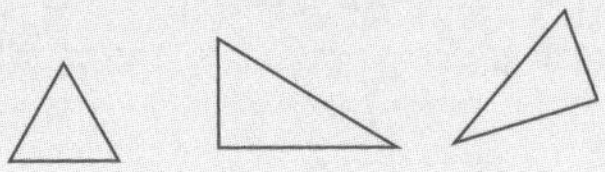

△ triangle

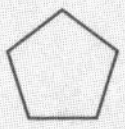

⬠ pentagon

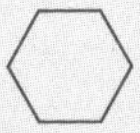

⬡ hexagon

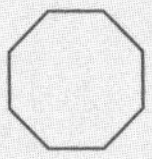

⯃ octagon

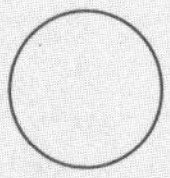

○ circle

⬭ oval

semicircle

3-dimensional shapes

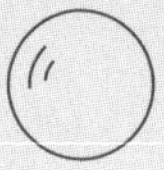

○ sphere

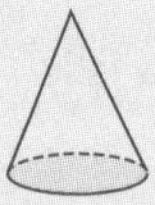

△ cone

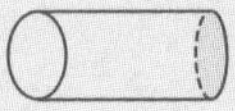

⬭ cylinder

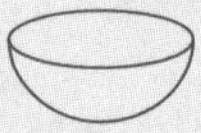

⌣ hemisphere

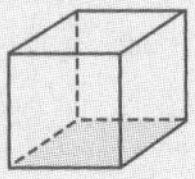

▱ cube

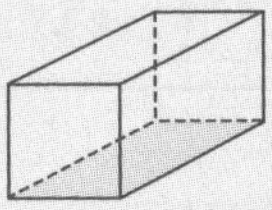

▱ square prism

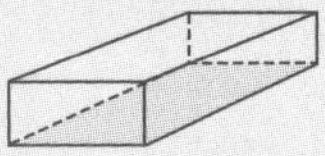

▱ rectangular prism

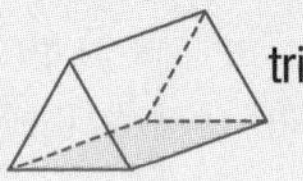

◺ triangular prism

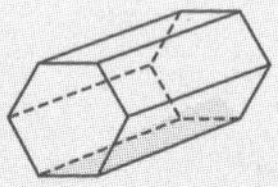

⬡ hexagonal prism

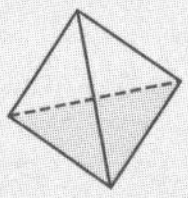

◬ triangular pyramid

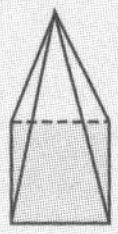

◭ square pyramid

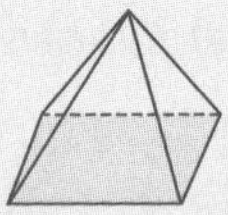

◭ rectangular pyramid

UNIT 1

See START UPS page 1

Numbers to 999

1 Write the **number** shown by the Base ten blocks:

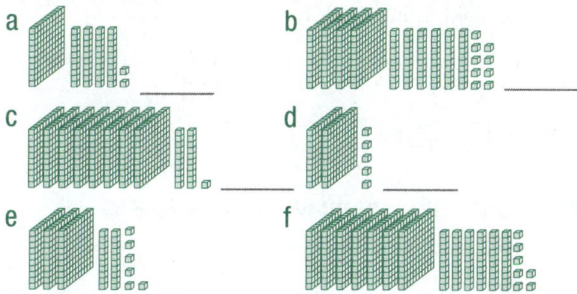

a _____

b _____

c _____

d _____

e _____

f _____

2 Write the **number** shown by the abacus:

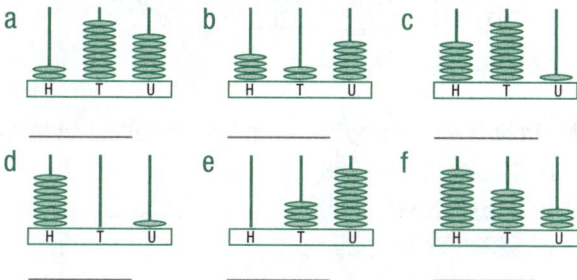

a _____ b _____ c _____

d _____ e _____ f _____

3 Write each of the following numbers in **words**:

a 226 _____

b 416 _____

c 325 _____

d 56 _____

e 989 _____

f 102 _____

4 Write each number as a **numeral**:

a one hundred and sixty-two _____

b eight hundred and twenty-one _____

c three hundred and ninety-nine _____

d eighty-six _____

e five hundred and thirteen _____

f nine hundred and two _____

5 Write the **number** shown by the Base ten blocks:

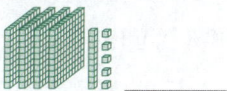

_____

6 Write the **number** shown by the abacus:

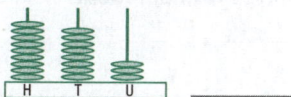

_____

7 Write 621 in **words**.

_____

8 Write three hundred and sixteen as a **numeral**.

_____

9 Circle the number which is **larger**:
two hundred and fifty or 215.

UNIT 2

See START UPS page 1

Place value

1 Write the **number** shown by the Base ten blocks or the abacus:

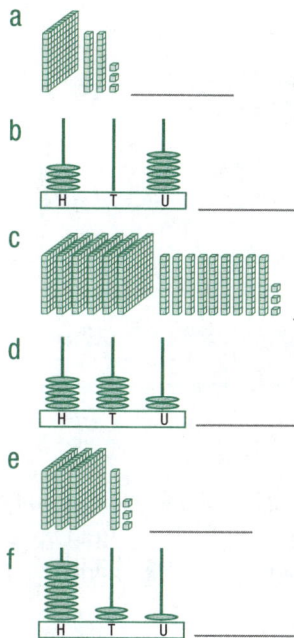

a _____

b _____

c _____

d _____

e

f _____

2 What is the **value** of the 5 in each of the following numbers?

a 215 _____   b 506 _____   c 352 _____

d 105 _____   e 659 _____   f 599 _____

3 Circle the **larger** number:

a 206 or 306   b 491 or 914   c 227 or 272

d 375 or 753   e 609 or 690   f 111 or 101

4 Write the **next** number after the one given:

a 206 _____   b 399 _____   c 429 _____

d 689 _____   e 901 _____   f 860 _____

5 Write the **number** shown by the abacus:

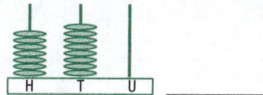

_____

6 What is the **value** of the 5 in the number 650?

_____

7 Circle the **larger** number of 215 or 251.

8 Write the **next** number after 309. _____

9 What is the **value** of the 8 in the following number:
six hundred and eighteen? _____

Numbers to 9999

1 Write the **numeral** for each of the following:

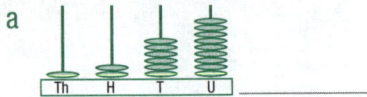

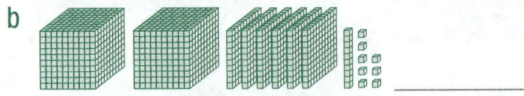

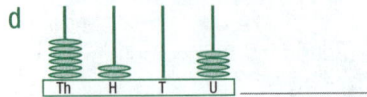

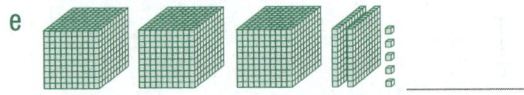

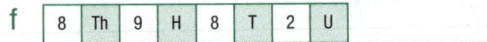

a

_____

b

_____

c

| 9 | Th | 3 | H | 4 | T | 6 | U |

_____

d

_____

e

_____

f

| 8 | Th | 9 | H | 8 | T | 2 | U |

_____

2 How many **digits** are in each of the following numbers?

a 26____   b 489____   c 1289____
d 1000____   e 4249____   f 8605____

3 Write as a **numeral**:

a five thousand, three hundred and seventy-two

_____

b two thousand, six hundred and eighty _____
c eight thousand, two hundred and ninety-five

_____

d six thousand, seven hundred and six _____
e two thousand, one hundred and fifty-nine

_____

f three thousand, four hundred and twenty-five

_____

4 Write in **words**:

a 6308 _____
b 5251 _____
c 1006 _____
d 1329 _____
e 9909 _____
f 3266 _____

5 Write the **numeral** for:

| 5 | Th | 0 | H | 2 | T | 1 | U |

_____

6 How many **digits** are there in the number 2603? ____

7 Write three thousand, and forty-nine as a **numeral**.

_____

8 Write 2346 in **words**. _____
_____

9 Draw a **picture** to represent
six thousand, and twenty-two.

Ordering numbers (1)

1 What is the **value** in the hundreds position in each of
the following numbers?

a 206 _____   b 2168 _____
c 4916 _____   d 4026 _____
e 1825 _____   f 39 _____

2 Write the **missing numbers** in the spaces:

a 408, 409, _____, 411
b 201, 211, 221, _____
c 887, 888, 889, _____
d 390, 380, _____, 360
e 501, 401, _____, 201
f 903, 902, 901, _____

3 Order the following numbers from **smallest to largest**:

a 220, 210, 236, 206 _____
b 326, 245, 691, 589 _____
c 529, 295, 952, 259 _____
d 786, 687, 678, 876 _____
e 503, 609, 805, 302 _____
f 989, 998, 976, 980 _____

4 Order the numbers from **largest to smallest**:

a 301, 205, 603, 103 _____
b 46, 64, 84, 44 _____
c 119, 125, 108, 132 _____
d 406, 605, 506, 305 _____
e 972, 876, 792, 899 _____
f 520, 580, 511, 536 _____

5 What is the **value** in the hundreds position in the
number 15 082? _____

6 Write the **missing number** in the space:
687, 688, 689, _____

7 Order the numbers from **smallest to largest**:
208, 691, 298, 198 _____

8 Order the numbers from **largest to smallest**:
526, 896, 325, 696 _____

9 Order the following numbers from **smallest to largest**:
four hundred and twenty-nine, three hundred and eleven,
four hundred and eight-five, five hundred and six,
two hundred and ninety-one

_____
_____
_____

Counting by tens (1)

1 **Count the total number** of pencils in each of the following:

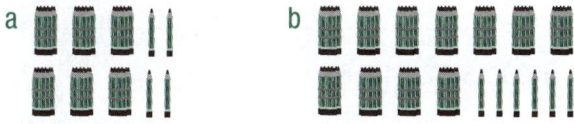

a

b

c

d

e

f

2 **Count forwards by tens** to complete the sequence:

a 10, 20, 30, _____, _____, _____
b 100, 110, 120, _____, _____, _____
c 70, 80, 90, _____, _____, _____
d 250, 260, 270, _____, _____, _____
e 3, 13, 23, _____, _____, _____
f 352, 362, 372, _____, _____, _____

3 **Count backwards by tens** to complete the sequence:

a 100, 90, 80, _____, _____, _____
b 500, 490, 480, _____, _____, _____
c 50, 40, 30, _____, _____, _____
d 370, 360, 350, _____, _____, _____
e 215, 205, 195, _____, _____, _____
f 437, 427, 417, _____, _____, _____

4 Write the **missing numbers** to complete the sequence:

a 82, 92, _____, 112, _____
b _____, 66, 76, _____, 96
c 403, 413, _____, _____, 443
d 295, _____, 275, 265, _____
e 350, _____, 330, _____, 310
f 97, _____, _____, 67, 57

5 **Count the total number** of pencils:

6 **Count forwards by tens** to complete the sequence:

56, 66, 76, _____, _____, _____

7 **Count backwards by tens** to complete the sequence:

122, 112, 102, _____, _____, _____

8 Write the **missing numbers** to complete the sequence:

94, _____, 114, _____, 134

9 What is the **next** number in the sequence?

1230, 1330, 1430, 1530, _____

Counting by tens (2)

1 **Complete**:

a 860 $\xrightarrow{+10}$ _____   b 430 $\xrightarrow{-10}$ _____
c 920 $\xrightarrow{+10}$ _____   d 65 $\xrightarrow{-10}$ _____
e 552 $\xrightarrow{+10}$ _____   e 741 $\xrightarrow{-10}$ _____

2 **Count forwards by tens** to complete the sequence:

a 40, 50, 60, _____, _____, _____
b 75, 85, 95, _____, _____, _____
c 33, 43, 53, _____, _____, _____
d 8, 18, 28, _____, _____, _____
e 156, 166, 176, _____, _____, _____
f 367, 377, 387, _____, _____, _____

3 **Count backwards by tens** to complete the sequence:

a 110, 100, 90, _____, _____, _____
b 150, 140, 130, _____, _____, _____
c 189, 179, 169, _____, _____, _____
d 83, 73, 63, _____, _____, _____
e 411, 401, 391, _____, _____, _____
f 856, 846, 836, _____, _____, _____

4 **Complete** the spaces:

a 120, _____, 140, _____, 160, 170, _____
b 325, 335, _____, _____, 365, _____, _____
c _____, 856, 866, _____, _____, 896, _____
d 400, 390, _____, _____, 360, _____, 340
e 555, _____, 535, _____, 515, _____, _____
f _____, 916, _____, 896, _____, _____, 866

5 **Complete**: 272 $\xrightarrow{+10}$ _____

6 **Count forwards by tens** to complete the sequence:

123, 133, 143, _____, _____, _____

7 **Count backwards by tens** to complete the sequence:

377, 367, 357, _____, _____, _____

8 **Complete** the sequence:

961, _____, 941, 931, _____, _____, 901

9 a **Count forwards by tens**, starting at 1065:

1065, _____, _____, _____, _____

b **Count backwards by tens**, starting at 1432:

1432, _____, _____, _____, _____

Counting by hundreds

1 **Complete** the table:

	100 less	Number	100 more
a		400	
b		550	
c		921	
d		763	
e		1230	
f		1569	

2 **Count forwards by hundreds** to complete the sequences:

a 100, 200, 300, _____, _____, _____

b 98, 198, 298, _____, _____, _____

c 451, 551, 651, _____, _____, _____

d 750, 850, 950, _____, _____, _____

e 1270, 1370, 1470, _____, _____

f 2896, 2996, 3096, _____, _____

3 **Count backwards by hundreds** to complete the sequences:

a 900, 800, 700, _____, _____, _____

b 801, 701, 601, _____, _____, _____

c 560, 460, 360, _____, _____, _____

d 799, 699, 599, _____, _____, _____

e 1845, 1745, 1645, _____, _____

f 3166, 3066, 2966, _____, _____

4 **Complete** the sequences:

a 117, _____, 317, _____, 517, _____

b 140, _____, _____, 440, _____, 640

c _____, 505, 605, _____, _____, 905

d 832, 732, _____, _____, 432, _____

e 516, _____, _____, 216, _____, 16

f _____, 625, 525, _____, _____, 225

5 **Complete:**

100 less	Number	100 more
	865	

6 **Count forwards by hundreds** to complete the sequences:

1485, 1585, 1685, _____, _____

7 **Count backwards by hundreds** to complete the sequences:

763, 663, 563, _____, _____, _____

8 **Complete** the sequence:

842, _____, _____, 1142, 1242

9 a **Count forwards by hundreds** starting at 1999:

1999, _____, _____, _____

b **Count backwards by hundreds** starting at 2555:

2555, _____, _____, _____

Ordering numbers (2)

1 Arrange the numbers from **smallest to largest**:

a 14, 19, 6, 7, 2

_____

b 26, 45, 32, 11, 18

_____

c 98, 75, 86, 66, 73

_____

d 486, 496, 346, 248, 325

_____

e 527, 752, 896, 666, 519

_____

f 1027, 1170, 1005, 1279, 1156

_____

2 Write the **smallest** possible number using all the digits given:

a 9, 6, 4 _____   b 3, 7, 5 _____

c 8, 1, 3 _____   d 8, 0, 2 _____

e 1, 5, 9, 3 _____   f 8, 7, 6, 1 _____

3 Write the **largest** possible number using all the digits given:

a 3, 2, 6 _____   b 4, 8, 6 _____

c 1, 0, 9 _____   d 1, 2, 2 _____

e 1, 0, 6, 5 _____   f 3, 9, 8, 6 _____

4 **True or false?**

a 426 > 416 _____   b 871 < 325 _____

c 872 < 596 _____   d 285 > 125 _____

e 1089 > 1000 _____   f 2467 < 2264 _____

5 Arrange the numbers from **smallest to largest**:

1269, 1437, 1186, 1286, 1372

_____

6 Write the **smallest** possible number using the digits:

6, 0, 4 _____

7 Write the **largest** possible number using the digits:

6, 8, 9, 7 _____

8 **True or false?** 989 < 998 _____

9 Add the sign, **< or > or =**, to make the number sentence correct:

one thousand five hundred and seventy-six _____ 1765

Counting forwards and backwards

1 **Start** at:

a 25 and count forwards 3 _____

b 25 and count forwards 8 _____

c 25 and count forwards 9 _____

d 25 and count forwards 11 _____

e 25 and count forwards 6 _____

f 25 and count forwards 5 _____

2 **Start** at:

a 39 and count backwards 5 _____

b 39 and count backwards 9 _____

c 39 and count backwards 7 _____

d 39 and count backwards 11 _____

e 39 and count backwards 3 _____

f 39 and count backwards 20 _____

3 **Start** at 51 and:

a go forwards 6 _____

b now go forwards 5 _____

c now go backwards 3 _____

d now go backwards 2 _____

e now go forwards 7 _____

f now go forwards 10 _____

4 **Start** at 89 and:

a go backwards 9 _____

b now go backwards 3 _____

c now go forwards 7 _____

d now go backwards 2 _____

e now go forwards 8 _____

f now go forwards 6 _____

5 **Start** at 36 and count forwards 7. _____

6 **Start** at 23 and count backwards 5. _____

7 **Start** at 42 and go forwards 6 and then backwards 8.

_____

8 **Start** at 55 and go backwards 3 and then forwards 10.

_____

9 I **start** at 45.

a How many do I need to go forwards to stop at 52?

_____

b How many do I need to go backwards to stop at 37?

_____

Patterns (1)

1 Continue the **pattern** modelled with the shapes:

a ▲ ■ ▲ ■   b ▲ ▼ ▲ ▼

c ● ◆ ♠ ● ◆ ♠   d

e

f

2 Complete each number **pattern**:

a 2, 4, 6, _____, _____, _____

b 8, 16, 24, _____, _____, _____

c 1, 3, 5, _____, _____, _____

d 10, 15, 20, _____, _____, _____

e 6, 9, 12, _____, _____, _____

f 21, 23, 25, _____, _____, _____

3 Write the **next five** numbers for each of the patterns by following the rules:

a Make a pattern by adding 4: 2, _____

b Make a pattern by adding 3: 1, _____

c Make a pattern by adding 4: 3, _____

d Make a pattern by adding 3: 10, _____

e Make a pattern by adding 2: 20, _____

f Make a pattern by adding 5:

100, _____

4 Use **words** to describe each pattern:

a 4, 8, 12, 16 _____

b 48, 24, 12, 6 _____

c 1, 2, 4, 8, 16 _____

d 100, 90, 80, 70 _____

e 200, 100, 50, 25 _____

f 7, 14, 21, 28 _____

5 Continue the **pattern**:

6 Complete the **pattern**: 20, 22, 24, _____, _____, _____

7 Write the **next five** numbers for the rule. Make a pattern by adding 5:   4, _____

8 Use **words** to describe the pattern: 7, 10, 13, 16, 19

_____

9 **Complete** the pattern: 2, 7, 22, 47, _____, _____

Expanding 3-digit numbers

1 Use the **number expander** to expand the following numbers:

a 226

	H	T		U

b 409

	H	T		U

c 670

	H	T		U

d 111

	H	T		U

e 80

	H	T		U

f 802

	H	T		U

2 Write the **numeral** for each of the following numbers:

a 600 + 20 + 5 _____

b 200 + 60 + 9 _____

c 300 + 7 _____

d 800 + 30 + 6 _____

e 400 + 80 _____

f 900 + 90 + 9 _____

3 **Expand** each of the following numbers:

a 826 _____

b 270 _____

c 402 _____

d 989 _____

e 725 _____

f 519 _____

4 Write the **value** of each underlined digit:

a 6̲46 _____

b 29̲3 _____

c 411̲ _____

d 85̲3 _____

e 1̲98 _____

f 260̲ _____

5 Use the **number expander** to expand the number 507.

	H	T		U

6 Write the **numeral** of 700 + 50 + 3. _____

7 **Expand** the number 613. _____

8 Write the **value** of the underlined digit: 31̲5 _____

9 What number comes just **before** 340? _____

Expanding 4-digit numbers

1 Write the **number** shown on each abacus:

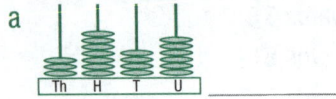

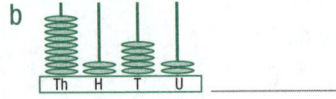

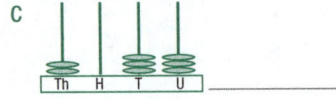

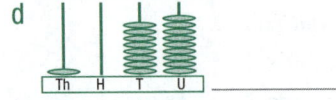

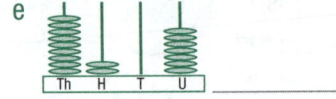

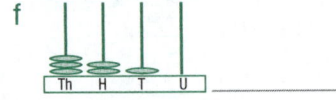

a

b

c

d

e

f

2 Write the **numeral** for:

a 1000 + 600 + 20 + 3 _____

b 4000 + 300 + 80 + 7 _____

c 2000 + 400 + 60 + 5 _____

d 8000 + 40 + 2 _____

e 5000 + 900 + 1 _____

f 7000 + 900 + 30 + 8 _____

3 **Expand** each of the following numbers:

a 6241 _____

b 7777 _____

c 2049 _____

d 1406 _____

e 3220 _____

f 9898 _____

4 Write the **value** of each underlined digit:

a 2̲689 _____   b 346̲8 _____

c 141̲1 _____   d 8̲309 _____

e 6̲440 _____   f 7̲877 _____

5 Write the **number** shown on the abacus:

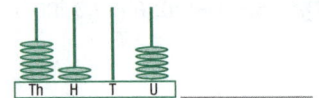

6 Write the **numeral** for:

3000 + 700 + 60 + 2 _____

7 **Expand** 5275. _____

8 Write the **value** of the underlined digit in 23̲07.

_____

9 What is the number that comes just **before,** and the number that comes just **after,** 3299?

_____ , _____

4-digit numbers

1 **Expand** each of the following numbers:

a 4526 _____

b 6849 _____

c 8407 _____

d 9260 _____

e 3066 _____

f 1299 _____

2 Write the numbers **before and after** the ones given:

a _____ , 97, _____

b _____ , 8460, _____

c _____ , 3426, _____

d _____ , 368, _____

e _____ , 8877, _____

f _____ , 649, _____

3 Write each set of numbers from **smallest to largest**:

a 8752, 7582, 8572, 2578

_____

b 1999, 3420, 2870, 2500

_____

c 870, 249, 1672, 972

_____

d 1111, 4213, 2671, 1098

_____

e 3264, 4628, 3999, 4086

_____

f 9989, 9685, 9990, 9329

_____

4 Write down the **largest** number possible using all the digits supplied:

a 1, 4, 9, 2 _____   b 3, 6, 7, 8 _____

c 3, 2, 4, 8 _____   d 2, 6, 6, 4 _____

e 1, 0, 9, 2 _____   f 1, 2, 4, 3 _____

5 **Expand** the number 2310.

_____

6 Write the numbers **before and after** the number 3099.

_____ , _____

7 Write the set of numbers from **smallest to largest**.
1021, 1051, 1161, 909, 1211

_____

8 Write the **largest** number possible with all the digits:
1, 8, 9, 3 _____

9 Write the **smallest** number possible in words using all the digits: 4, 3, 2, 5 _____

Ordering numbers (3)

1 Arrange each set of numbers from **largest to smallest**:

a 62, 85, 36, 95, 72

_____

b 110, 115, 135, 102, 127

_____

c 121, 563, 273, 429, 333

_____

d 926, 852, 608, 739, 886

_____

e 1026, 1139, 1485, 1269, 1312

_____

f 1789, 1990, 1995, 1852, 1763

_____

2 Write the **largest** possible number with all the given digits:

a 1, 4, 6 _____   b 5, 3, 6 _____

c 8, 9, 7 _____   d 6, 5, 7 _____

e 1, 7, 7, 9 _____   f 1, 3, 0, 5 _____

3 Write the **smallest** possible number with all the given digits:

a 3, 2, 9 _____   b 6, 7, 4 _____

c 5, 2, 5 _____   d 1, 3, 2 _____

e 1, 4, 6, 3 _____   f 4, 1, 9, 3 _____

4 Circle the **larger** number in each pair:

a 94 or 82   b 110 or 101

c 805 or 914   d 583 or 538

e 1935 or 1906   f 1628 or 1529

5 Arrange the numbers from **largest to smallest**:
15, 106, 94, 32, 87

_____

6 Write the **largest** possible number with all the digits:
8, 7, 1, 3 _____

7 Write the **smallest** possible number with all the digits:
7, 9, 8 _____

8 Circle the **larger** number in the pair:
1048 or 1408

9 Write all of the different **combinations** of 3-digit numbers with the following digits: 4, 3, 2.

_____

Odd and even numbers

1 Which of the following numbers are **odd**? Circle them.

a 25　　　　b 210　　　　c 386

d 18　　　　e 147　　　　f 56

2 Which of the following numbers are **even**? Circle them.

a 14　　　　　　b 351

c 568　　　　　d 56

e 315　　　　　f 90

3 Complete the following patterns by **counting by twos**:

a 2, 4, 6, _____, _____, _____

b 20, 22, 24, _____, _____, _____

c 58, 60, 62, _____, _____, _____

d 102, 104, 106, _____, _____, _____

e 128, 130, 132, _____, _____, _____

f 148, 150, 152, _____, _____, _____

4 Group the following items into **groups of two**:

a △ △ △ △ △
　△ △ △ △ △

b ☆ ☆ ☆
　☆ ☆ ☆

c ○ ○ ○ ○
　○ ○ ○ ○

d ☐ ☐
　☐ ☐

e ♡ ♡ ♡ ♡
　♡ ♡ ♡ ♡
　♡ ♡ ♡ ♡

f ○ ○ ○ ○
　○ ○ ○ ○
　○ ○ ○ ○
　○ ○ ○ ○

5 Is 48 an **odd** number? _____

6 Is 60 an **even** number? _____

7 Complete the pattern **counting by twos**:

190, 192, 194, _____, _____, _____

8 Group the stars into **groups of 2**.

☆ ☆ ☆ ☆ ☆ ☆ ☆ ☆ ☆ ☆ ☆ ☆ ☆ ☆ ☆ ☆ ☆ ☆

9 All of the numbers that end in 0, 2, 4, 6 and 8 are _____. All of the numbers that end in 1, 3, 5, 7 and 9 are _____. Explain why:

_____

_____

_____

Looking for ten when adding

1 Look for **combinations of 10** first when adding the following numbers:

a $4 + 2 + 6 =$ _____　　b $7 + 3 + 5 =$ _____

c $9 + 8 + 1 =$ _____　　d $8 + 2 + 4 =$ _____

e $5 + 3 + 5 =$ _____　　f $9 + 1 + 5 =$ _____

2 Look for **combinations of 10** first when adding the following numbers:

a	b	c	d	e	f
3	7	9	8	5	1
4	3	6	2	6	3
+6	+5	+1	+2	+5	+9

3 Look for **combinations** first when adding:

a $4 + 3 + 16 =$ _____　　b $15 + 7 + 5 =$ _____

c $12 + 2 + 8 =$ _____　　d $13 + 7 + 9 =$ _____

e $18 + 3 + 2 =$ _____　　f $14 + 8 + 6 =$ _____

4 a There are 3 pencils, 6 textas and 7 crayons on the table. How many items are there **altogether**? _____

b There are 6 trucks, 4 cars and 7 motorbikes in the car park. How many vehicles are there **altogether**?

_____

c There are 5 apples, 2 pears and 5 oranges on the bench. How many pieces of fruit are there **altogether**? _____

d There are 6 chickens, 2 parrots and 4 ducks on the farm. How many birds are there **altogether**? _____

e There are 8 footballs, 9 soccer balls and 2 volleyballs on the field. How many balls are there **altogether**?

_____

f There are 9 DVDs, 5 videos and 1 CD on the shelf. How many items are there **altogether**? _____

5 Look for **combinations of 10** first when adding:

$7 + 6 + 4 =$ _____

6 Look for **combinations of 10** first when adding:

8
2
+9
—

7 Look for **combinations** first when adding:

$15 + 6 + 5 =$ _____

8 There are 3 toy sheep, 8 toy horses and 7 toy cars on the floor. How many toys are there **altogether**? _____

9 A doll costs $8, a ball costs $4, a teddy costs $7 and a hat costs $3. If a hat, teddy and ball were purchased, what would be the **total** cost? _____

Adding to 20

1 **Complete**:

a | +   b   +

_____ + _____ = _____   _____ + _____ = _____

c   + | d   +

_____ + _____ = _____   _____ + _____ = _____

e   +   f | + |

_____ + _____ = _____   _____ + _____ = _____

2 **Complete**:

a   8 + 11 = _____   b   7 + 5 = _____
c   9 + 6 = _____   d   10 + 7 = _____
e   8 + 8 = _____   f   6 + 7 = _____

3 Write **number sentences** and find the answer to:

a   six plus five equals _____
b   thirteen plus six equals _____
c   three plus seven equals _____
d   nine plus four equals _____
e   five plus twelve equals _____
f   seven plus two equals _____

4 **Complete** the following:

a   + | 3   b   + | 8   c   + | 11

4		7		2
5		8		3
6		9		4
7		10		5

d   + | 5   e   + | 15   f   + | 7

1		2		3
6		1		5
9		4		11
14		3		8

5 **Complete**: | +

_____ + _____ = _____

6 **Complete**: 15 + 3 = _____

7 Write a **number sentence** and find the answer to:
fourteen plus three equals _____

8 **Complete**:   + | 4

| 8 |
| 6 |
| 12 |
| 15 |

9 Write the **answer** to: 3 + 4 + 7 + 5 = _____

Adding to 50

1 Write and **solve** the number sentences for each of the following:

a   +   b   +

_____   _____

c | +   d   +

_____   _____

e   +   f   + |

_____   _____

2 **Complete** the following:

a   12 + 15 = _____   b   27 + 11 = _____
c   36 + 12 = _____   d   40 + 9 = _____
e   17 + 22 = _____   f   25 + 13 = _____

3 **Find** the correct answer for each question:

18   44   37   38   29   46

a   21 + 23 = _____
b   13 + 25 = _____
c   16 + 13 = _____
d   8 + 10 = _____
e   34 + 12 = _____
f   24 + 13 = _____

4 Find the **missing numbers**:

a   20 + _____ = 35
b   36 + _____ = 38
c   11 + _____ = 32
d   12 + _____ = 35
e   24 + _____ = 48
f   36 + _____ = 47

5 Write and **solve** the number sentence for:

| +

_____

6 **Complete**:   23 + 14 = _____

7 **Find** the correct answer for 32 + 14:

36   46   40   42   44   30

8 Find the **missing number**:   21 + _____ = 35

9 Draw a **picture** to
show the number
sentence and
solve it:

16 + 12 = _____

Adding to 99 (1)

1 Write and **solve** the number sentences for each of the following:

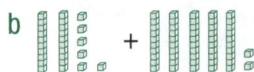

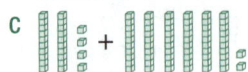

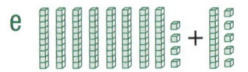

a +

b +

_____   _____

c +

d +

_____   _____

e +

f +

_____   _____

2 **Complete** each of the following:

a
T	U
4	6
+ 1	2

b
T	U
7	2
+ 2	6

c
T	U
6	0
+ 3	9

d
T	U
8	4
+ 1	2

e
T	U
4	5
+ 4	3

f
T	U
5	2
+ 3	7

3 **Solve** the following:

a $50 + 25 =$ _____   b $28 + 11 =$ _____

c $73 + 14 =$ _____   d $36 + 41 =$ _____

e $26 + 52 =$ _____   f $84 + 15 =$ _____

4 **Find** the correct answer for each question:

93   56   78   87   74   75

a $24 + 32 =$ b $34 + 53 =$

c $61 + 17 =$ d $32 + 43 =$

e $53 + 21 =$ f $61 + 32 =$

5 Write and **solve** the number sentence for:

 + _____

6 **Complete**:

T	U
6	5
+ 2	3

7 **Solve**: $56 + 31 =$ _____

8 **Find** the correct answer for $17 + 62$:

77   83   73   89   79   85   91

9 Selecting from the following numbers, write two **sums** that equal 48.

24   34   14   40   18   30   32

_____ , _____

Adding to 99 (2)

1 **Complete** the following:

a   4 tens and 6 units   b   2 tens and 3 units
     + 3 tens and 2 units   + 4 tens and 6 units
     _____   _____

c   8 tens and 2 units   d   5 tens and 5 units
     + 1 ten and 2 units   + 2 tens and 3 units
     _____   _____

e   7 tens and 7 units   f   5 tens and 4 units
     + 2 tens and 1 unit   + 1 ten and 5 units
     _____   _____

2 **Complete**:

a
T	U
3	0
+ 1	5

b
T	U
4	4
+ 1	3

c
T	U
5	6
+ 2	3

d
T	U
4	8
+ 1	1

e
T	U
7	2
+ 1	7

f
T	U
8	6
+ 1	2

3 **Find** the following:

a $14 + 31 =$ _____   b $28 + 41 =$ _____

c $83 + 15 =$ _____   d $62 + 35 =$ _____

e $43 + 50 =$ _____   f $80 + 9 =$ _____

4 **Solve** number sentences to find the total number of each of the items altogether:

a 15 apples and 23 apples _____

b 23 sweets and 71 sweets _____

c 36 buttons and 22 buttons _____

d 85 paperclips and 13 paperclips _____

e 32 pencils and 47 pencils _____

f 63 books and 14 books _____

5 **Complete**:   5 tens and 3 units
                          + 4 tens and 1 unit
                          _____

6 **Complete**:

T	U
3	4
+ 2	3

7 **Find**: $65 + 22 =$ _____

8 **Solve** a number sentence for:
56 mice and 23 mice—how many mice altogether?

_____

9 There are 14 boys, 13 girls and the teacher in a class. **How** many people in the class room? _____

Adding to 99 (3)

1 Write **number sentences** and find the answer to each of the following:

a thirty-seven add twenty-one _____

b fifty-five plus thirteen _____

c add twenty-five to forty _____

d the total of thirty-three and sixty-five _____

e seventy-six plus twenty-two _____

f the total of twelve and eighty _____

2 **Complete** each of the following:

a
```
  T | U
  9 | 1
+   | 8
```

b
```
  T | U
  6 | 3
+ 1 | 4
```

c
```
  T | U
  5 | 4
+ 3 | 3
```

d
```
  T | U
  2 | 6
+ 4 | 3
```

e
```
  T | U
  1 | 7
+ 7 | 2
```

f
```
  T | U
  2 | 0
+ 6 | 9
```

3 **Find** the following:

a $48 + $31 = _____   b $66 + $22 = _____

c $35 + $43 = _____   d $15 + $52 = _____

e $27 + $41 = _____   f $73 + $25 = _____

4 **Complete** the boxes:

a
```
  7 2
+ 1 □
  □ 6
```

b
```
  2 □
+ 3 7
  □ 9
```

c
```
  4 0
+ 2 □
  □ 8
```

d
```
  1 2
+ □ 2
  6 □
```

e
```
  □ 5
+ 3 □
  7 8
```

f
```
  □ □
+ 4 4
  9 9
```

5 Write a **number sentence** and find the answer to forty-one plus twenty-seven. _____

6 **Complete**:
```
  T | U
  2 | 6
+ 7 | 1
```

7 **Find**: $23 + $53 = _____

8 **Complete** the boxes:
```
    2 □
+ □ 6
  7 9
```

9 **Complete**:

Wheel: centre + 12; segments: 72 8, 14, 23, 35, 41, 57, 66

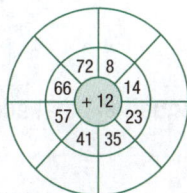

Adding with trading to 99 (1)

1 **Complete** the number sentence using the models:

a _____ + ___ = _____   b _____ + ___ = _____

c _____ + ___ = _____   d _____ + ___ = _____

e _____ + ___ = _____   f _____ + ___ = _____

2 **Estimate** each sum by first rounding each number to the **nearest ten**:

a 18 + 15 _____

b 28 + 35 _____

c 52 + 39 _____

d 17 + 37 _____

e 63 + 28 _____

f 46 + 29 _____

3 Use the **jump strategy** to complete the spaces:

a 38 + 19 = 38 + 10 + 9 = _____

b 45 + 28 = 45 + 20 + 8 = _____

c 27 + 36 = 27 + 30 + ___ = _____

d 48 + 15 = 48 + 10 + ___ = _____

e 67 + 24 = 67 + _____ + ___ = _____

f 58 + 34 = 58 + _____ + ___ = _____

4 Complete each of the following using the **jump strategy**:

a 38 + 16 = _____   b 46 + 15 = _____

c 83 + 9 = _____   d 65 + 18 = _____

e 79 + 15 = _____   f 58 + 25 = _____

5 **Complete** the number sentence using the models:

_____ + _____ = _____

6 **Estimate** the sum by first rounding each number to the **nearest ten**:

76 + 17 _____

7 Use the **jump strategy** to complete the spaces:

56 + 37 = 56 + _____ + ___ = _____

8 Complete using the **jump strategy**: 78 + 13 _____

9 What is the **total** cost of buying a tennis ball which costs 35c and a yoyo which costs 28c?

_____

Adding with trading to 99 (2)

1 Use the models to complete the **number sentences**:

a _____ + _____ = _____   b _____ + _____ = _____

c _____ + _____ = _____   d _____ + _____ = _____

e _____ + _____ = _____   f _____ + _____ = _____

2 Complete each of the following using the **jump strategy**:

a 65 + 18 = _____   b 47 + 35 = _____

c 28 + 58 = _____   d 35 + 29 = _____

e 53 + 19 = _____   f 34 + 37 = _____

3 **Complete** each of the following:

a	T	U
	7	7
+		9

b	T	U
	4	5
+		8

c	T	U
	6	6
+		5

d	T	U
	8	8
+		4

e	T	U
	7	9
+		3

f	T	U
	5	7
+		7

4 **Complete** each of the following:

a	T	U
	6	5
+	2	8

b	T	U
	3	7
+	2	7

c	T	U
	3	6
+	5	7

d	T	U
	4	9
+	1	1

e	T	U
	3	4
+	4	8

f	T	U
	5	5
+	1	6

5 Complete the **number sentence** using the models:

_____ + _____ = _____

6 Use the **jump strategy** for: 55 + 28 = _____

7 **Complete**:

	T	U
	4	5
+		8

8 **Complete**:

	T	U
	4	3
+	2	9

9 Thirty-five cows and twenty-seven sheep were in the paddock. How many animals were there **altogether**?

_____

Adding with trading to 99 (3)

1 **Complete** each of the following:

a	3	8
+	5	6

b	3	6
+	5	6

c	5	9
+	2	7

d	7	6
+	1	5

e	5	6
+	2	8

f	2	5
+	5	9

2 **Complete** each of the following:

a $56
  + $ 8

b $89
  + $ 7

c $36
  + $44

d $19
  + $53

e $38
  + $38

f $49
  + $32

3 Find the **total** number of:

a 28 pencils and 53 pencils _____

b 25 hats and 36 hats _____

c 54 counters and 27 counters _____

d 15 ducks and 19 swans _____

e 36 trees and 47 trees _____

f 27 beads and 48 beads _____

4 Complete each of the following **addition wheels**:

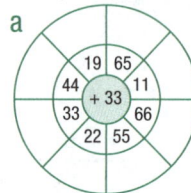

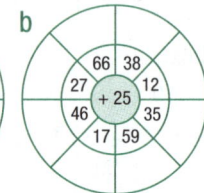

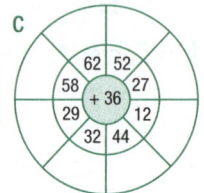

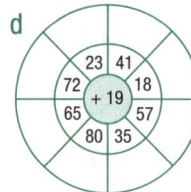

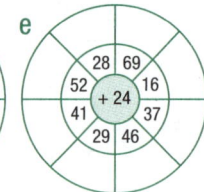

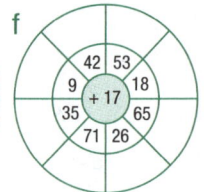

a (+ 33): 19, 65, 11, 66, 55, 22, 33, 44

b (+ 25): 66, 38, 12, 35, 59, 17, 46, 27

c (+ 36): 62, 52, 27, 12, 44, 32, 29, 58

d (+ 19): 23, 41, 18, 57, 35, 80, 65, 72

e (+ 24): 28, 69, 16, 37, 46, 29, 41, 52

f (+ 17): 42, 53, 18, 65, 26, 71, 35, 9

5 **Complete**:

	6	3
+	2	9

6 **Complete**:

    $46
  + $29

7 John paid 39c for an apple and 27c for a banana. How much did he spend in **total**? _____

8 Complete the **addition wheel**:

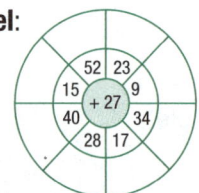

(+ 27): 52, 23, 9, 34, 17, 28, 40, 15

9 Create four different **equations** that add to 52.

_____ , _____ ,

_____ , _____

Adding three or more numbers

1 **Complete** each of the following:

a	T	U		b	T	U		c	T	U
	3	9			1	6			3	0
	2	4			2	8			3	4
+ 1		3		+ 3		9		+ 1		7

d	T	U		e	T	U		f	T	U
	1	4			4	0			2	6
	3	6			1	9			2	7
+ 2		3		+ 2		6		+ 2		8

2 **Complete** each of the following:

a 14 + 18 + 26 + 32 _____

b 12 + 25 + 16 + 25 _____

c 12 + 13 + 14 + 15 _____

d 17 + 19 + 25 + 32 _____

e 30 + 14 + 17 + 9 _____

f 8 + 16 + 23 + 7 _____

3 Find the **total** number of:

a 27 eggs, 25 eggs and 29 eggs _____

b 15 fish, 23 fish and 19 fish _____

c 22 sweets, 19 sweets and 30 sweets _____

d 23 bees, 36 bees and 28 bees _____

e 27 L, 17 L and 19 L of water _____

f 16 cars, 12 cars and 15 cars _____

4 Complete each **magic square**:

a 15
4	9	2
8		6

b 33
14	9	10
12		8

c 36
11		
		12
15		13

d 21
	7	
10	3	8

e 75
20		
	25	
40		30

f 30
13		11
8		12
		7

5 **Complete**:

	T	U
	1	7
	1	6
+ 2		5

6 **Complete**: 9 + 25 + 17 + 32 _____

7 What was the **total** cost of $22, $14 and $28? _____

8 Complete the **magic square**: 66
28	18	20
		16

9 You have $100 to spend. Work out the different **combinations** of 3 items from the following that you could buy.

hat $26   game $22   book $36   tape deck $76   CD $19   calculator $23

_____

_____

Adding 3-digit numbers

1 **Complete** each of the following:

a	H	T	U		b	H	T	U		c	H	T	U
	1	4	2			5	1	3			3	4	6
+ 2	3	1		+ 2	2	5		+ 5	2	3

d	H	T	U		e	H	T	U		f	H	T	U
	1	0	7			5	0	7			4	3	2
+ 6	9	2		+ 4	2	2		+ 4	6	3

2 Complete the following with **trading** in the units:

a	H	T	U		b	H	T	U		c	H	T	U
	7	0	8			4	3	6			6	2	8
+ 2	0	6		+ 4	3	6		+ 3	0	4

d	H	T	U		e	H	T	U		f	H	T	U
	7	3	9			2	0	7			2	0	9
+ 2	4	6		+ 3	7	5		+ 7	2	8

3 Complete the addition with **trading** in the tens and units:

a 372
+ 259

b 688
+ 185

c 173
+ 258

d 238
+ 398

e 239
+ 397

f 178
+ 84

4 Find the **cost** of:

$155 Game console $180 TV $376 Bed $567 Couch $298 DVD player $265 Desk

a a TV and a DVD player _____

b a game console and desk _____

c a couch and a bed _____

d a bed and a DVD player _____

e a game console and a couch _____

f a TV and a desk _____

5 **Complete**:

	H	T	U
	2	3	2
+ 1	4	6	

6 Complete with **trading** in the units:

	H	T	U
	4	5	6
+ 1	2	8	

7 Complete with **trading** in the tens and units:

438
+ 296

8 Find the **cost** of: a DVD player $298 and speakers $325

_____

9 Write a **problem** and **solve** it for: 176 + 208

_____

UNIT 27

See START UPS page 3

Mental strategies for adding

1 Find the following by making **patterns**:

a 200 + 700 = _____

b 800 + 300 = _____

c 900 + 800 = _____

d 600 + 500 = _____

e 700 + 700 = _____

f 500 + 900 = _____

2 Find the following by looking for **tens**:

a 7 + 3 + 4 = _____

b 12 + 6 + 8 = _____

c 4 + 3 + 16 = _____

d 19 + 8 + 1 = _____

e 5 + 7 + 15 = _____

f 7 + 6 + 13 = _____

3 **Find** the following:

a 37 + 6 = _____

b 28 + 8 = _____

c 42 + 9 = _____

d 38 + 5 = _____

e 29 + 7 = _____

f 64 + 7 = _____

4 **Find** the following:

a 32 + 41 = _____

b 26 + 43 = _____

c 36 + 31 = _____

d 42 + 52 = _____

e 19 + 20 = _____

f 23 + 26 = _____

5 Find 600 + 300 = _____ by making **patterns**.

6 Find 11 + 8 + 9 = _____ by looking for **tens**.

7 **Find**: 26 + 9 _____

8 **Find**: 21 + 33 _____

9 Draw a **number line** to show the addition of 52 + 23 and find the answer.

UNIT 28

See START UPS page 3

Rounding numbers (1)

1 Answer the following:

a Is 196 **closer to** 100 or 200? _____

b Is 722 closer to 700 or 800? _____

c Is 464 closer to 400 or 500? _____

d Is 612 closer to 600 or 700? _____

e Is 873 closer to 800 or 900? _____

f Is 111 closer to 100 or 200? _____

2 Round each number to the **nearest hundred**:

a 215 _____

b 329 _____

c 476 _____

d 190 _____

e 520 _____

f 388 _____

3 Round each number to the **nearest ten**:

a 172 _____

b 429 _____

c 863 _____

d 411 _____

e 397 _____

f 208 _____

4 Answer **true or false**:

a 325 rounded to the nearest hundred is 300. _____

b 1459 rounded to the nearest hundred is 1400. _____

c 689 rounded to the nearest hundred is 700. _____

d 1590 rounded to the nearest hundred is 1500. _____

e 2395 rounded to the nearest hundred is 2400. _____

f 1475 rounded to the nearest hundred is 1500. _____

5 Is 821 **closer to** 800 or 900? _____

6 Round 482 to the **nearest hundred**. _____

7 Round 822 to the **nearest ten**. _____

8 Answer **true or false**:
779 rounded to the nearest hundred is 800. _____

9 Is 5416 **closer to** 5400 or 5500? Explain.

_____

Subtraction

1 **Answer** the following questions:
a 10 take away 6 _____
b 17 minus 5 _____
c the difference between 12 and 2 _____
d subtract 8 from 10 _____
e 14 take away 3 _____
f 9 minus 7 _____

2 Use the number line to help find the **differences**:

a 14 − 9 = _____   b 12 − 4 = _____
c 18 − 12 = _____   d 19 − 7 = _____
e 16 − 7 = _____   f 15 − 11 = _____

3 Write a **number sentence** for each of the following pictures:

a

apples
_____

b
trees
_____

c
peaches
_____

d
sweets
_____

e

cherries
_____

f

peanuts
_____

4 Find how many **are left**:
a There are 10 crayons, 3 broke. _____
b There are 15 books, 8 were borrowed. _____
c There are 20 biscuits, 12 were eaten. _____
d There were 12 shirts in the sale, 6 were sold. _____
e There were 18 sheets of paper, 7 were drawn on.
_____
f There were 9 mice in the cage, 6 escaped. _____

5 **Subtract** 4 from 14: _____

6 Find the **difference**: 13 − 7 ____
(Use the number line in question 2 to help.)

7 Write a **number sentence** for:

 _____

8 There are 20 chocolates in a box, 15 were eaten. How many **are left**? _____

9 **Complete**:

Subtraction patterns

1 **Complete** the following:
a 9 − 4 = ____   b 8 − 1 = ____
90 − 40 = _____   80 − 10 = _____
900 − 400 = _____   800 − 100 = _____
c 8 − 4 = ____   d 7 − 5 = ____
80 − 40 = _____   70 − 50 = _____
800 − 400 = _____   700 − 500 = _____
e 6 − 3 = ____   f 9 − 7 = ____
60 − 30 = _____   90 − 70 = _____
600 − 300 = _____   900 − 700 = _____

2 **Complete**:
a 9 − 2 = _____   9 − 7 = _____
b 9 − 4 = _____   9 − 5 = _____
c 11 − 5 = _____   11 − 6 = _____
d 10 − 4 = _____   10 − 6 = _____
e 12 − 9 = _____   12 − 3 = _____
f 13 − 5 = _____   13 − 8 = _____

3 **Complete** in order:

a _____   b _____

c _____   d _____

e _____   f _____

4 **Complete**:
a 8 + 3 = 11,   11 − ____ = 8,   11 − ____ = 3
b 12 + 8 = 20,   20 − ____ = 8,   20 − ____ = 12
c 14 + 5 = 19,   19 − ____ = 5,   19 − ____ = 14
d 9 + 6 = 15,   15 − ____ = 6,   15 − ____ = 9
e 6 + 7 = 13,   13 − ____ = 7,   13 − ____ = 6
f 5 + 11 = 16,   16 − ____ = 11,   16 − ____ = 5

5 **Complete**:   7 − 5 = ____
70 − 50 = _____
700 − 500 = _____

6 **Complete**:   7 + 4 = _____   4 + 7 = _____
11 − 7 = ____   11 − 4 = ____

7 **Complete**:

_____

8 **Complete**:
8 + 7 = 15,   15 − ____ = 7,   15 − ____ = 8

9 Charles has $20 in his bank account. He spends $12. How much does he have **left** in the account? _____

2-digit subtraction to 50

1 **Complete** the following:

a $35 - 8 =$ _____

b $24 - 9 =$ _____

c $32 - 3 =$ _____

d $19 - 7 =$ _____

e $27 - 8 =$ _____

f $38 - 4 =$ _____

2 Use the **jump strategy** to answer these questions:

a $30 - 12$ think $30 - 10 - 2 =$ _____

b $24 - 11$ think $24 - 10 - 1 =$ _____

c $46 - 13$ think $46 -$ _____ $- 3 =$ _____

d $47 - 22$ think $47 -$ _____ $- 2 =$ _____

e $39 - 25$ think $39 -$ _____ $-$ _____ $=$ _____

f $36 - 23$ think $36 -$ _____ $-$ _____ $=$ _____

3 **Answer** the following questions:

a $45 - 13 =$ _____

b $50 - 16 =$ _____

c $29 - 17 =$ _____

d $38 - 23 =$ _____

e $44 - 8 =$ _____

f $29 - 15 =$ _____

4 **Complete**:

a
T	U
2	7
− 1	2

b
T	U
4	9
−	7

c
T	U
1	9
−	8

d
T	U
3	6
− 1	4

e
T	U
4	6
− 2	4

f
T	U
3	6
− 2	0

5 **Complete**: $26 - 8 =$ _____

6 Use the **jump strategy** to complete:

$49 - 28$ think $49 -$ _____ $-$ _____ $=$ _____

7 **Find**: $49 - 17 =$ _____

8 **Complete**:

T	U
3	6
− 1	4

9 Draw a **diagram** to illustrate $46 - 13 =$ _____ and **solve**.

2-digit subtraction to 99

1 **Complete**:

a
T	U
9	6
− 1	5

b
T	U
7	7
− 3	5

c
T	U
6	3
− 4	1

d
T	U
8	9
− 4	7

e
T	U
5	6
− 2	5

f
T	U
4	4
− 3	2

2 **Complete**:

a
T	U
5	9
− 2	☐
3	3

b
T	U
9	9
− ☐	8
2	1

c
T	U
6	6
− 4	☐
2	4

d
T	U
8	5
− ☐	1
1	4

e
T	U
7	9
− ☐	☐
2	4

f
T	U
9	4
− ☐	☐
3	2

3 **Complete**:

a $79 - 36 =$ _____   b $89 - 57 =$ _____

c $57 - 26 =$ _____   d $75 - 21 =$ _____

e $98 - 55 =$ _____   f $64 - 43 =$ _____

4 Complete:

a   55 birds, 24 flew away. How many **left**? _____

b   79 candles, 38 used. How many **remain**? _____

c   98 flowers, 76 picked. How many **left**? _____

d   52 boxes, 41 sold. How many are **left**? _____

e   39 girls and 14 boys. How many **more** girls are there than boys? _____

f   46 cats and 21 dogs. How many **more** cats are there than dogs? _____

5 **Complete**:

T	U
8	4
− 2	3

6 **Complete**:

T	U
7	7
− ☐	☐
2	5

7 **Complete**: $66 - 54 =$ _____

8 Complete: 49 apples, 23 picked. **How many are left**?

_____

9 Yuko had 37 marbles. She gave 6 away and had 43 left. What is **wrong** with Yuko's story? _____

How many did she really have? _____

Subtraction with trading (1)

1 **Complete** each of the following:

a
T	U
2	4
−	8

b
T	U
4	2
−	9

c
T	U
7	1
−	8

d
T	U
5	3
−	9

e
T	U
4	2
−	4

f
T	U
6	1
−	5

2 **Complete** each of the following:

a
T	U
7	4
− 1	6

b
T	U
6	5
− 3	7

c
T	U
9	1
− 7	6

d
T	U
8	3
− 2	5

e
T	U
5	3
−	9

f
T	U
4	1
− 2	6

3 **Check** Malek's **subtraction** equations by repeating them yourself:

a 86 − 27 = 69   b 32 − 19 = 13   c 45 − 38 = 3
d 92 − 67 = 25   e 81 − 14 = 67   f 25 − 18 = 17

4 **Check** Tiana's **subtraction** equations by doing addition:

a
5	9	→	3	4
− 2	5		+ 2	5
3	4			

b
8	3	→	3	7
− 4	6		+ 4	6
3	7			

c
8	5	→	☐	☐
− 1	4		+ 1	4
7	1		☐	☐

d
⁸9̸	¹2	→	☐	☐
− 7	5		+ 7	5
1	7		☐	☐

e
7	5	→	☐	☐
− 2	9		+ 2	9
4	6		☐	☐

f
6	3	→	☐	☐
− 4	5		+ 4	5
1	8		☐	☐

5 **Complete**:

T	U
− 5	2
	8

6 **Complete**:

T	U
5	3
− 2	6

7 **Check** Anthony's **subtraction** equation by repeating it yourself: 63 − 48 = 15

8 **Check** Linda's **subtraction** equation by doing addition:

9	1	→	☐	☐
− 6	4		+ 6	4
2	7		☐	☐

9 Amelia bought a calculator and a book for a total of $83. If she had $91 to begin with, how much did she have **left**? _____

Subtraction with trading (2)

1 **Complete** each of the following:

a
```
  4 0
−   6
```

b
```
  6 0
−   9
```

c
```
  7 0
−   3
```

d
```
  9 0
−   8
```

e
```
  8 0
−   4
```

f
```
  5 0
−   7
```

2 **Complete** each of the following:

a
```
  8 2
− 3 8
```

b
```
  4 3
− 2 6
```

c
```
  5 5
− 3 6
```

d
```
  4 0
− 1 3
```

e
```
  9 0
− 7 5
```

f
```
  6 7
− 5 8
```

3 **Check** to see if the answer is right or wrong for each of the following equations:

a
```
  5 0
− 1 9
  3 1
```

b
```
  2 6
− 1 7
  1 1
```

c
```
  9 4
− 6 2
  3 2
```

d
```
  7 0
− 5 3
  2 7
```

e
```
  6 5
− 3 6
  3 9
```

f
```
  7 1
− 4 3
  2 8
```

4 **Complete** the boxes:

a
```
  6 7
− 1 ☐
  5 4
```

b
```
  9 7
− 3 ☐
  6 2
```

c
```
  8 5
− 6 ☐
  ☐ 7
```

d
```
  7 2
− ☐ 3
  2 ☐
```

e
```
  5 5
− ☐ ☐
  2 1
```

f
```
  7 3
− ☐ ☐
  5 8
```

5 **Complete**:
```
  9 0
−   9
```

6 **Complete**:
```
  7 3
− 5 6
```

7 **Check** the answer to:
```
  7 5
− 6 9
    6
```

8 **Complete** the boxes:
```
  6 2
− 1 ☐
  ☐ 8
```

9 Fill in the **missing boxes**:

a
```
  ☐ ☐
− 2 4
  1 2
```

b
```
  7 0
− ☐ ☐
  3 7
```

Subtraction with trading (3)

1 **Complete** each of the following:

	T	U
a	3	2
−		8

	T	U
b	4	0
−		4

	T	U
c	9	2
−		3

	T	U
d	7	6
−		8

	T	U
e	5	5
−		6

	T	U
f	3	3
−		7

2 **Complete** each of the following:

	T	U
a	5	2
− 2	7

	T	U
b	8	1
− 2	6

	T	U
c	7	3
− 4	6

	T	U
d	5	3
− 2	8

	T	U
e	7	7
− 1	9

	T	U
f	6	0
− 4	4

3 **Complete** each of the following:

a $89
   − $27

b $55
   − $29

c $80
   − $53

d $78
   − $29

e $71
   − $36

f $90
   − $11

4 Solve the following to find **how many are left**:

a   83 children went to the park, 39 caught the bus home. _____
b   70 cars were in the car park, 48 drove off. _____
c   There were 58 pens in a jar, 29 were removed. _____
d   In the first round of a singing contest 65 out of 91 contestants were asked to leave. _____
e   45 birds were in a cage, 28 were sold. _____
f   35 loaves of bread were taken to the canteen, 27 loaves were used. _____

5 **Complete**:

	T	U
	6	5
−		8

6 **Complete**:

	T	U
	5	2
− 2	7

7 **Complete**:

  $25
− $16

8 53 DVDs were on sale, 47 were bought. **How many are left**? _____

9 Find four pairs of numbers with a **difference** of 37.

_____   _____

_____   _____

Subtraction with 3-digit numbers

1 **Complete** each of the following:

a	9	8	5
−	1	2	0

b	8	7	9
−	5	3	4

c	6	7	5
−	3	6	1

d	8	7	6
−	6	5	4

e	4	7	9
−	1	2	5

f	2	7	8
−	1	6	3

2 Find the **missing digits** in the following subtraction equations:

a	9	3	5
−	☐	2	☐
	2	1	3

b	4	9	9
−	3	4	☐
	☐	5	6

c	7	5	6
−	☐	☐	5
	2	1	☐

d	☐	☐	6
−	6	4	☐
	2	5	3

e	☐	☐	8
−	2	6	☐
	5	1	5

f	☐	4	7
−	5	☐	1
	4	3	☐

3 The following children have been saving for a television. Find **how much more** each person needs to save before the television is theirs.

a   Steve has saved $345 _____
b   Coral has saved $479 _____
c   Chris has saved $185 _____
d   Anton has saved $517 _____
e   Annita has saved $395 _____
f   Corrine has saved $267 _____

$529

4 What is the **difference** in price between:

a   A12 and B69? _____
b   D50 and P80? _____
c   G16 and D50? _____

What **change** would I get from:

d $250 if I bought the B69? _____
e $350 if I bought the A12? _____
f $500 if I bought the D50? _____

A12 $290
B69 $169
D50 $427
G16 $399
P80 $345

5 **Complete**:

	9	8	7
−	2	6	5

6 Find the **missing digits**:

	3	☐	8
−	2	4	☐
	☐	5	6

7 **How much more** does Morgan have to save if she has $375 towards the $529 television? _____

8 For the printers in question 4, what is the **difference** in price between P80 and B69? _____

9 If Mark bought two computer games each costing $89, how much **change** would he have from $200?

_____

Patterns with subtraction

1 Use the chart to **find** the number:

1	2	3	4	5	6	7	8	9	10
11	12	13	14	15	16	17	18	19	20
21	22	23	24	25	26	27	28	29	30
31	32	33	34	35	36	37	38	39	40
41	42	43	44	45	46	47	48	49	50

a 5 less than 22 _____   b 5 less than 12 _____
c 7 less than 34 _____   d 7 less than 44 _____
e 8 less than 26 _____   f 8 less than 46 _____

2 Use the chart to **find** the number:

51	52	53	54	55	56	57	58	59	60
61	62	63	64	65	66	67	68	69	70
71	72	73	74	75	76	77	78	79	80
81	82	83	84	85	86	87	88	89	90
91	92	93	94	95	96	97	98	99	100

a 9 less than 74 _____   b 9 less than 84 _____
c 6 less than 91 _____   d 6 less than 61 _____
e 8 less than 85 _____   f 8 less than 75 _____

3 Find the answers by **counting back**:

a Damon needs 65 cents. He has 50 cents. How much more does he need? _____

b 43 drawing pins were lost, Kobi found 37. How many were still missing? _____

c Mel dropped 75 pencils. She picked up 57. How many are still on the floor? _____

d Kylie has 25 baby pins. How many more does she need, to have a total of 33? _____

e Ajit needs 72 nails. He has 56. How many more does he need? _____

f A box of 35 matches was dropped. Leah has found 18 matches. How many are still missing? _____

4 Complete the **pattern**:

a 15 − 7 = 8   b 13 − 6 = _____
   25 − 7 = _____   23 − 6 = _____
   35 − 7 = _____   33 − _____ = 27

c 11 − 5 = _____   d 12 − 7 = _____
   _____ − 5 = 16   22 − _____ = 15
   31 − _____ = 26   _____ − 7 = 25

e 14 − 9 = _____   f 16 − _____ = 9
   _____ − 9 = 15   26 − 7 = _____
   34 − 9 = _____   _____ − 7 = 29

5 Use the chart in question 1 to **find** the number 9 less than 32. _____

6 Use the chart in question 2 to **find** the number 5 less than 71. _____

7 Eddie needed 27 nails. He has 18. By **counting back**, find how many more he needs. _____

8 Complete the **pattern**: 17 − 9 = _____
                  27 − _____ = 18
                  _____ − 9 = 28

9 Write as many different **subtraction equations** as possible using the numbers 9, 11 and 20.

_____

Checking subtraction by adding

1 **Complete** each question and **check** the answer.

a 24 − 13 ⟶ [ ]   + 13   b 46 − 34 ⟶ [ ]   + 34

c 39 − 17 ⟶ [ ]   + 17   d 32 − 9 ⟶ [ ]   + 9

e 42 − 16 ⟶ [ ]   + 16   f 51 − 29 ⟶ [ ]   + 29

2 **Complete** each question and **check** the answers.

a 59 − 36   b 74 − 51   c 85 − 23

d 46 − 37   e 52 − 25   f 76 − 48

3 From the information on the signpost, are the following **distances** correct? **Check** by adding.

Beach	5 km
Shop	14 km
Viewing platform	22 km
Petrol	55 km

a Beach to Shop is 9 km _____
b Shop to Petrol is 49 km. _____
c Viewing platform to Petrol is 34 km. _____
d Beach to Viewing platform is 17 km. _____
e Shop to Viewing platform is 8 km. _____
f Beach to Petrol is 60 km. _____

4 Complete each question to find **how many are left**. **Check** the answers by adding.

a Meg had 25 books. She gave 17 to the library. _____
b There are 47 frogs in the pond. 28 swam away. _____
c Mark saved $93. He spent $48. _____
d The farm had 45 cows. 18 were sold. _____
e Alf had 25 sweets and Joe ate 19 of them. _____
f Pat has 42 pens. She gave 26 away. _____

5 **Complete and check** the answer: 5 2 − 2 9 ⟶ [ ]   + 2 9

6 **Complete** the question and **check**: 41 − 17 = _____

7 From the information on the signpost, is the **distance** from Vincent to Newton 24 km? **Check** by adding.

| Vincent | 18 km |
| Newton | 42 km |

_____

8 There were 31 mice in the cage and 17 escaped. **How many mice** are **left**? _____

9 **Complete** and **check** the following subtraction equation.   1265 − 391

Estimating

1 Circle the best **estimate** (use nearest ten):

a	9 + 6 + 15 + 20	20 or 60 or 100
b	15 + 20 + 25 + 30	10 or 50 or 100
c	10 + 11 + 12 + 13	20 or 40 or 60
d	21 + 35 + 14 + 2	50 or 70 or 90
e	8 + 2 + 6 + 5	30 or 40 or 50
f	15 + 21 + 13 + 5	30 or 60 or 90

2 Circle the best **estimate** (use nearest ten):

a	30 + 60 + 50 + 21	130 or 160 or 190
b	90 + 100 + 20 + 40	150 or 200 or 250
c	46 + 24 + 59 + 63	150 or 190 or 230
d	112 + 14 + 110 + 21	250 or 290 or 330
e	92 + 56 + 108 + 29	250 or 290 or 340
f	121 + 205 + 36 + 50	420 or 440 or 460

3 Circle the best **estimate** (use nearest ten):

a	14 + 14 + 14	30 or 70 or 100
b	8 + 8 + 8 + 8 + 8	20 or 50 or 80
c	21 + 21 + 21 + 21	60 or 80 or 100
d	32 + 32 + 32 + 32	100 or 120 or 140
e	53 + 53 + 53	100 or 150 or 200
f	19 + 19 + 19 + 19 + 19	100 or 110 or 120

4 Circle the best **estimate** (use nearest ten):

a	90 − 1 − 1 − 1 − 1	90 or 70 or 50
b	140 − 8 − 8 − 8 − 8 − 8	120 or 90 or 60
c	130 − 9 − 9 − 9 − 9	100 or 90 or 70
d	150 − 1 − 1 − 1 − 1 − 1	150 or 120 or 100
e	200 − 9 − 9 − 9 − 9	220 or 190 or 160
f	190 − 7 − 7 − 7 − 7 − 7	220 or 180 or 140

5 Circle the best **estimate** (use nearest ten):
8 + 5 + 7 + 21   20 or 50 or 70

6 Circle the best **estimate** (use nearest ten):
19 + 76 + 25 + 37   90 or 130 or 170

7 Circle the best **estimate** (use nearest ten):
22 + 22 + 22 + 22 + 22   70 or 100 or 130

8 Circle the best **estimate** (use nearest ten):
130 − 7 − 7 − 7 − 7   120 or 90 or 60

9 **Estimate** by rounding the first number to the nearest ten, and then check with a **calculator**:
a 28 × 5 _____   b 48 × 7 _____
c 71 × 9 _____   d 82 × 4 _____

Rounding numbers (2)

1 Round each of the following numbers to the **nearest hundred**:

a 72 _____   b 126 _____
c 185 _____   d 236 _____
e 398 _____   f 572 _____

2 Round each of the following numbers to the **nearest hundred**:

a 1126 _____
b 4739 _____
c 6285 _____
d 3572 _____
e 5821 _____
f 4011 _____

3 Round each of the following numbers to the **nearest ten**:

a 13 _____   b 29 _____
c 47 _____   d 92 _____
e 88 _____   f 53 _____

4 Round each of the following numbers to the **nearest ten**:

a 121 _____
b 173 _____
c 206 _____
d 498 _____
e 263 _____
f 341 _____

5 Round 565 to the **nearest hundred**. _____

6 Round 3990 to the **nearest hundred**. _____

7 Round 98 to the **nearest ten**. _____

8 Round 325 to the **nearest ten**. _____

9 Greg planted 54 seeds in the morning and 39 seeds in the afternoon.

a **Round** each number to the nearest ten and estimate the total number of seeds Greg planted.

_____

The next day Greg planted a further 85 seeds.

b Using **estimation**, did Greg plant more or less than 200 seeds in the two days?

_____

Rounding numbers (3)

1 Round each of the following numbers to the **nearest ten**:

a 1285 _____   b 1346 _____
c 1192 _____   d 4829 _____
e 3635 _____   f 2014 _____

2 Round each of the numbers to the **nearest ten** and use these to **estimate** the answer:

a 31 + 62 _____   b 39 + 41 _____
c 81 + 22 _____   d 79 + 13 _____
e 61 + 49 _____   f 51 + 38 _____

3 Round each of the numbers to the **nearest ten** and use these to **estimate** the answer:

a 59 − 22 _____   b 87 − 31 _____
c 71 − 28 _____   d 69 − 17 _____
e 82 − 38 _____   f 91 − 58 _____

4 Use a **calculator** to complete the table:

	Equation	Dad's estimate	Actual answer	Difference
a	129 + 38	170		
b	489 − 51	440		
c	66 + 38	110		
d	88 − 69	20		
e	176 + 139	320		
f	82 − 36	40		

5 Round 3985 to the **nearest ten**. _____

6 Round each number to the **nearest ten** and use these to **estimate** the answer of 69 + 23.

_____

7 Round each number to the **nearest ten** and use these to **estimate** the answer of 97 − 48.

_____

8 Use a **calculator** to find the difference between Dad's estimate and the actual answer to: 72 − 29 = _____
Dad's estimate: 40   Difference is _____

9 **Estimate** (use nearest ten) the answer to this problem. At Kangaroo Primary School there are three classes of Year 3:

	3A	3B	3C
	27	22	29

Roughly how many children are in Year 3 at Kangaroo Primary School? _____

Multiplication with modelling

1 Complete a **number sentence** for each of the following:

a
3 rows of 4 = ____

b
2 rows of 5 = ____

c
____ rows of 5 = ____

d
____ rows of 7 = ____

e
____ rows of ____ = ____

f
____ row of ____ = ____

2 **Complete** each of the following:

a 5 rows of 8 = _____   b 8 rows of 2 = _____
c 3 rows of 5 = _____   d 6 lots of 3 = _____
e 10 lots of 1 = _____   f 4 lots of 6 = _____

3 **Complete** the following:

a 4 groups of 7 hats = _____
b 9 groups of 2 fish = _____
c 4 groups of 10 pens = _____
d 4 girls in a row. 5 rows. How many girls? _____
e 7 boys in a team. 6 teams. How many boys? _____
f 8 nails in a packet. 4 packets. How many nails? _____

4 Answer **yes or no** to each of the following:

a 6 × 3 equals 3 × 6 _____
b 3 × 9 equals 9 + 9 + 9 _____
c 5 × 2 equals 10 × 1 _____
d 4 × 6 equals 3 × 8 _____
e 5 × 7 equals 7 + 7 + 7 + 7 + 7 _____
f 8 × 9 equals 9 × 8 _____

5 Complete the **number sentence** for:

____ rows of ____ = _____

6 **Complete**: 2 lots of 7 = _____

7 **Complete**: 3 groups of 5 cups = _____

8 **Yes or no**?
4 × 6 equals 6 + 6 + 6 + 6 _____

9 Draw pictures to show all of the different **combinations** of multiplication equations that equal 12.

1 Complete the **number sentences** using the pictures:

a

b

3 groups of 4 = _____   7 groups of 4 = _____

c    d

9 groups of 4 = _____   _____ groups of 4 = 8

e   f

_____ group of 4 = ____   _____ groups of 4 = ____

2 Use the array to complete the **number sentences**:

a $4 \times 2 =$ _____   b $10 \times 2 =$ _____
c $7 \times 2 =$ _____   d _____ $\times 2 = 10$
e _____ $\times 2 = 16$ f _____ $\times 2 = 12$

3 Study the arrays to complete the **number sentences**:

a   b

$3 \times 2 =$ _____ $5 \times 4 =$ _____

c 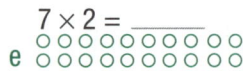   d

$7 \times 2 =$ _____ $6 \times 4 =$ _____

e   f

$10 \times 2 =$ _____ $8 \times 4 =$ _____

4 Draw **diagrams** of your own to model the given number sentences:

a 3×2 b 4×4 c 2×2

d 9×4 e 8×2 f 7×4

5 Complete the **number sentence** using:

 4 groups of 4 = _____

6 Use the array
to complete the **number sentence**: ____ $\times 2 = 18$

7 Study the array and complete the **number sentence**:
$4 \times 2 =$ _____

8 Draw a **diagram** for the number sentence 5×4.

9 Complete the multiplication **wheel**:

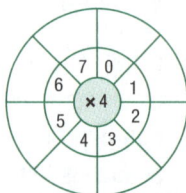

---

1 Use the diagrams to **complete** the number sentences:

a   b

6 groups of 10 = _____   9 groups of 10 = _____

c   d

4 groups of 10 = _____   7 groups of 10 = _____

e   f

2 groups of 10 = _____   10 groups of 10 = _____

2 Use the **array** to complete the number sentences:

a $8 \times 5 =$ _____   b $5 \times 5 =$ _____
c $2 \times 5 =$ _____   d _____ $\times 5 = 35$
e _____ $\times 5 = 50$ f _____ $\times 5 = 45$

3 Draw **diagrams** to model the number sentences:

a 5×3 b 10×8 c 5×10

d 10×7 e 5×4 f 10×3

4 Complete the following **grids**:

a
×	1	2	3	4
5				

b
×	1	2	3	4
10				

c
×	9	10	7	4
5				

d
×	5	6	7	8
10				

e
×	5	6	7	8
5				

f
×	9	10	5	3
10				

5 Use the diagram  to **complete**:

5 groups of 10 = _____

6 Use the **array** to complete:

 _____ $\times 5 = 40$

7 Draw a **diagram** to model 6×10.

8 Complete the **grid**:

×	3	4	5	6
5				

9 Write a word problem for: $5 \times 6 =$ _____

_____

× 0, × 1, × 2 and × 4

1 Complete the following **number sentences** by using the diagrams:

a

b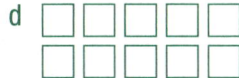

6 groups of 1 = ____   3 groups of 0 = ____

c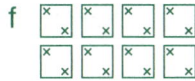

d

9 groups of 1 = ____   10 groups of 0 = ____

e

f

5 groups of 4 = ____   8 groups of 2 = ____

2 **Complete** the following:

a $7 \times 0 =$ ____   b $4 \times 1 =$ ____   c $6 \times 0 =$ ____
d $10 \times 1 =$ ____   e $9 \times 0 =$ ____   f $5 \times 1 =$ ____

3 Complete the following **grids**:

a
×	4	5	6	7
4				

b
×	7	8	9	10
1				

c
×	8	9	10	3
0				

d
×	1	2	3	4
1				

e
×	5	6	7	8
2				

f
×	3	4	5	6
4				

4 Complete the following pairs of **equations**:

a $2 \times 1 =$ ____ $= 1 \times 2$ b $4 \times 0 =$ ____ $= 6 \times 0$
c $3 \times 4 =$ ____ $= 6 \times 2$ d $10 \times 2 =$ ____ $= 5 \times 4$
e $4 \times 4 =$ ____ $= 8 \times 2$ f $10 \times 1 =$ ____ $= 5 \times 2$

5 Complete the **number sentence**:

8 groups of 0 = _____

6 **Complete**: ____ $\times 1 = 7$

7 Complete the grid:
×	7	8	9	10
1				

8 Complete the **equation**: $3 \times 2 =$ ____ $= 6 \times 1$

9 a Shade the **tables of 2**.   b Circle the **tables of 4**.

c What did you **discover**? _____

1	2	3	4	5	6	7	8	9	10
11	12	13	14	15	16	17	18	19	20
21	22	23	24	25	26	27	28	29	30
31	32	33	34	35	36	37	38	39	40

× 3 and × 6

1 Write a number sentence to describe the **arrays**:

a    b

_____   _____

c    d

_____   _____

e   f

_____   _____

2 **Complete** the spaces:

a $1 \times 6 =$ ____ $= 6 \times 1$

b $10 \times 6 =$ _____ $=$ _____ $\times 10$

c ____ $\times 6 =$ _____ $= 6 \times 5$

d ____ $\times 6 = 54 = 6 \times$ ____

e $8 \times 6 =$ _____ $=$ ____ $\times 8$

f $3 \times 6 =$ _____ $=$ _____ $\times 3$

3 Find how many **points** there are on:

a 1 triangle _____   b 4 triangles _____
c 8 triangles _____   d 2 triangles _____
e 7 triangles _____   f 10 triangles _____

4 **Complete** the spaces:

a $5 \times 6 =$ _____   b ____ $\times 3 = 18$
c $9 \times 6 =$ _____   d $5 \times$ ____ $= 15$
e ____ $\times 6 = 42$ f $9 \times 3 =$ _____

5 Write a number sentence to describe the **array**:

_____

6 **Complete** the spaces: ____ $\times 3 =$ _____ $= 3 \times 6$

7 Find how many **points** there are on 5 triangles.

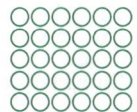 ____

8 **Complete** the space: $6 \times$ ____ $= 36$

9 What is the **cost** of 8 movie tickets at $6 each?

_____

× 9

1 Use the diagram to help **answer** the following questions:

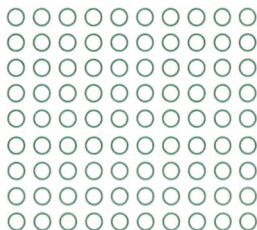

a 3 groups of 9 = _____   b 8 groups of 9 = _____
c 2 rows of 9 = _____   d 10 rows of 9 = _____
e 7 groups of 9 = _____   f 9 rows of 9 = _____

2 **Complete** the spaces:

a 1 × 9 = 10 − ___ = _____
b 2 × 9 = 20 − ___ = _____
c 3 × 9 = 30 − ___ = _____
d 4 × 9 = 40 − ___ = _____
e 5 × 9 = 50 − ___ = _____
f 6 × 9 = 60 − ___ = _____

3 Write the **equation** for each of the answers from the 9 times table:

a 27 = _____   b 18 = _____
c 63 = _____   d 36 = _____
e 9 = _____   f 45 = _____

4 **Complete** the spaces:

a 9 × 2 = 18 = _____ × 6
b 4 × ___ = 36 = 6 × ___
c 9 × 10 = _____ = _____ × 9
d ___ × 9 = 9 = 3 × ___
e 6 × 9 = _____ = 9 × _____
f ___ × 9 = 63 = 9 × ___

5 Use the diagram to **answer**:

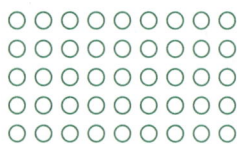

5 groups of 9 = _____

6 **Complete** the spaces: 8 × 9 = 80 − ___ = _____

7 Write the **equation** for the answer 54 from the 9 times table. _____

8 **Complete** the spaces: 3 × ___ = _____ = 9 × 1

9 If 9 friends ate 3 biscuits each, how many biscuits were eaten in **total**? _____

× 3, × 6 and × 9

1 Using the **arrays**,

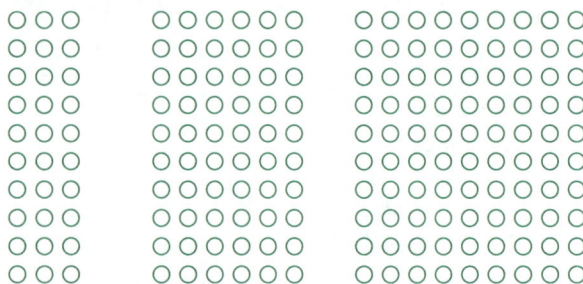

complete the following:

a 7 × 3 = _____   b 9 × 6 = _____
c 5 × 9 = _____   d 6 × 3 = _____
e 4 × 6 = _____   f 2 × 9 = _____

2 Complete the following:

a The **product** of 4 and 3 = _____
b The product of 8 and 6 = _____
c The product of 8 and 9 = _____
d The product of 10 and 3 = _____
e The product of 7 and 6 = _____
f The product of 7 and 9 = _____

3 **Complete**:

a   5   b   6   c   7
    × 3   × 2   × 9
  _____   _____   _____

d   8   e   7   f   9
    × 3   × 6   × 9
  _____   _____   _____

4 **Complete** the spaces:

a 3 × 2 = ___ = ___ × 1
b 6 × ___ = 36 = 9 × ___
c 3 × ___ = 24 = 6 × ___
d ___ × 6 = 18 = 2 × ___
e 3 × ___ = 12 = ___ × 2
f 6 × 5 = _____ = 3 × _____

5 Using the **array**, complete:

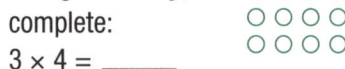

3 × 4 = _____

6 Complete: the **product** of 6 and 9 = _____

7 **Complete**:   9
                       × 3
                     _____

8 **Complete** the spaces: 4 × ___ = 36 = ___ × 6

9 **Complete**:

×	2	4	5	6	8	10
3						
6						

Excel Start Up Maths Year 3

☞ Answers on page 123

× 8

❶

How many legs are there on:

a　10 spiders? _____　　b　6 spiders? _____

c　7 spiders? _____　　d　9 spiders? _____

e　3 spiders? _____　　f　5 spiders? _____

❷ Complete:

a　6 **groups of** 8 = _____

b　0 groups of 8 = _____

c　4 groups of 8 = _____

d　2 groups of 8 = _____

e　5 groups of 8 = _____

f　8 groups of 8 = _____

❸ **Complete** the spaces:

a　$1 \times 8 =$ _____　　　　b　_____ $\times 8 = 32$

c　_____ $\times 8 = 56$　　　d　$6 \times$ _____ $= 48$

e　$3 \times$ _____ $= 24$　　　f　_____ $\times 8 = 64$

❹ **Complete**:

a　　8　　b　　8　　c　　5
　　$\times 2$　　　　$\times 8$　　　　$\times 8$
　　_____　　　　_____　　　　_____

d　　10　　e　　8　　f　　9
　　$\times 8$　　　　$\times 4$　　　　$\times 8$
　　_____　　　　_____　　　　_____

❺

How many legs are there on 4 spiders? _____

❻ Complete: 7 **groups** of 8 = _____

❼ **Complete** the space: _____ $\times 8 = 80$

❽ **Complete**:　　　3
　　　　　　　　　$\times 8$
　　　　　　　　　_____

❾ **Complete**:

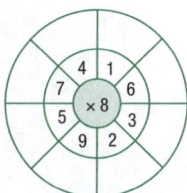

× 2, × 4 and × 8

❶ Using the **arrays,**

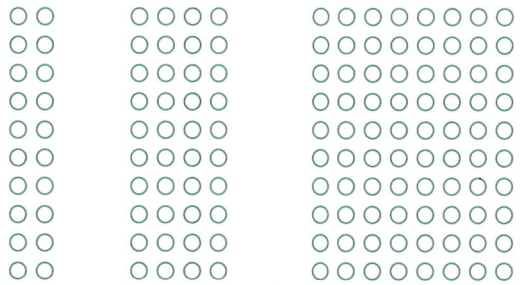

complete the following:

a　$7 \times 2 =$ _____　　b　$7 \times 4 =$ _____

c　$3 \times 8 =$ _____　　d　$6 \times 2 =$ _____

e　$5 \times 4 =$ _____　　f　$6 \times 8 =$ _____

❷ Complete the following:

a　The **product of** 3 and 2 = _____.

b　The product of 8 and 4 = _____.

c　The product of 7 and 8 = _____.

d　The product of 9 and 2 = _____.

e　The product of 2 and 4 = _____.

f　The product of 9 and 8 = _____.

❸ **Complete**:

a

×	7	8	9	10
2				

b

×	3	4	5	6
4				

c

×	9	10	5	8
8				

d

×	3	6	5	4
2				

e

×	2	8	10	7
4				

f

×	3	7	4	8
8				

❹ **Complete** the spaces:

a　$4 \times 2 =$ _____ $= 8 \times 1$

b　$6 \times 4 =$ _____ $= 8 \times$ _____

c　$5 \times$ _____ $= 40 = 10 \times$ _____

d　$10 \times$ _____ $= 20 = 4 \times$ _____

e　$6 \times$ _____ $=$ _____ $= 4 \times 3$

f　$6 \times$ _____ $=$ _____ $= 3 \times 8$

❺ Using the **arrays,** complete:

$5 \times 4 =$ _____

$5 \times 2 =$ _____

❻ Complete: the **product** of 9 and 4 = _____.

❼ **Complete**:

×	1	3	5	7
4				

❽ **Complete** the spaces: $4 \times$ _____ $= 16 =$ _____ $\times 2$

❾ One teddy bear costs $8. **How much** will three teddy bears cost? _____

× 7

1

January						
S	M	T	W	T	F	S
		1	2	3	4	5
6	7	8	9	10	11	12
13	14	15	16	17	18	19
20	21	22	23	24	24	26
27	28	29	30	31		

February						
S	M	T	W	T	F	S
					1	2
3	4	5	6	7	8	9
10	11	12	13	14	15	16
17	18	19	20	21	22	23
24	25	26	27	28		

March						
S	M	T	W	T	F	S
31					1	2
3	4	5	6	7	8	9
10	10	12	13	14	15	16
17	18	19	20	21	22	23
24	25	26	27	28	29	30

How many **days** are there in:

a 3 weeks? _____   b 1 week? _____

c 6 weeks? _____   d 4 weeks? _____

e 8 weeks? _____   f 5 weeks? _____

2 **Complete**:

a 0 groups of 7 = _____   b 6 groups of 7 = _____

c 4 groups of 7 = _____   d 10 groups of 7 = _____

e 2 groups of 7 = _____   f 9 groups of 7 = _____

3 **Complete** the spaces:

a $7 \times 7 =$ _____   b $7 \times$ _____ $= 35$

c $9 \times 7 =$ _____   d _____ $\times 7 = 21$

e $7 \times$ _____ $= 56$ f _____ $\times 7 = 0$

4 **Complete**:

a $\begin{array}{r} 3 \\ \times 7 \\ \hline \end{array}$ b $\begin{array}{r} 7 \\ \times 4 \\ \hline \end{array}$ c $\begin{array}{r} 8 \\ \times 7 \\ \hline \end{array}$

d $\begin{array}{r} 7 \\ \times 2 \\ \hline \end{array}$ e $\begin{array}{r} 6 \\ \times 7 \\ \hline \end{array}$ f $\begin{array}{r} 7 \\ \times 9 \\ \hline \end{array}$

5 How many **days** are there in 7 weeks?

_____

6 Complete: 3 **groups** of 7 = _____

7 **Complete** the space: ___ $\times 7 = 42$

8 **Complete**: $\begin{array}{r} 7 \\ \times 7 \\ \hline \end{array}$

9 Write a word problem for: $7 \times 8 =$ _____

_____

Multiplication tables

1 **Complete** the following:

a 6 groups of 4 = _____   b 4 groups of 2 = _____

c 8 groups of 6 = _____   d 5 groups of 5 = _____

e 3 groups of 8 = _____   f 9 groups of 7 = _____

2 **Complete**:

a $1 \times 5 =$ _____   b $10 \times 3 =$ _____

c $8 \times 9 =$ _____   d $2 \times 10 =$ _____

e $6 \times 7 =$ _____   f $4 \times 4 =$ _____

3 **Complete**:

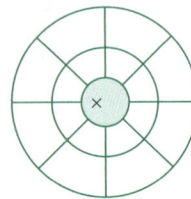

(a) × 5: 8 5 0 6 1 3 2 4

(b) × 6: 9 2 8 7 3 4 6 5

(c) × 2: 9 10 4 3 7 8 6 5

(d) × 10: 1 8 2 7 3 10 4 5

(e) × 2: 8 1 3 6 2 7 5 10

(f) × 7: 9 8 6 7 5 0 2 3

4 **Complete**:

a $\begin{array}{r} 10 \\ \times 8 \\ \hline \end{array}$ b $\begin{array}{r} 0 \\ \times 6 \\ \hline \end{array}$ c $\begin{array}{r} 5 \\ \times 3 \\ \hline \end{array}$

d $\begin{array}{r} 7 \\ \times 2 \\ \hline \end{array}$ e $\begin{array}{r} 7 \\ \times 5 \\ \hline \end{array}$ f $\begin{array}{r} 8 \\ \times 9 \\ \hline \end{array}$

5 **Complete**: 10 groups of 8 = _____

6 **Complete**: $4 \times 6 =$ _____

7 **Complete**:

8 **Complete**: $\begin{array}{r} 7 \\ \times 9 \\ \hline \end{array}$

9 **Factors** are numbers that when multiplied together give another number. So 2 and 3 are factors of 6 as $2 \times 3 = 6$. List all of the factors of:

a 12 _____

b 18 _____

c 20 _____

Square numbers

❶ Complete the labels for the **square numbers**:

a $1^2 = 1 \times 1 =$ ____ b $2^2 = 2 \times 2 =$ ____

c $3^2 = 3 \times 3 =$ ____ d $4^2 = 4 \times 4 =$ _____

e $5^2 = 5 \times 5 =$ _____ f $6^2 = 6 \times 6 =$ _____

❷ Draw a **square** on each side:

a 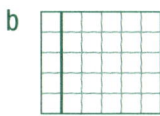 b

area = ____ squares area = _____ squares

c d

area = ____ squares area = ____ square

e f

area = ____ squares area = ____ squares

❸ Draw a square of counters of the following **square numbers** and state the **total number** of counters used:

a 3×3 b 2×2 c 4×4

d 1×1 e 5×5 f 6×6

❹ Which of the following numbers are **square numbers**?

a 25 _____ b 49 _____ c 50 _____

d 100 _____ e 75 _____ f 81 _____

❺ Complete the label for the **square number**:

$7^2 = 7 \times 7 =$ _____

❻ Draw a **square** on each side:

area = _____ squares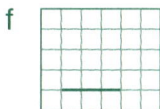

❼ Draw a square of counters of the **square number** 8×8 and state the **total number** of counters used. _____

❽ Is 99 a **square number**? _____

❾ List all of the **square numbers** up to 100. _____

_____

Multiples

❶

1	2	3	4	5	6	7	8	9	10
11	12	13	14	15	16	17	18	19	20
21	22	23	24	25	26	27	28	29	30
31	32	33	34	35	36	37	38	39	40
41	42	43	44	45	46	47	48	49	50

a Circle the **multiples** of 2.

b Shade the **multiples** of 4.

c Put a cross on the **multiples** of 8.

d Are the **multiples** of 2, 4 and 8 related? _____

e Did the multiples from each number form a **pattern**?

_____

f Why was the **number** 50 not crossed? _____

❷ Complete the following **multiples** of 5:

a $1 \times 5 =$ ____ b $2 \times 5 =$ ____ c $3 \times 5 =$ ____

d $4 \times 5 =$ ____ e $5 \times 5 =$ ____ f $6 \times 5 =$ ____

❸ List the first ten **multiples** of:

a	2									

b	3									

c	9									

d	5									

e	6									

f	7									

❹ Shade the **multiples** of the middle number:

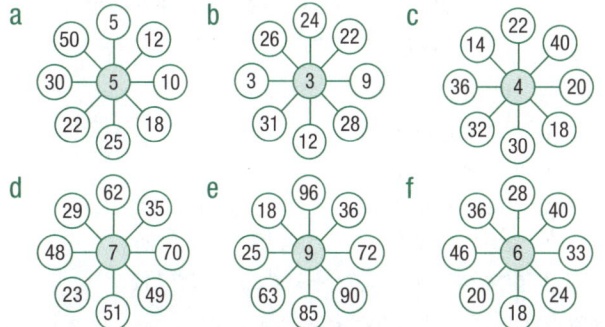

❺ On the completed grid from question 1, why was the **number** 30 not shaded? _____

❻ Complete the **multiple** of 5: $9 \times 5 =$ _____

❼ List the first ten **multiples** of:

10										

❽ Shade the **multiples** of 8: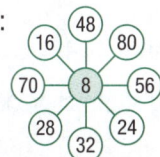

❾ Lisa has twice as much money as Joe. Joe has twice as much as Liam. If Liam has $20, **how much** money do Lisa and Joe have? _____

Sharing

1 Use the pictures to **share**:

a 10 shared by 2

b 12 shared by 3

c 9 shared by 3

d 6 shared by 2

e 16 shared by 4

f 8 shared by 4

2 Complete:

a 21 **shared** among 3 = ____

b 12 **shared** among 6 = ____

c 18 **shared** among 9 = ____

d 20 **shared** among 5 = ____

e 15 **shared** among 3 = ____

f 2 **shared** among 2 = ____

3 Complete:

a 4 boys **share** 20 apples. One share = _____

b 6 girls **share** 30 oranges. One share = _____

c 10 children **share** 40 stickers. One share = _____

d 5 teachers **share** 30 biscuits. One share = _____

e 9 doctors **share** 18 charts. One share = _____

f 7 builders **share** 21 boxes. One share = _____

4 10 pieces of toast:

a **shared** by 5 = ____

b **shared** by 2 = ____

c **shared** by 1 = ____

d **shared** by 3 = ____ and ____ left over.

e **shared** by 4 = ____ and ____ left over.

f **shared** by 6 = ____ and ____ left over.

5 Use the picture to **share** 12 by 6.

6 Complete: 25 **shared** among 5 = ____

7 5 children **share** 25 cupcakes.
One share = _____

8 9 cups **shared** by 4 = ____ and ____ left over.

9 Show using subtraction how 6 children would **share** 48 pens.

Division (1)

1 Complete each of the following:

a 15 **shared** among 5 = ____
Groups of 5 in 15 = ____

b 12 **shared** among 4 = ____
Groups of 4 in 12 = ____

c 20 **shared** among 5 = ____
Groups of 5 in 20 = ____

d 18 **shared** among 3 = ____
Groups of 3 in 18 = ____

e 6 **shared** among 3 = ____
Groups of 3 in 6 = ____

f 7 **shared** among 1 = ____
Groups of 1 in 7 = ____

2 Complete each of the following:

a **Divide** by 2

____ ÷ ____ = ____

b **Divide** by 6

____ ÷ ____ = ____

c **Divide** by 3

____ ÷ ____ = ____

d **Divide** by 9

____ ÷ ____ = ____

e **Divide** by 4

____ ÷ ____ = ____

f **Divide** by 1

____ ÷ ____ = ____

3 Use the picture to help solve the division equations:

a 24 **divided** by 6 is 24 ÷ 6 = ____

b 24 divided by 4 is 24 ÷ ____ = ____

c 24 divided by 3 is 24 ÷ ____ = ____

d 24 divided by 8 is 24 ÷ ____ = ____

e 24 divided by 2 is 24 ÷ ____ = ____

f 24 divided by 12 is 24 ÷ ____ = ____

4 **Try** these questions; you could use counting materials to help:

a 20 ÷ 4 = ____

b 16 ÷ 4 = ____

c 18 ÷ 2 = ____

d 14 ÷ 2 = ____

e 30 ÷ 3 = ____

f 32 ÷ 4 = ____

5 Complete:

4 **shared** among 4 = ____
Groups of 4 in 4 = ____

6 **Divide** by 3:

____ ÷ ____ = ____

7 Use the picture in question 3 to help solve:
24 **divided** by 1 is 24 ÷ ____ = ____

8 **Try**: 35 ÷ 5 = ____

9 Write all of the different **division equations** for 12 that you can. ____

Division as repeated subtraction

1 How many **groups of** 2 could be made from each of the following?

a ✿✿✿
✿✿✿
✿✿ ___

b ♡♡♡
♡♡♡
♡ ___

c ▢▢
▢▢ ___

d ⵔⵔⵔⵔⵔⵔⵔⵔ
ⵔⵔⵔⵔⵔ ___

e ▤▤▤
▤▤▤
▤▤▤ ___

f △△ ___

2 There are 12 apples in the bowl:
a **How many times** can I take 2 apples? _____ times
b How many times can I take 4 apples? _____ times
c How many times can I take 3 apples? _____ times
d How many times can I take 1 apple? _____ times
e How many times can I take 6 apples? _____ times
f How many times can I take 12 apples? _____ times

3 a **How many times** can I take 5 candles from 10? ___
b How many times can I take 6 books from 30? ___
c How many times can I take 4 balls from 20? ___
d How many times can I take 2 pens from 24? ___
e How many times can I take 10 pins from 90? ___
f How many times can I take 3 cherries from 18? ___

4 a Twelve marbles were **shared** between 2 girls. How many did each girl receive? ___
b Ten stickers were **shared** between 5 children. How many did each child receive? ___
c Nine toys were **shared** between 3 toddlers. How many did each child receive? ___
d Eight pieces of fruit were **shared** between 2 children. How many did each child receive? ___
e Six books were **shared** between 3 children. How many did each child receive? ___
f Fourteen pencils were **shared** between 2 boys. How many did each boy receive? ___

5 How many **groups of** 2 could be made from
∞∞ ∞∞ ∞∞
∞∞ ∞∞ ? ___

6 There are 15 oranges in the bowl. **How many times** can I take 3 oranges? ___ times

7 **How many times** can I take 4 grapes from 16? ___

8 Fifteen pieces of paper were **shared** between 3 girls. How many did each girl receive? ___

9 Draw a **picture** for the number sentence:
$20 \div 5 = 4$

Division (2)

1 Use the **arrays** to answer the following division questions:

a ⚬⚬
⚬⚬
⚬⚬

$6 \div 3 =$ ___

b ⚬⚬⚬⚬
⚬⚬⚬⚬

$8 \div 4 =$ ___

c ⚬⚬⚬⚬⚬
⚬⚬⚬⚬⚬
⚬⚬⚬⚬⚬
⚬⚬⚬⚬⚬
⚬⚬⚬⚬⚬

$25 \div 5 =$ ___

d ⚬⚬⚬⚬⚬
⚬⚬⚬⚬⚬
⚬⚬⚬⚬⚬

$15 \div 3 =$ ___

e ⚬⚬⚬
⚬⚬⚬
⚬⚬⚬

$9 \div 3 =$ ___

f ⚬⚬⚬⚬⚬⚬
⚬⚬⚬⚬⚬⚬

$12 \div 4 =$ ___

2 Draw **arrays** to model the division number sentences:
a $18 \div 6 = 3$ b $10 \div 2 = 5$ c $9 \div 1 = 9$

d $21 \div 3 = 7$ e $16 \div 4 = 4$ f $30 \div 6 = 5$

3 **Complete**:
a $20 \div 10 =$ ___   b $40 \div 5 =$ ___
c $28 \div 4 =$ ___   d $32 \div 8 =$ ___
e $70 \div 10 =$ ___   f $3 \div 3 =$ ___

4 Answer:
a **How many** 5s in 25? ___
b How many 3s in 21? ___
c How many 10s in 100? ___
d How many 8s in 48? ___
e How many 7s in 49? ___
f How many 9s in 27? ___

5 ⚬⚬⚬⚬
⚬⚬⚬⚬
⚬⚬⚬⚬
⚬⚬⚬⚬   Use this **array** to find the answer to:

$16 \div 8 =$ ___

6 Draw an **array** to model the division equation:
$14 \div 7 = 2$

7 **Complete**: $45 \div 5 =$ ___

8 **How many** 4s in 28? ___

9 Scarlet bought 50 apples. She put the same number of apples in each of 5 fruit bowls. **How many** apples did Scarlet put in each fruit bowl? ___

Division with number lines

1 Use the number line to find the answers:

```
0  1  2  3  4  5  6  7  8  9  10 11 12 13 14 15
```

a **How many** 2s are in 4? _____
b How many 2s are in 6? _____
c How many 2s are in 8? _____
d How many 2s are in 12? _____
e How many 1s are in 4? _____
f How many 1s are in 3? _____

2 Use the number line to find the answers:

```
0  1  2  3  4  5  6  7  8  9  10 11 12 13 14 15
```

a **How many** 3s are in 3? $3 \div 3 =$ _____
b How many 3s are in 6? $6 \div 3 =$ _____
c How many 3s are in 12? $12 \div 3 =$ _____
d How many 4s are in 4? $4 \div 4 =$ _____
e How many 4s are in 8? $8 \div 4 =$ _____
f How many 4s are in 12? $12 \div 4 =$ _____

3 Use the **number line** to find the answers:

```
0        5        10        15        20
```

a $5 \div 5 =$ _____   b $10 \div 5 =$ _____
c $15 \div 5 =$ _____   d $20 \div 5 =$ _____
d $10 \div 2 =$ _____   e $8 \div 2 =$ _____

4 Use the **number line** to find the answers:

```
0        5        10        15        20
```

a $4 \div 2 =$ _____   b $10 \div 2 =$ _____
c $12 \div 2 =$ _____   d $6 \div 6 =$ _____
e $18 \div 6 =$ _____   f $12 \div 6 =$ _____

5 Use the number line to find:
how many 2s are in 10? _____

```
0     2     4     6     8     10
```

6 Use the number line to find:
how many 3s are in 9? $9 \div 3 =$ _____

```
0     3     6     9
```

7 Use the **number line** in question 3 to find:
$6 \div 2 =$ _____

8 Use the **number line** in question 4 to find:
$15 \div 3 =$ _____

9 Draw a **number line and use jumps** to solve the division equations:
$15 \div$ ___ $= 5$ $18 \div$ ___ $= 2$ $18 \div$ ___ $= 6$

Division (3)

1 Use the multiplication table to answer each of the following **division** equations:

a $6 \times 5 = 30$ b $8 \times 10 = 80$

$6 \overline{)30}$ $10 \overline{)80}$

c $7 \times 9 = 63$ d $9 \times 5 = 45$

$9 \overline{)63}$ $5 \overline{)45}$

e $9 \times 8 = 72$ f $7 \times 6 = 42$

$8 \overline{)72}$ $6 \overline{)42}$

2 Amy only ever bought 5c stamps. Find **how many** stamps she could buy for:

a 30c _____   b 15c _____
c 50c _____   d 45c _____
e 25c _____   f 35c _____

3 John only ever bought 10c stamps. Find **how many** stamps he could buy for:

a 50c _____   b 90c _____
c 40c _____   d 60c _____
e 80c _____   f 100c _____

4 **Complete** each of the following:

a $48 \div 8 =$ _____   b $36 \div 4 =$ _____
c $90 \div 10 =$ _____   d $9 \div 3 =$ _____
e $12 \div 6 =$ _____   f $12 \div 3 =$ _____

5 Use the multiplication table to answer the **division** equation: $5 \times 7 = 35$

$5 \overline{)35}$

6 If Amy only ever bought 5c stamps, find **how many** stamps she could buy for 40c. _____

7 If John only ever bought 10c stamps, find **how many** stamps he could buy for 70c. _____

8 **Complete**: $50 \div 5 =$ _____

9 Four men **shared** 24 keys. How many keys did each man receive? Draw a picture to answer the question. _____

Division with remainders (1)

1 Make the following **groups**:

a groups of 3 circles

○ ○ ○ ○ ○
○ ○ ○ ○ ○

____ groups
____ circle left over

b groups of 2 squares

□ □ □ □ □
□ □ □ □ □ □

____ groups
____ square left over

c groups of 4 triangles

△ △ △ △ △
△ △ △ △ △
△ △ △ △ △

____ groups
____ triangles left over

d groups of 3 stars

☆ ☆ ☆ ☆ ☆
☆ ☆ ☆

____ groups
____ stars left over

e groups of 5 ovals

○○○○○○○○
○○○○○○○○

____ groups
____ oval left over

f groups of 6 hearts

♡ ♡ ♡ ♡ ♡
♡ ♡ ♡ ♡

____ group
____ hearts left over

2 Answer the following questions using the diagram:

a **How many** groups of 6? ____

△ △ △ △ △ △
△ △ △ △ △ △
△ △ △ △ △ △

b How many groups of 3? ____
c How many groups of 9? ____
d How many groups of 5? ____ remainder ____
e How many groups of 7? ____ remainder ____
f How many groups of 4? ____ remainder ____

3 Answer the following questions using the diagram:

a **How many** groups of 4? ____

□ □ □ □ □
□ □ □ □ □
□ □ □ □ □
□ □ □ □ □

b How many groups of 10? ____
c How many groups of 2? ____
d How many groups of 3? ____ remainder ____
e How many groups of 6? ____ remainder ____
f How many groups of 7? ____ remainder ____

4 Answer:

a $10 \div 3 =$ ____ **remainder** ____
b $16 \div 5 =$ ____ remainder ____
c $21 \div 4 =$ ____ remainder ____
d $13 \div 2 =$ ____ remainder ____
e $17 \div 8 =$ ____ remainder ____
f $23 \div 5 =$ ____ remainder ____

5 Make **groups** of 4 stars:

____ groups
____ star left over

☆ ☆ ☆ ☆ ☆
☆ ☆ ☆ ☆

6 **How many** groups of 4?
____ remainder ____

□ □ □ □ □
□ □ □ □ □

7 **How many** groups of 3? ____ remainder ____

△ △ △ △
△ △ △ △

8 Answer: $40 \div 7 =$ ____ **remainder** ____

9 38 balls are packed into boxes of 6. Draw a **diagram** showing the number of boxes needed.

Division with remainders (2)

1 Answer the following questions:

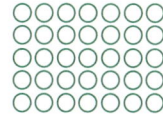

○○○○○○○○
○○○○○○○○
○○○○○○○○
○○○○○○○○
○○○○○○○○

a **How many groups of** 5 are there? ____
b How many groups of 7 are there? ____
c How many groups of 10 are there? ____ r ____
d How many groups of 4 are there? ____ r ____
e How many groups of 6 are there? ____ r ____
f How many groups of 8 are there? ____ r ____

2 There are 27 frogs.

a **How many** ponds are needed if 10 frogs are put into each pond? ____
b **How many** frogs are left over from the ponds? ____
c $27 \div 10 =$ ____ remainder ____
d **How many** buckets are needed if 5 frogs are put into each bucket? ____
e **How many** frogs are left over from the buckets? ____
f $27 \div 5 =$ ____ remainder ____

3 a **How many groups of** 8 footballs in 20? ____ r ____
b How many groups of 7 buttons in 30? ____ r ____
c How many groups of 6 pens in 10? ____ r ____
d How many groups of 5 fish in 12? ____ r ____
e How many groups of 4 rulers in 30? ____ r ____
f How many groups of 9 dogs in 40? ____ r ____

4 **Answer** each of the following:

a $8 \div 3 =$ ____ r ____
b $15 \div 6 =$ ____ r ____
c $12 \div 5 =$ ____ r ____
d $11 \div 4 =$ ____ r ____
e $20 \div 7 =$ ____ r ____
f $22 \div 8 =$ ____ r ____

5 **How many groups of** 7 are there in:

○○○○○○
○○○○○○
○○○○○○

____ r ____

6 There are 14 ants. **How many** boxes are needed if 6 ants are put into each box? ____ remainder ____

7 **How many groups of** 7 hats in 20? ____ r ____

8 **Answer**: $19 \div 4 =$ ____ r ____

9 33 comics are in sets of 4. **How many** sets are there?

____

Division practice

1 Use the multiplication table to answer the **division** questions:

a $5 \times 9 = 45$

b $8 \times 7 = 56$

$9 \overline{)\, 45}$ 　　　　 $8 \overline{)\, 56}$

c $6 \times 7 = 42$

d $4 \times 8 = 32$

$7 \overline{)\, 42}$ 　　　　 $4 \overline{)\, 32}$

e $9 \times 9 = 81$

f $8 \times 10 = 80$

$9 \overline{)\, 81}$ 　　　　 $10 \overline{)\, 80}$

2 Complete:

a $40 \div 10 = \underline{\quad}$

b $64 \div 8 = \underline{\quad}$

c $35 \div 7 = \underline{\quad}$

d $49 \div 7 = \underline{\quad}$

e $54 \div 6 = \underline{\quad}$

f $63 \div 9 = \underline{\quad}$

3
a **Divide** 30 marbles into 4 groups: $\underline{\quad}$ r $\underline{\quad}$

b **Share** 32 chocolates among 5 ladies: $\underline{\quad}$ r $\underline{\quad}$

c **Divide** 16 dogs into 3 groups: $\underline{\quad}$ r $\underline{\quad}$

d **Share** 20 lollies between 6 children: $\underline{\quad}$ r $\underline{\quad}$

e **Divide** 22 fish into 7 fish bowls: $\underline{\quad}$ r $\underline{\quad}$

f **Share** 18 snacks between 4 boys: $\underline{\quad}$ r $\underline{\quad}$

4
a $9 \div 4 = \underline{\quad}$ r $\underline{\quad}$

b $15 \div 6 = \underline{\quad}$ r $\underline{\quad}$

c $14 \div 5 = \underline{\quad}$ r $\underline{\quad}$

d $30 \div 9 = \underline{\quad}$ r $\underline{\quad}$

e $20 \div 8 = \underline{\quad}$ r $\underline{\quad}$

f $36 \div 7 = \underline{\quad}$ r $\underline{\quad}$

5 Use the multiplication table $9 \times 8 = 72$ to answer the **division** question:

$8 \overline{)\, 72}$

6 Complete: $16 \div 8 = \underline{\quad}$

7 **Divide** 17 toy trucks among 5 girls: $\underline{\quad}$ r $\underline{\quad}$

8 $26 \div 8 = \underline{\quad}$ r $\underline{\quad}$

9 Farmer Fred wants to put 26 sheep into 4 paddocks. Draw a picture to show **how many** sheep go in each paddock and how many are **left over**.

Multiplication and division

1 Find **how many groups of**:

a 4 buttons can be made from 24 buttons $\underline{\quad}$

b 3 hats can be made from 15 hats $\underline{\quad}$

c 3 fish can be made from 6 fish $\underline{\quad}$

d 2 balls can be made from 10 balls $\underline{\quad}$

e 2 apples can be made from 8 apples $\underline{\quad}$

f 4 coins can be made from 12 ten cent coins $\underline{\quad}$

2 Use the first number sentence to **fill in** the other two:

a $5 \times 3 = 15$ 　 $15 \div 3 = \underline{\quad}$ 　 $15 \div 5 = \underline{\quad}$

b $6 \times 4 = 24$ 　 $24 \div 4 = \underline{\quad}$ 　 $24 \div 6 = \underline{\quad}$

c $10 \times 9 = 90$ 　 $90 \div 9 = \underline{\quad}$ 　 $90 \div 10 = \underline{\quad}$

d $8 \times 7 = 56$ 　 $56 \div 7 = \underline{\quad}$ 　 $56 \div 8 = \underline{\quad}$

e $7 \times 9 = 63$ 　 $63 \div 9 = \underline{\quad}$ 　 $63 \div 7 = \underline{\quad}$

f $9 \times 6 = 54$ 　 $54 \div 6 = \underline{\quad}$ 　 $54 \div 9 = \underline{\quad}$

3 Use the first number sentence to **fill in** the other two:

a $24 \div 6 = 4$ 　 $\underline{\quad} \times 6 = 24$ 　 $6 \times \underline{\quad} = 24$

b $45 \div 5 = 9$ 　 $\underline{\quad} \times 5 = 45$ 　 $5 \times \underline{\quad} = 45$

c $18 \div 3 = 6$ 　 $\underline{\quad} \times 3 = 18$ 　 $3 \times \underline{\quad} = 18$

d $70 \div 7 = 10$ 　 $\underline{\quad} \times 7 = 70$ 　 $7 \times \underline{\quad} = 70$

e $27 \div 9 = 3$ 　 $\underline{\quad} \times 9 = 27$ 　 $9 \times \underline{\quad} = 27$

f $48 \div 8 = 6$ 　 $\underline{\quad} \times 8 = 48$ 　 $8 \times \underline{\quad} = 48$

4 Write two multiplication and two division facts to describe each of the following **arrays**:

a ⭕⭕⭕⭕

b ⭕⭕⭕⭕⭕ ⭕⭕⭕⭕⭕

c ⭕⭕⭕⭕⭕⭕⭕

d ⭕⭕⭕⭕ ⭕⭕⭕⭕ ⭕⭕⭕⭕

e (array)

f (array)

5 There are 18 golf balls. Find **how many groups of** 6 golf balls can be made. $\underline{\quad}$

6 Use the first number sentence to **fill in** the other two:

$7 \times 5 = 35$ 　 $35 \div 7 = \underline{\quad}$ 　 $35 \div 5 = \underline{\quad}$

7 Use the first number sentence to **fill in** the other two:

$63 \div 9 = 7$ 　 $\underline{\quad} \times 9 = 63$ 　 $9 \times \underline{\quad} = 63$

8 Write two multiplication and two division facts to describe the **array**: ⭕⭕⭕⭕⭕⭕⭕⭕⭕⭕

9 Cross off all of the winning **numbers** to find which row (A, B or C) wins. $\underline{\quad}$

A	20	42	10	36
B	4	12	6	2
C	16	8	7	32

a 5×2 　 b 4×4 　 c $24 \div 4$ 　 d $40 \div 10$

e 6×7 　 f $6 \div 2$ 　 g 4×8 　 h $16 \div 8$

Using number lines

1 Use the **jump strategy** to solve the addition equations:

a $32 + 19 =$ _____   b $31 + 28 =$ _____
c $36 + 17 =$ _____   d $42 + 18 =$ _____
e $39 + 13 =$ _____   f $34 + 21 =$ _____

2 Use the **jump strategy** to solve the subtraction equations:

a $50 - 13 =$ _____   b $29 - 7 =$ _____
c $43 - 15 =$ _____   d $49 - 23 =$ _____
e $45 - 18 =$ _____   f $46 - 18 =$ _____

3 Use the **number line** to find the answers:

a $5 \times 3 =$ _____   b $4 \times 6 =$ _____
c $7 \times 4 =$ _____   d $3 \times 9 =$ _____
e $3 \times 10 =$ _____   f $2 \times 7 =$ _____

4 Use the **number line** to find the answers:

a $20 \div 5 =$ _____   b $18 \div 9 =$ _____
c $21 \div 7 =$ _____   d $24 \div 6 =$ _____
e $30 \div 5 =$ _____   f $27 \div 3 =$ _____

5 Use the **jump strategy** to solve: $79 + 14 =$ _____

6 Use the **jump strategy** to solve: $94 - 16 =$ _____

7 Use the **number line** to find: 3×8 _____

8 Use the **number line** to find: $28 \div 4$ ____

9 Write four questions based around the following **number line**:

_____   _____
_____   _____

Inverse operations

1 Check the addition facts by using **subtraction**:

a $8 + 6 = 14$ $14 -$ _____ $=$ _____
b $9 + 15 = 24$ $24 -$ _____ $=$ _____
c $24 + 7 = 31$ $31 -$ _____ $=$ _____
d $17 + 8 = 25$ $25 -$ _____ $=$ _____
e $26 + 5 = 31$ $31 -$ _____ $=$ _____
f $35 + 8 = 43$ $43 -$ _____ $=$ _____

2 Check the subtraction facts by using **addition**:

a $14 - 6 = 8$ $8 +$ _____ $=$ _____
b $21 - 8 = 13$ $13 +$ _____ $=$ _____
c $25 - 19 = 6$ $6 +$ _____ $=$ _____
d $36 - 17 = 19$ $19 +$ _____ $=$ _____
e $37 - 28 = 9$ $9 +$ _____ $=$ _____
f $23 - 6 = 17$ $17 +$ _____ $=$ _____

3 Write a **division** fact from each multiplication fact:

a $7 \times 5 = 35$ $35 \div$ _____ $=$ _____
b $9 \times 3 = 27$ $27 \div$ _____ $=$ _____
c $4 \times 9 = 36$ $36 \div$ _____ $=$ _____
d $8 \times 6 = 48$ $48 \div$ _____ $=$ _____
e $2 \times 9 = 18$ $18 \div$ _____ $=$ _____
f $3 \times 10 = 30$ $30 \div$ _____ $=$ _____

4 Write a **multiplication** fact from each division fact:

a $16 \div 4 = 4$ $4 \times$ _____ $=$ _____
b $21 \div 7 = 3$ $3 \times$ _____ $=$ _____
c $18 \div 6 = 3$ $3 \times$ _____ $=$ _____
d $20 \div 4 = 5$ $5 \times$ _____ $=$ _____
e $42 \div 6 = 7$ $7 \times$ _____ $=$ _____
f $50 \div 5 = 10$ $10 \times$ _____ $=$ _____

5 Check the addition facts by using **subtraction**:

$29 + 17 = 46$ $46 -$ _____ $=$ _____

6 Check the subtraction facts by using **addition**:

$24 - 16 = 8$ $8 +$ _____ $=$ _____

7 Write a **division** fact from the multiplication fact:

$8 \times 7 = 56$ $56 \div$ ____ $=$ ____

8 Write a **multiplication** fact from the division fact:

$27 \div 9 = 3$ $3 \times$ _____ $=$ _____

9 Write: 2 addition _____ , _____
          2 subtraction _____ , _____
          2 multiplication _____ , _____
   and   2 division _____ , _____
facts that give the **answer 10**.

Which order?

1 Rewrite each **number sentence** to make it easier to solve:

a $6 + 7 + 4 =$ _____

b $18 + 4 + 2 =$ _____

c $17 + 6 + 3 =$ _____

d $7 + 8 + 3 =$ _____

e $5 + 8 + 15 =$ _____

f $12 + 9 + 8 =$ _____

2 **Add** the following sets of numbers:

a $6 + 4 =$ _____ $4 + 6 =$ _____

b $10 + 12 =$ _____ $12 + 10 =$ _____

c $6 + 9 =$ _____ $9 + 6 =$ _____

d $8 + 5 =$ _____ $5 + 8 =$ _____

e $13 + 6 =$ _____ $6 + 13 =$ _____

f $18 + 7 =$ _____ $7 + 18 =$ _____

3 **Multiply** the following sets of numbers:

a $3 \times 6 =$ _____ $6 \times 3 =$ _____

b $4 \times 2 =$ _____ $2 \times 4 =$ _____

c $6 \times 7 =$ _____ $7 \times 6 =$ _____

d $5 \times 8 =$ _____ $8 \times 5 =$ _____

e $9 \times 10 =$ _____ $10 \times 9 =$ _____

f $8 \times 4 =$ _____ $4 \times 8 =$ _____

4 **Complete** the spaces:

a $9 + 7 =$ _____ $7 +$ _____ $= 16$

b $13 + 5 =$ _____ $5 +$ _____ $= 18$

c $11 + 9 =$ _____ $9 +$ _____ $= 20$

d $7 \times 6 =$ _____   _____ $\times 7 = 42$

e $3 \times 8 =$ _____   _____ $\times 3 = 24$

f $10 \times 8 =$ _____   _____ $\times 10 = 80$

5 Rewrite the **number sentence** $14 + 9 + 6 =$ to make it easier to solve. _____

6 **Add** the following numbers:

$18 + 3 =$ _____ $3 + 18 =$ _____

7 **Multiply** the following numbers:

$8 \times 6 =$ _____ $6 \times 8 =$ _____

8 **Complete** the spaces:

$4 \times 10 =$ _____   _____ $\times 4 = 40$

9 Bert had a box of chocolates with 6 rows of 4 chocolates.

Greg had a box of chocolates with 4 rows of 6 chocolates.

Who had the **most** chocolates? _____

Bingo!

1 Mark off the numbers to find the **winning row**:

17	4	6	15
3	8	11	2
10	16	7	14

a $4 + 3$ b $8 + 7$
c $10 + 6$ d $3 + 11$
e $6 + 5$ f $1 + 9$

2 Mark off the numbers to find the **winning row**:

5	12	8	4
6	10	1	2
3	11	7	9

a $8 - 7$ b $11 - 5$
c $15 - 7$ d $16 - 9$
e $7 - 5$ f $18 - 8$

3 Mark off the numbers to find the **winning row**:

6	16	15	4
10	14	9	8
2	18	12	20

a 4×5 b 3×6
c 2×1 d 5×2
e 3×3 f 4×3

4 Mark off the numbers to find the **winning row**:

10	2	8	9
12	3	5	6
1	16	4	7

a $16 \div 2$ b $12 \div 3$
c $20 \div 2$ d $14 \div 7$
e $18 \div 6$ f $9 \div 1$

5 Mark off the numbers to find the **winning row**:

10	8	5
6	4	7

$3 + 5$ $2 + 2$ $6 + 4$ $4 + 1$ _____

6 Mark off the numbers to find the **winning row**:

8	6	3
5	1	7

$11 - 4$ $8 - 3$ $7 - 1$ $9 - 8$ _____

7 Mark off the numbers to find the **winning row**:

5	8	16
3	12	10

2×5 3×1 8×2 2×6 _____

8 Mark off the numbers to find the **winning row**:

5	2	4
7	3	6

$6 \div 3$ $14 \div 2$ $16 \div 4$ $10 \div 2$ _____

9 Circle the **winning Bingo card**.

11	7	1	28
8	25	26	30

17	15	4	14
3	24	5	22

20	15	14	2
6	17	9	10

$2 + 5$ $8 + 6$ $10 + 14$ $1 + 1$

$26 - 9$ $19 - 11$ $30 - 20$ $28 - 2$

3×5 4×7 $20 + 2$ 3×3

$22 - 11$ $18 \div 3$ $20 \div 4$ 4×5

Missing numbers

❶ Supply the **missing numbers** for the spaces:
  a 8 + _____ = 14
  b 35 + _____ = 50
  c 42 + _____ = 56
  d 17 − _____ = 9
  e 26 − _____ = 13
  f 46 − _____ = 12

❷ Supply the **missing numbers** for the spaces:
  a 7 × _____ = 28
  b 6 × _____ = 30
  c 9 × _____ = 54
  d _____ × 2 = 6
  e _____ × 10 = 100
  f _____ × 9 = 72

❸ Supply the **missing numbers** for the spaces:
  a 8 ÷ _____ = 4
  b 9 ÷ _____ = 3
  c 24 ÷ _____ = 6
  d 50 ÷ _____ = 5
  e 18 ÷ _____ = 9
  f 36 ÷ _____ = 6

❹ Use +, − or × **symbols** to make the number sentences correct:
  a 4 ☐ 7 = 11
  b 4 ☐ 3 = 12
  c 18 ☐ 12 = 6
  d 13 ☐ 11 = 24
  e 20 ☐ 13 = 7
  f 8 ☐ 4 = 32

❺ Supply the **missing number** for the space:
  25 + _____ = 47

❻ Supply the **missing number** for the space:
  ___ × 3 = 21

❼ Supply the **missing number** for the space:
  80 ÷ _____ = 8

❽ Use +, − or × **symbols** to make 15 ☐ 12 = 27 correct.

❾ Use +, − or × **symbols** to make the following number sentences correct:
  a 3 ☐ 4 ☐ 5 = 17
  b 5 ☐ 4 ☐ 3 = 4
  c 8 ☐ 9 ☐ 10 = 62
  d 5 ☐ 10 ☐ 15 = 65

Patterns (2)

❶ Complete each **pattern**:
  a 0, 2, 4, 6, _____, _____, _____
  b 0, 3, 6, 9, 12, _____, _____, _____
  c 0, 6, 12, 18, 24, _____, _____, _____
  d 0, 5, 10, 15, 20, _____, _____, _____
  e 0, 4, 8, 12, 16, _____, _____, _____
  f 0, 7, 14, 21, 28, _____, _____, _____

❷ Complete each **pattern** and then write a **rule** for it:
  a 50, 55, 60, 65, _____, _____, _____; _____
  b 50, 60, 70, 80, _____, _____, _____; _____
  c 50, 52, 54, 56, _____, _____, _____; _____
  d 30, 36, 42, 48, _____, _____, _____; _____
  e 40, 48, 56, 64, _____, _____, _____; _____
  f 11, 22, 33, 44, _____, _____, _____; _____

❸ For each of the following patterns, state what the **tenth number** would be:
  a 2, 4, 6, 8, ... _____   b 3, 6, 9, 12, ... _____
  c 20, 24, 28, 32, ... _____   d 10, 15, 20, 25, ... _____
  e 100, 101, 102, 103, ... _____
  f 100, 105, 110, 115, ... _____

❹ Complete the following **grids**:

a
+	4	14	24	34	44
4					

b
+	6	16	26	36	46
6					

c
+	5	15	25	35	45
3					

d
+	4	14	24	34	44
6					

e
+	8	18	28	38	48
8					

f
+	9	19	29	39	49
9					

❺ Complete the **pattern**:
  0, 9, 18, 27, 36, 45, _____, _____, _____

❻ Complete the **pattern** and write a **rule** for it:
  30, 33, 36, 39, _____, _____, _____; _____

❼ For the pattern 40, 44, 48, 52, ... state what the **tenth number** would be. _____

❽ Complete the **grid**:
+	11	21	31	41	51
6					

❾ Create two number **patterns** starting at 100.

  _____

  _____

Rules for patterns

1 Write the **next number** in each of the following patterns:

a 10, 20, 30, _____   b 99, 88, 77, _____

c 3, 6, 9, _____   d 50, 45, 40, _____

e 10, 17, 24, _____   f 49, 48, 47, _____

2 Continue each **pattern** by following the rule:

a Add 5:   25, _____, _____, _____

b Subtract 10:   100, _____, _____, _____

c Multiply by 2:   4, _____, _____, _____

d Add 8:   20, _____, _____, _____

e Subtract 7:   49, _____, _____, _____

f Multiply by 3:   1, _____, _____, _____

3 Write a **rule** for each of the following:

a 2, 4, 6, 8 _____

b 20, 17, 14, 11 _____

c 10, 20, 30, 40 _____

d 9, 15, 21, 27 _____

e 50, 46, 42, 38 _____

f 4, 12, 36, 108 _____

4 Write the **rule** for the number of dots used in each of the following patterns:

a
_____

b
_____

c
_____

d
_____

e
_____

f
_____

5 Write the **next number** in: 20, 18, 16, _____

6 Continue the **pattern** of adding 6:
11, _____, _____, _____

7 Write a **rule** for: 5, 50, 500, 5000
_____

8 Write a **rule** for the number of dots used:
_____

9 Write two different **rules** for your own patterns starting at 100.
_____
_____

Calculator – place value

1 Write the **calculator sentence** you would use to change:

a 54 to 50   b 35 to 30
_____   _____

c 91 to 90   d 180 to 187
_____   _____

e 230 to 236   f 720 to 726
_____   _____

2 Write the **calculator sentence** you would use to change:

a 86 to 6   b 49 to 9
_____   _____

c 35 to 5   d 106 to 186
_____   _____

e 508 to 558   f 402 to 492
_____   _____

3 Write the **calculator sentence** you would use to change:

a 427 to 27   b 960 to 60
_____   _____

c 829 to 29   d 73 to 473
_____   _____

e 20 to 120   f 14 to 214
_____   _____

4 Write the **calculator sentence** you would use to change:

a 1426 to 426   b 2385 to 385
_____   _____

c 4520 to 520   d 291 to 3291
_____   _____

e 160 to 5160   f 945 to 8945
_____   _____

5 Write the **calculator sentence** you would use to change 419 to 410. _____

6 Write the **calculator sentence** you would use to change 906 to 946. _____

7 Write the **calculator sentence** you would use to change 73 to 573. _____

8 Write the **calculator sentence** you would use to change 491 to 6491. _____

9 Use your **calculator** to find the answer to:

4) + 6   × 10   ÷ 2   − 2   ÷ 2

UNIT 73
See START UPS page 5
Calculator – addition and subtraction

1 Using a **calculator**, find the answer to each of the following:

   a 438 + 279 _____   b 562 + 893 _____

   c 729 + 579 _____   d 1236 + 1499 _____

   e 2365 + 4852 _____

   f 2895 + 5876 _____

2 Using a **calculator**, find the answer to each of the following:

   a 479 − 389 _____   b 725 − 699 _____

   c 852 − 376 _____   d 1254 − 879 _____

   e 4689 − 3927 _____

   f 8492 − 7836 _____

3 Using a calculator, find the answer to each of the following:

   a **add** 529 and 678 _____

   b 326 **minus** 198 _____

   c 1426 **plus** 2875 _____

   d the **difference between** 812 and 485 _____

   e the **sum** of 1276 and 987 _____

   f 841 **take away** 273 _____

4 **Write** a calculator sentence for each of the following and find the **answer**:

   a Sophie has 324 stamps and 479 cards. How many items does she have? _____

   b Neil had 441 nails but used 279. How many did he have left? _____

   c Jake had 872 $1 coins in one jar and 584 $1 coins in another. How many $1 coins? _____

   d Kim had picked 1424 strawberries. She gave away 956. How many left? _____

   e Jodie had 235 jelly beans in one bag and 198 in the other. What was the total number of jelly beans? _____

   f Josh counted 275 pieces of Lego in one tub and 349 in another. What was the total number of pieces? _____

5 Use a **calculator** to find the answer to:
2926 + 1462 = _____

6 Use a **calculator** to find the answer to:
6426 − 2872 = _____

7 Use a calculator to find the **sum** of 621 and 1856. _____

8 George needed 945 bricks for the paving. He has 489 already. **Write** a calculator sentence to find **how many more** bricks were needed. _____

9 **Find**: one thousand six hundred and fifty two **plus** two thousand, four hundred and seventy-six. _____

UNIT 74
See START UPS page 5
Calculator – multiplication and division

1 Using a **calculator**, find the answer to each of the following:

   a $33 \times 9 =$ _____   b $48 \times 3 =$ _____

   c $110 \times 4 =$ _____   d $214 \times 7 =$ _____

   e $239 \times 5 =$ _____   f $412 \times 6 =$ _____

2 Using a **calculator**, find the answer to each of the following:

   a $510 \div 5 =$ _____   b $102 \div 3 =$ _____

   c $198 \div 2 =$ _____   d $136 \div 4 =$ _____

   e $360 \div 6 =$ _____   f $245 \div 7 =$ _____

3 Using a calculator, find the answer to each of the following:

   a 8 **times** 91 _____

   b 6 **multiplied** by 52 _____

   c 9 **groups** of 14 _____

   d 126 **divided** by 3 _____

   e 171, **how many** 9s are there? _____

   f **how many groups** of 8 in 136? _____

4 Write a **calculator sentence** for each of the following and find the **answer**:

   a Ben has 12 boxes of 15 apples. How many apples in total? _____

   b David has 25 boxes of 35 matches. How many matches altogether? _____

   c Anita has 5 packets of 155 sheets of paper. How many sheets of paper altogether? _____

   d Sue needs to put 198 brochures into 6 boxes. How many brochures in each box? _____

   e Chris has 136 nails to put in 4 buckets. How many nails in each bucket? _____

   f Helen needs to sort 612 oranges into 12 boxes. How many oranges in each box? _____

5 Use a **calculator** to find the answer to:
$412 \times 7 =$ _____

6 Use a **calculator** to find the answer to: $195 \div 5 =$ _____

7 Use a **calculator** to find the answer to:
424, how many groups of 4? _____

8 Write a **calculator sentence** and find the **answer** for: There are 9 classes of 25 students at the school. How many students are at the school? _____

9 Write five different **calculator sentences** which have the answer of 1000.

_____

_____

_____

_____

_____

Fraction names

1 **Complete**:

a $\frac{2}{3}$ is ___ out of 3 equal parts.

b $\frac{1}{4}$ is ___ out of 4 equal parts.

c $\frac{3}{6}$ is ___ out of 6 equal parts.

d $\frac{4}{10}$ is ___ out of _____ equal parts.

e $\frac{6}{8}$ is ___ out of ___ equal parts.

f $\frac{3}{5}$ is ___ out of ___ equal parts.

2 Write the following fractions as **numbers**:

a two fifths ___   b seven eighths ___   c four sixths ___

d three tenths ___   e one third ___   f three quarters ___

3 Write the fraction numbers in **words**:

a $\frac{1}{2}$ _____   b $\frac{4}{5}$ _____

c $\frac{2}{6}$ _____   d $\frac{3}{8}$ _____

e $\frac{2}{3}$ _____   f $\frac{7}{10}$ _____

4 Draw a **picture** to show:

a nine tenths   b two quarters

c five sixths   d one fifth

e two eighths   f seven tenths

5 **Complete**: $\frac{5}{8}$ is ___ out of ___ equal parts.

6 Write the fraction two tenths as a **number**. ___

7 Write the fraction $\frac{1}{6}$ in **words**.
_____

8 Draw a **picture** to show eight tenths.

9 Write the fraction in **words** to describe each of the following diagrams:

a _____

b _____

Naming fractions (1)

1 Complete the **labels** to represent the shaded part of each shape:

a ___ out of ___   b ___ out of ___

c ___ out of ___   d ___ out of ___

e ___ out of ___   f ___ out of ___

2 Complete the **fractions** to represent the shaded part of each shape:

a $\frac{\square}{4}$ b $\frac{3}{\square}$

c $\frac{\square}{\square}$ d $\frac{\square}{9}$

e $\frac{7}{\square}$ f $\frac{\square}{\square}$

3 **What part** of each shape has been shaded?

a $\frac{\square}{\square}$ b $\frac{\square}{\square}$

c $\frac{\square}{\square}$ d $\frac{\square}{\square}$

e $\frac{\square}{\square}$ f $\frac{\square}{\square}$

4 **What part** of each group has been shaded?

a $\frac{\square}{\square}$ b $\frac{\square}{\square}$

c $\frac{\square}{\square}$ d $\frac{\square}{\square}$

e $\frac{\square}{\square}$ f $\frac{\square}{\square}$

5 Complete the **label** for: ___ out of ___

6 Write a **fraction** for: $\frac{\square}{\square}$

7 **What part** of △ has been shaded? $\frac{\square}{\square}$

8 **What part** of ☆☆☆ ★★ has been shaded? $\frac{\square}{\square}$

9 Is ⊞ the **same** as ⊞ ? ___

Naming fractions (2)

1 What **part** of each of the following has been shaded?

a   b

c   d ☆☆☆☆☆ ☆☆☆☆☆

e   f

2 Colour **part** of each shape to match the given fraction:

a $\frac{1}{2}$ b $\frac{2}{3}$ c $\frac{3}{4}$

d $\frac{5}{6}$ e $\frac{3}{8}$ f $\frac{4}{5}$

3 Colour **part** of each group to match the given fraction:

a $\frac{6}{7}$ b $\frac{1}{10}$ c $\frac{1}{6}$

d $\frac{5}{8}$ e $\frac{1}{3}$ f $\frac{3}{4}$

4 **Shade** the given fraction:

a $\frac{2}{5}$ of the boxes   b $\frac{1}{2}$ of the circle

c $\frac{1}{8}$ of the square   d $\frac{1}{10}$ of the triangles

e $\frac{3}{4}$ of the group   f $\frac{5}{8}$ of the block

5 What **part** of ●●● has been shaded?
      ○○○

6 Colour **part** of ▭ to show $\frac{3}{8}$.

7 Colour **part** of △△△△△ to show $\frac{7}{9}$.
              △△△△

8 **Colour** $\frac{5}{6}$ of the pizza.

9 Draw a **picture** to show $\frac{3}{4}$ of a circle.

Naming fractions (3)

1 What **part** of each of the following has been shaded?

a   b   c

d   e   f

2 **Colour part** of each shape to match the given fraction:

a $\frac{1}{2}$ b $\frac{3}{4}$ c $\frac{5}{8}$

d $\frac{1}{8}$ e $\frac{3}{6}$ f $\frac{2}{4}$

3 Write **another name** for the shaded part, other than the one given:

a $\frac{3}{6}$ ____   b $\frac{2}{2}$ ____

c $\frac{2}{8}$ ____   d $\frac{2}{4}$ ____

e $\frac{2}{6}$ ____   f $\frac{6}{10}$ ____

4 **Colour part** of each group to match the fraction:

a $\frac{1}{2}$ b $\frac{3}{4}$ c 1

d $\frac{1}{3}$ e $\frac{1}{5}$ f $\frac{1}{4}$

5 What **part** of ◇ has been shaded?

6 **Colour part** of ▭ to show $\frac{3}{10}$.

7 Write **another name** for the shaded part of ▦ other than $\frac{4}{4}$. ____

8 **Colour part** of △△△△△ to show $\frac{2}{3}$.
              △△△△

9 $\frac{4}{8}$ $\frac{6}{8}$ $\frac{1}{2}$ $\frac{2}{4}$

Colour the **fraction** of each of the pizzas. Which pizza does not have the same amount coloured? ____

Comparing fractions

1 Circle the **larger** fraction:

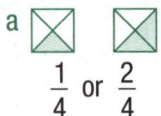

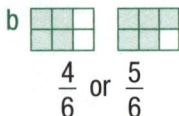

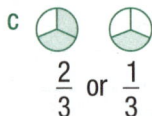

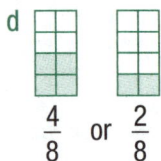

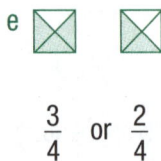

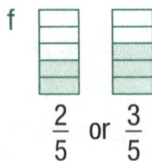

a ⊠ ⊠ $\frac{1}{4}$ or $\frac{2}{4}$ b ▦ ▦ $\frac{4}{6}$ or $\frac{5}{6}$ c ◔ ◔ $\frac{2}{3}$ or $\frac{1}{3}$

d ▦ ▦ $\frac{4}{8}$ or $\frac{2}{8}$ e ⊠ ⊠ $\frac{3}{4}$ or $\frac{2}{4}$ f ▤ ▤ $\frac{2}{5}$ or $\frac{3}{5}$

2 Colour the **larger** fraction for the following groups:

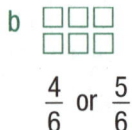

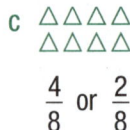

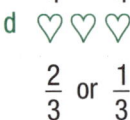

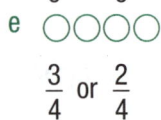

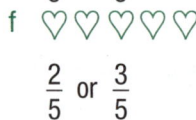

a ◇◇ ◇◇ $\frac{1}{4}$ or $\frac{2}{4}$ b ☐☐☐ ☐☐☐ $\frac{4}{6}$ or $\frac{5}{6}$ c △△△△ △△△△ $\frac{4}{8}$ or $\frac{2}{8}$

d ♡♡♡ $\frac{2}{3}$ or $\frac{1}{3}$ e ○○○○ $\frac{3}{4}$ or $\frac{2}{4}$ f ♡♡♡♡♡ $\frac{2}{5}$ or $\frac{3}{5}$

3 Order the following sets of fractions from **smallest to largest**.

a $\frac{1}{4}, \frac{4}{4}, \frac{2}{4}, \frac{3}{4}$ b $\frac{2}{5}, \frac{4}{5}, \frac{1}{5}, \frac{3}{5}$ c $\frac{1}{8}, \frac{3}{8}, \frac{4}{8}, \frac{2}{8}$

d $\frac{4}{6}, \frac{2}{6}, \frac{3}{6}, \frac{6}{6}$ e $\frac{3}{10}, \frac{9}{10}, \frac{7}{10}, \frac{5}{10}$ f $\frac{8}{8}, \frac{3}{8}, \frac{6}{8}, \frac{5}{8}$

4 Circle the **smaller** fraction:

a $\frac{2}{10}$ or $\frac{9}{10}$ b $\frac{3}{4}$ or $\frac{1}{4}$ c $\frac{4}{5}$ or $\frac{2}{5}$

d $\frac{3}{3}$ or $\frac{1}{3}$ e $\frac{3}{8}$ or $\frac{5}{8}$ f $\frac{4}{6}$ or $\frac{2}{6}$

5 Circle the **larger** fraction: △ $\frac{1}{3}$ or △ $\frac{2}{3}$

6 Colour the **larger** fraction: ○○○ ○○ $\frac{4}{5}$ or $\frac{2}{5}$

7 Order the fractions $\frac{1}{5}, \frac{4}{5}, \frac{3}{5}, \frac{5}{5}$ from **smallest to largest**.

8 Circle the **smaller** fraction $\frac{3}{4}$ or $\frac{1}{4}$.

9 Draw a **picture** to show the fractions $\frac{1}{8}$ and $\frac{3}{8}$, and circle the **smaller** fraction.

Fractions of a collection

1 **Find** the fraction of each collection:

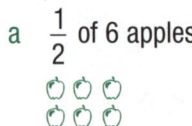

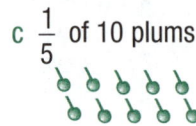

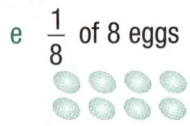

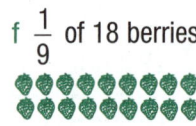

a $\frac{1}{2}$ of 6 apples b $\frac{1}{4}$ of 8 cakes c $\frac{1}{5}$ of 10 plums

d $\frac{1}{3}$ of 9 pears e $\frac{1}{8}$ of 8 eggs f $\frac{1}{9}$ of 18 berries

2 Draw a **picture** to show:

a $\frac{1}{2}$ of 8 tennis balls   b $\frac{1}{4}$ of 12 basketballs

c $\frac{1}{3}$ of 3 volleyballs   d $\frac{1}{10}$ of 20 golf balls

e $\frac{1}{8}$ of 16 baseballs   f $\frac{1}{5}$ of 10 cricket balls

3 **Find** the fraction of each collection:

a $\frac{1}{4}$ of 16 triangles ____ b $\frac{1}{2}$ of 10 squares ____

c $\frac{1}{3}$ of 6 circles ____ d $\frac{1}{5}$ of 5 trapeziums ____

e $\frac{1}{8}$ of 16 rectangles ____ f $\frac{1}{10}$ of 40 ovals ____

4 **How many** points did each person score if they scored:

a Ash: $\frac{1}{4}$ of 20 points? ____

b Victoria: $\frac{1}{3}$ of 18 points? ____

c George: $\frac{1}{10}$ of 50 points? ____

d Izzy: $\frac{1}{5}$ of 25 points? ____

e Alex: $\frac{1}{2}$ of 20 points? ____

f John: $\frac{1}{8}$ of 40 points? ____

5 **Find** $\frac{1}{5}$ of 15 oranges.

6 Draw a **picture** to show $\frac{1}{2}$ of 14 cricket balls.

7 **Find** $\frac{1}{3}$ of 12 diamonds. _____

8 **How many** points? Polly scored $\frac{1}{8}$ of 16 points. ____

9 There were 20 biscuits in the tray. Alf took $\frac{1}{4}$ of the biscuits. How many were **left**? ____

Equivalent fractions

1 **Colour part** of each shape to match the given fraction:

a $\frac{1}{2}$　　b $\frac{1}{2}$　　c $\frac{1}{2}$

d $\frac{1}{4}$　　e $\frac{1}{4}$　　f $\frac{1}{4}$

2 Circle the **larger** fraction in each pair:

a $\frac{4}{10}$ or $\frac{5}{10}$　　b $\frac{1}{4}$ or $\frac{3}{4}$　　c $\frac{4}{5}$ or $\frac{2}{5}$

d $\frac{1}{3}$ or $\frac{2}{3}$　　e $\frac{5}{8}$ or $\frac{3}{8}$　　f $\frac{9}{10}$ or $\frac{7}{10}$

3 **Match** the fractions which are equal by drawing lines:

a $\frac{2}{8}$　b $\frac{1}{2}$　c $\frac{1}{5}$　d $\frac{3}{4}$　e $\frac{6}{10}$　f $\frac{1}{3}$

$\frac{2}{10}$　$\frac{6}{8}$　$\frac{1}{4}$　$\frac{2}{6}$　$\frac{5}{10}$　$\frac{3}{5}$

4 Write **true or false** for each of the following statements:

a $\frac{1}{2} = \frac{3}{4}$ ____　b $\frac{5}{10} = \frac{1}{2}$ ____　c $\frac{1}{3} = \frac{2}{4}$ ____

d $\frac{3}{4} = \frac{6}{8}$ ____　e $\frac{2}{5} = \frac{4}{10}$ ____　f $\frac{1}{8} = \frac{1}{4}$ ____

5 **Colour part** of ▢▢▢▢▢▢ to show $\frac{1}{2}$.

6 Circle the **larger** fraction of: $\frac{9}{10}$ or $\frac{3}{10}$

7 **Match** the fractions which are equal by drawing lines:

a $\frac{1}{4}$　　b $\frac{2}{10}$　　c $\frac{2}{3}$

$\frac{4}{6}$　　$\frac{2}{8}$　　$\frac{1}{5}$

8 Write **true or false** for:

$\frac{9}{10} = \frac{3}{5}$ _____

9 Complete each counting **pattern**:

a $\frac{1}{5}, \frac{2}{5}$, ___, ___, ___

b $\frac{1}{8}, \frac{2}{8}$, ___, ___, ___

c $\frac{5}{10}, \frac{6}{10}$, ___, ___, ___

Hundredths (1)

1 Write the **number** out of 100 for each of the following hundredths grids:

a　　b　　c

___ out of 100　___ out of 100　___ out of 100

d　　e　　f

___ out of 100　___ out of 100　___ out of 100

2 What **part** of each hundredths square has been coloured? Write your answer as a fraction.

a ____　b ____　c ____

d ____　e ____　f ____

3 **Colour** the hundredths square to match the hundredths:

a　　b　　c

12 out of 100　36 out of 100　23 out of 100

d　　e　　f

57 out of 100　94 out of 100　72 out of 100

4 **Colour** the hundredths square to match the given fraction:

a $\frac{5}{100}$　b $\frac{45}{100}$　c $\frac{51}{100}$

d $\frac{63}{100}$　e $\frac{80}{100}$　f $\frac{100}{100}$

5 Write the **number** out of 100 for:

_____ out of 100

6 What **part** of the hundredths square has been coloured? Write the answer as a fraction. ____

7 **Colour** $\frac{47}{100}$ on the hundredths square.

8 **Colour** $\frac{29}{100}$ on the hundredths square.

9 Order the hundredths from **smallest to largest**:

___ ___ ___ ___

Hundredths (2)

1 What **part** of each hundredths square has been coloured?

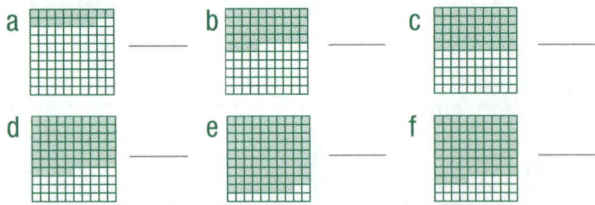

a _____   b _____   c _____

d _____   e _____   f _____

2 **Colour** the hundredths square to match the given fraction:

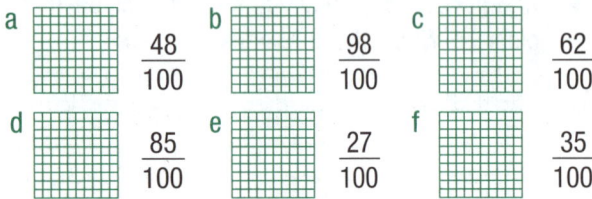

a $\dfrac{48}{100}$ b $\dfrac{98}{100}$ c $\dfrac{62}{100}$

d $\dfrac{85}{100}$ e $\dfrac{27}{100}$ f $\dfrac{35}{100}$

3 Circle the **larger** amount in each pair:

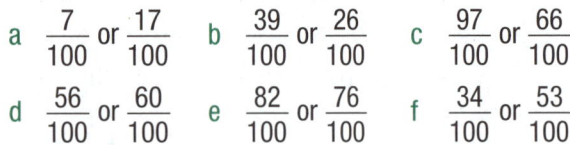

a $\dfrac{7}{100}$ or $\dfrac{17}{100}$ b $\dfrac{39}{100}$ or $\dfrac{26}{100}$ c $\dfrac{97}{100}$ or $\dfrac{66}{100}$

d $\dfrac{56}{100}$ or $\dfrac{60}{100}$ e $\dfrac{82}{100}$ or $\dfrac{76}{100}$ f $\dfrac{34}{100}$ or $\dfrac{53}{100}$

4 **Complete** the **grids**:

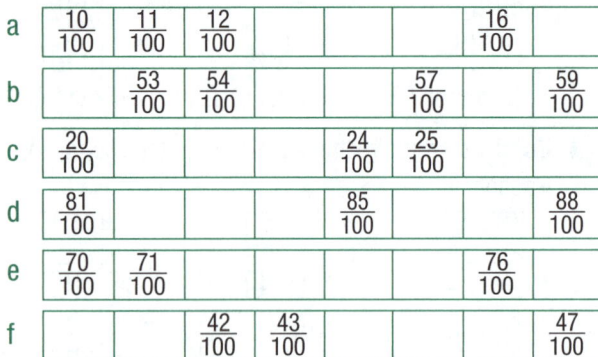

a

| $\dfrac{10}{100}$ | $\dfrac{11}{100}$ | $\dfrac{12}{100}$ | | | $\dfrac{16}{100}$ | |

b

| | $\dfrac{53}{100}$ | $\dfrac{54}{100}$ | | $\dfrac{57}{100}$ | | $\dfrac{59}{100}$ |

c

| $\dfrac{20}{100}$ | | | $\dfrac{24}{100}$ | $\dfrac{25}{100}$ | | |

d

| $\dfrac{81}{100}$ | | | $\dfrac{85}{100}$ | | | $\dfrac{88}{100}$ |

e

| $\dfrac{70}{100}$ | $\dfrac{71}{100}$ | | | | $\dfrac{76}{100}$ | |

f

| | | $\dfrac{42}{100}$ | $\dfrac{43}{100}$ | | | $\dfrac{47}{100}$ |

5 What **part** of [grid] has been coloured? _____

6 **Colour** $\dfrac{19}{100}$ on the hundredths square.

7 Circle the **larger** amount in the pair: $\dfrac{9}{100}$ $\dfrac{91}{100}$

8 **Complete** the **gride**:

| $\dfrac{90}{100}$ | | | $\dfrac{93}{100}$ | | $\dfrac{95}{100}$ | | |

9 What **fractions** are shown on the models?

_____   _____

Tenths (1)

1 **Shade** each hundredths square to represent the tenths:

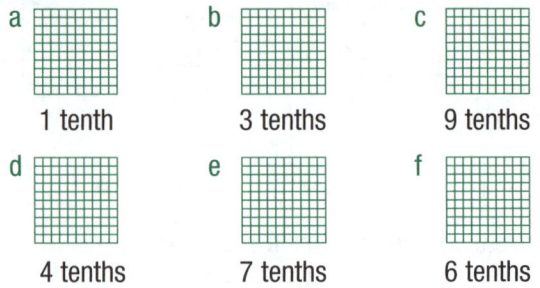

a 1 tenth   b 3 tenths   c 9 tenths

d 4 tenths   e 7 tenths   f 6 tenths

2 Record the shaded fraction of each hundredths grid in **tenths**:

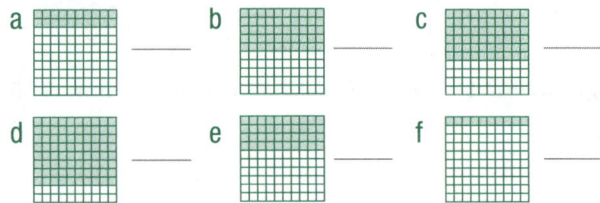

a _____   b _____   c _____

d _____   e _____   f _____

3 Record the shaded fraction of each hundredths grid as a **decimal**:

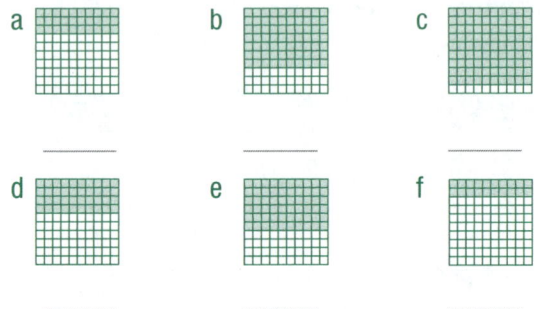

a   b   c

_____

d   e   f

_____

4 Use **decimals** to write:

a one tenth _____   b five tenths _____

c eight tenths _____   d three tenths _____

e nine tenths _____   f four tenths _____

5 **Shade** the hundredths square to represent 2 tenths.

6 Record the shaded fraction [grid] in **tenths**.

_____

7 Record the shaded fraction [grid] as a **decimal**.

_____

8 Use **decimals** to write seven tenths. _____

9 On the **number line** complete the empty boxes to show the matching decimal for each fraction.

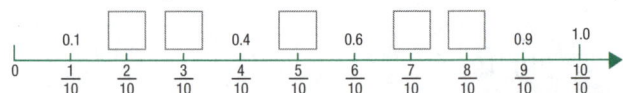

0.1 [ ] [ ] 0.4 [ ] 0.6 [ ] [ ] 0.9 1.0

0   $\dfrac{1}{10}$ $\dfrac{2}{10}$ $\dfrac{3}{10}$ $\dfrac{4}{10}$ $\dfrac{5}{10}$ $\dfrac{6}{10}$ $\dfrac{7}{10}$ $\dfrac{8}{10}$ $\dfrac{9}{10}$ $\dfrac{10}{10}$

Tenths (2)

1 Use **decimals** to write:
- a 5 tenths _____
- b 9 tenths _____
- c 2 tenths _____
- d 7 tenths _____
- e 3 tenths _____
- f 6 tenths _____

2 Write the **decimal** for each fraction:

a $\frac{1}{10}$ _____   b $\frac{4}{10}$ _____   c $\frac{8}{10}$ _____

d $\frac{3}{10}$ _____   e $\frac{6}{10}$ _____   f $\frac{9}{10}$ _____

3 Match the **decimal** with the correct fraction:

a
$\frac{1}{10}$	0.9
$\frac{3}{10}$	0.1
$\frac{9}{10}$	0.3

b
$\frac{4}{10}$	0.4
$\frac{6}{10}$	0.8
$\frac{8}{10}$	0.6

c
$\frac{2}{10}$	0.7
$\frac{5}{10}$	0.2
$\frac{7}{10}$	0.5

d
$\frac{2}{10}$	0.5
$\frac{3}{10}$	0.2
$\frac{5}{10}$	0.3

e
$\frac{3}{10}$	0.2
$\frac{2}{10}$	0.5
$\frac{5}{10}$	0.3

f
$\frac{3}{10}$	0.9
$\frac{7}{10}$	0.3
$\frac{9}{10}$	0.7

4 Write the **fraction** for each decimal:
- a 0.6
- b 0.3
- c 0.8
- d 1.5
- e 1.2
- f 2.4

5 Use **decimals** to write 4 tenths. _____

6 Write the **decimal** for $1\frac{7}{10}$. _____

7 Match the **decimal** with the correct fraction.

$\frac{2}{10}$	0.1
$\frac{4}{10}$	0.2
$\frac{1}{10}$	0.4

8 Write the **fraction** for: 0.7 _____

9 Complete the counting **patterns**:

a 0.2, 0.4, 0.6, _____, _____, _____

b $\frac{32}{100}, \frac{36}{100}, \frac{40}{100},$ _____, _____, _____

c $\frac{65}{100}, \frac{70}{100}, \frac{75}{100},$ _____, _____, _____

Counting forwards and backwards with decimals

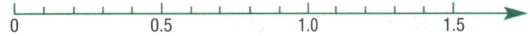

1 Start at:
- a 0.5 and **go forwards** 0.1 _____
- b 0.5 and go forwards 0.2 _____
- c 0.5 and go forwards 0.4 _____
- d 0.5 and go forwards 0.5 _____
- e 0.5 and go forwards 0.7 _____
- f 0.5 and go forwards 1.0 _____

2 Start at:

- a 0.9 and **go backwards** 0.1 _____
- b 0.9 and go backwards 0.2 _____
- c 0.9 and go backwards 0.4 _____
- d 0.9 and go backwards 0.8 _____
- e 0.9 and go backwards 0.5 _____
- f 0.9 and go backwards 0.9 _____

3 Start at 0.1 and:
- a **go forwards** 0.5 _____
- b then **go backwards** 0.2 _____
- c then **go backwards** 0.3 _____
- d then **go backwards** 0.1 _____
- e then **go forwards** 0.6 _____
- f then **go forwards** 0.5 _____

4 Start at 1.5 and:
- a **go backwards** 0.4 _____
- b then **go forwards** 0.7 _____
- c then **go backwards** 0.2 _____
- d then **go backwards** 0.1 _____
- e then **go backwards** 0.4 _____
- f then **go forwards** 0.9 _____

5 Start at 0.6 and **go forwards** 0.3: _____

6 Start at 0.6 and **go backwards** 0.4: _____

7 Start at 0.4 and **go forwards** 0.2 and **then go backwards** 0.3: _____

8 Start at 1.8 and **go backwards** 0.8 and **then go forwards** 0.4: _____

9 If I start at 1.6:
- a **how many** do I need to go forwards to stop at 2.3? _____
- b **how many** do I need to go backwards to stop at 0.8? _____

Decimals

1 What **decimal** is shown on the hundredths square?

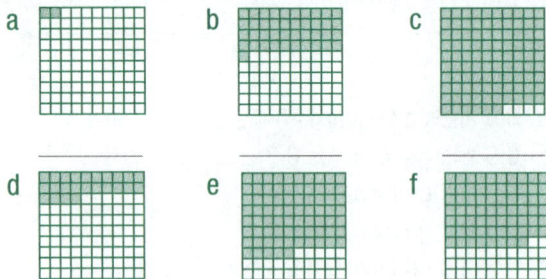

a   b   c

_____   _____   _____

d   e   f

_____   _____   _____

2 **Colour** part of each hundredths square to match the given decimal.

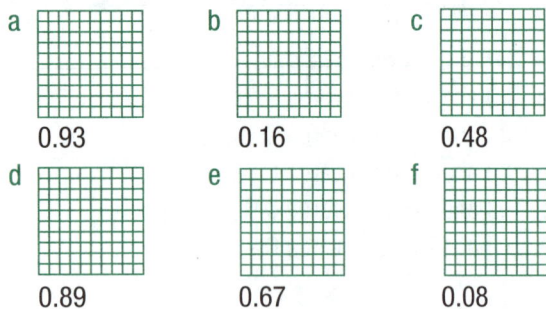

a   b   c

0.93   0.16   0.48

d   e   f

0.89   0.67   0.08

3 Complete the **numeral expander** for each decimal:

a 0.73 [tenths] [hundredths]

b 0.11 [tenths] [hundredths]

c 0.86 [tenths] [hundredths]

d 0.43 [tenths] [hundredths]

e 0.22 [tenths] [hundredths]

f 0.38 [tenths] [hundredths]

4 Complete the **decimals** from the stories:

a 100 animals, 62 are cats _____

b 100 people, 29 are male _____

c 100 parrots, 15 are blue _____

d 100 pencils, 75 are broken _____

e 100 biscuits, 41 are chocolate _____

f 100 cars, 36 are white _____

5 The **decimal** shown is:

_____

6 **Colour** the hundredths square to show: 0.64

7 Complete the **numeral expander** for: 0.84

[tenths] [hundredths]

8 Complete the **decimal**: 100 fish, 83 are orange. _____

9 Draw a **picture** to show: 1.86

Fractions to decimals

1 Write the **decimal** for each fraction:

a $\frac{4}{10}$ _____   b $\frac{6}{10}$ _____   c $\frac{8}{10}$ _____

d $\frac{37}{100}$ _____   e $\frac{61}{100}$ _____   f $\frac{87}{100}$ _____

2 Write the **decimal** for each fraction:

a $1\frac{1}{10}$ _____   b $2\frac{1}{10}$ _____   c $3\frac{3}{10}$ _____

d $2\frac{71}{100}$ _____   e $1\frac{33}{100}$ _____   f $1\frac{54}{100}$ _____

3 Use **decimals** to write:

a 2 tenths _____   b 5 tenths _____

c 9 tenths _____   d 21 hundredths _____

e 59 hundredths _____   f 84 hundredths _____

4 **Match** each decimal with the correct fraction:

a $\frac{4}{10}$ 0.6   b $\frac{3}{10}$ 0.8   c $\frac{61}{100}$ 0.99

$\frac{6}{10}$ 0.9 $\frac{2}{10}$ 0.3 $\frac{99}{100}$ 0.55

$\frac{9}{10}$ 0.4 $\frac{8}{10}$ 0.2 $\frac{55}{100}$ 0.61

d $\frac{92}{100}$ 0.30   e $1\frac{9}{100}$ 2.66   f $1\frac{70}{100}$ 1.97

$\frac{30}{100}$ 0.92 $2\frac{28}{100}$ 1.09 $1\frac{43}{100}$ 1.70

$\frac{81}{100}$ 0.81 $2\frac{66}{100}$ 2.28 $1\frac{97}{100}$ 1.43

5 Write the **decimal** for: $\frac{85}{100}$ _____

6 Write the **decimal** for: $1\frac{34}{100}$ _____

7 Use **decimals** to write 51 hundredths. _____

8 **Match** each decimal with the correct fraction:

$\frac{93}{100}$ $\frac{26}{100}$ $1\frac{76}{100}$

0.26   1.76   0.93

9 Order the following from **smallest to largest** by first making them all fractions **or** all decimals:

0.7 $\frac{3}{10}$ 0.5   0.2 $\frac{9}{10}$

Decimals and fractions

1 Write the **fraction** for:

a 6 tenths _____   b 9 tenths _____

c 2 tenths _____   d 8 tenths _____

e 1 tenth _____   f 5 tenths _____

2 Write the **fraction** for:

a 81 hundredths _____   b 69 hundredths _____

c 14 hundredths _____   d 48 hundredths _____

e 72 hundredths _____   f 57 hundredths _____

3 Write the **decimal** for:

a $\frac{3}{10}$ _____   b $\frac{4}{10}$ _____   c $\frac{7}{10}$ _____

d $\frac{23}{100}$ _____   e $\frac{74}{100}$ _____   f $\frac{62}{100}$ _____

4 Arrange in order from **smallest to largest**:

a 0.2   0.4   0.3 _____
b 0.9   0.6   0.8 _____
c 0.3   0.5   0.4 _____
d 0.9   0.3   0.1 _____
e 1.6   1.7   1.2 _____
f 1.9   2.2   1.5 _____

5 Write the **fraction** for 7 tenths. _____

6 Write the **fraction** for 58 hundredths. _____

7 Write the **decimal** for $\frac{89}{100}$. _____

8 Arrange in order from **smallest to largest**:
1.9   2.7   1.6 _____

9 a Which calculator screen displays the **largest** number?

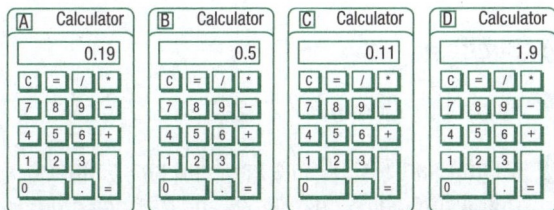

b Order the numbers from **smallest to largest**.

_____

Less than and greater than and rounding decimals

1 Write **true or false** for each fraction statement:

a $\frac{1}{8} < \frac{3}{8}$ _____   b $\frac{1}{5} > \frac{2}{5}$ _____

c $\frac{1}{10} > \frac{5}{10}$ _____   d $\frac{3}{4} > \frac{1}{4}$ _____

e $\frac{2}{4} < \frac{1}{4}$ _____   f $\frac{2}{5} > \frac{1}{5}$ _____

2 Use the correct sign, **< or >**, to make the fraction statements true:

a $\frac{1}{3} \square \frac{2}{3}$ b $\frac{3}{10} \square \frac{1}{10}$ c $\frac{4}{8} \square \frac{1}{8}$

d $\frac{2}{10} \square \frac{1}{10}$ e $\frac{1}{5} \square \frac{2}{5}$ f $\frac{6}{10} \square \frac{1}{10}$

3 Round each of the following decimals to the **nearest whole number**:

a 3.4 _____   b 6.7 _____

c 5.6 _____   d 4.27 _____

e 7.81 _____   f 0.87 _____

4 Use the correct sign, **< or >**, to make the decimal statements true:

a 0.5 $\square$ 0.9   b 0.3 $\square$ 0.1

c 0.8 $\square$ 0.4   d 0.7 $\square$ 1.0

e 0.25 $\square$ 0.75   f 0.5 $\square$ 0.6

5 Write **true or false** for: $\frac{2}{10} < \frac{1}{10}$ _____

6 Use the correct sign, **< or >**, to make the fraction statement true: $\frac{2}{3} \square \frac{1}{3}$

7 Round 2.73 to the **nearest whole number**.

_____

8 Use the correct sign, **< or >**, to make the decimal statement true: 0.4 $\square$ 0.2

9 Place the following fractions on the **number line**:

$\frac{1}{10}, \frac{1}{2}, \frac{2}{5}, \frac{7}{10}, \frac{1}{5}, \frac{3}{10}, \frac{3}{5}$

Decimal addition

1 **Add** the following decimals:

a	U	Tenths	b	U	Tenths	c	U	Tenths
	0	2		0	6		0	1
+	0	3	+	0	2	+	0	2

d	U	Tenths	e	U	Tenths	f	U	Tenths
	0	4		0	3		0	4
+	0	4	+	0	6	+	0	5

2 **Add** the following decimals:

a   1.5   b   3.2   c   1.4
   + 0.4   + 1.5   + 2.4

d   1.63   e   3.51   f   4.64
+ 2.12   + 2.32   + 0.31

3 **Add** the following decimals:

a   0.31 and 2.42 _____   b   0.43 and 0.25 _____
c   1.08 and 2.11 _____   d   5.61 and 2.27 _____
e   2.76 and 1.22 _____   f   3.65 and 2.23 _____

4 a   **Add:**   0.46 and 3.21 _____
   b   Find the **sum** of: 1.86 and 2.11 _____
   c   Find the **total** of: 9.03 and 0.46 _____
   d   **Add:**   1.48 and 2.51 _____
   e   Find the **sum** of: 6.25 and 3.03 _____
   f   Find the **total** of: 8.52 and 1.37 _____

5 **Add:**

	U	Tenths
	0	3
+	0	5

6 **Add:**   1.26
       + 3.43

7 **Add:**   1.09 and 2.90 _____

8 Find the **sum** of: 1.63 and 2.16 _____

9 Calculate the **total** of Mr Brown's lunch:

$1.55 $1.80 $0.80

_____

Decimal subtraction

1 **Subtract** the following decimals:

a	U	Tenths	b	U	Tenths	c	U	Tenths
	0	6		0	8		0	9
−	0	2	−	0	6	−	0	8

d	U	Tenths	e	U	Tenths	f	U	Tenths
	0	5		0	7		0	9
−	0	2	−	0	3	−	0	4

2 **Subtract** the following decimals:

a   1.8   b   6.9   c   9.4
   − 0.5   − 5.2   − 3.2

d   8.64   e   5.33   f   2.94
− 0.51   − 1.12   − 0.72

3 **Subtract** the following decimals:

a   0.86 − 0.25 _____   b   0.54 − 0.41 _____
c   6.25 − 4.12 _____   d   7.34 − 4.13 _____
e   6.59 − 3.26 _____   f   2.79 − 1.37 _____

4 a   **Subtract** 1.63 from 2.98 _____
   b   Find the **difference** between 3.59 and 2.46 _____
   c   Find 4.36 **minus** 1.24 _____
   d   Find 25.32 **take away** 14.11 _____
   e   **Subtract** 1.25 from 3.99 _____
   f   Find the **difference** between 4.68 and 4.34 _____

5 **Subtract:**

	U	Tenths
	0	8
−	0	7

6 **Subtract:**   4.93
           − 1.32

7 **Subtract:**   8.34 − 6.21

8 Find: 18.75 **minus** 12.32 _____

9 Megan had $10.00 to spend and she bought a magazine which cost $5.75 and a chocolate bar which cost $1.20. **How much change** did Megan receive?

_____

Decimal addition and subtraction with trading

1 **Add** the following decimals:

a   4.6
   + 2.9

b   4.2
   + 3.9

c   2.8
   + 4.6

d   6.35
   + 2.49

e   4.15
   + 4.27

f   2.72
   + 1.61

2 **Subtract** the following decimals:

a   7.2
   − 4.4

b   8.5
   − 5.6

c   9.3
   − 3.9

d   7.34
   − 2.16

e   5.29
   − 2.43

f   6.84
   − 2.55

3 **Find**

a   3.16
   + 2.75

b   4.81
   − 2.65

c   7.35
   + 2.17

d   2.59
   − 1.96

e   4.70
   + 1.38

f   3.65
   − 2.39

4 Find the:

a **total** length of 1.55 m and 2.35 m _____
b **difference** between 0.85 m and 0.59 m _____
c **sum** of 1.63 L and 2.41 L _____
d **change** from $5.00 after spending $3.54 _____
e **total** distance of 4.71 km and 2.87 km _____
f **difference** between 1.76 m and 0.49 m _____

5 **Add**:   2.73
      + 5.63

6 **Subtract**:   7.33
        − 2.15

7 **Find**:   2.63
      + 3.45

8 Find the **difference** between: 1.25 L and 0.71 L _____

9 Write one addition and one subtraction **word question** which gives the answer 1.06.

_____ , _____

Simple percentages

1 Look at the following signs.

50% off	100% guaranteed	15% off storewide	20% free	5% new
A	B	C	D	E

a Which is the **largest** percentage? ____
b Which is the **smallest** percentage? ____
c Which percentage is the **same** as a half? ____
d Which percentage is **twenty percent**? ____
e Is 20% **more or less** than 15%? ____
f What is the **percentage** of sign B? ____

2 Write in its **short form**:

a ten percent _____
b twenty-five percent _____
c twelve percent _____
d ninety-five percent _____
e twenty percent _____
f thirty percent _____

3 Write in **words**:

a 50% _____
b 75% _____
c 17% _____
d 2% _____
e 98% _____
f 60% _____

4 Write the sign, **< or >**, in the boxes to complete the number sentences:

a 20% ☐ 25%
b 15% ☐ 10%
c 5% ☐ 15%
d 90% ☐ 70%
e 95% ☐ 30%
f 95% ☐ 100%

5 Look at the following labels:

95% wheat	60% cream	5% pure juice
A	B	C

Which is the **largest** percentage? _____

6 Write in its **short form**: forty-five percent _____

7 Write in **words**: 35% _____

8 Write the sign, **< or >**, in the box to complete the number sentence: 50% ☐ 35%

9 **Draw** a label for a fruit juice container that has 15% pure juice.

Money — coins

1 **How many** of each coin are needed to make $2?
a $1 coins ____   b 50c coins ____   c 20c coins ____
d 10c coins ____   e 5c coins ____   f $2 coins ____

2 Write down the **smallest number** of coins needed to buy these items:

a
$1.45 ____

b
$1.25 ____

c
$1.95 ____

d
$2.25 ____

e
$1.50 ____

f
$1.85 ____

3 Write down the **smallest number** of coins needed for change from $5.00 for each of the following items:

a
$4.30 ____

b
$2.40 ____

c
$4.35 ____

d
$2.95 ____

e
$3.95 ____

f
$4.45 ____

4 6 children each bought a toy ball which cost $5.25. They all used different sets of coins. Complete the grid, the **different coins** they used:

		$2	$1	50c	20c	10c	5c
a	Jane						
b	William						
c	Yana						
d	Violet						
e	Trent						
f	Jay						

5 **How many** 20c coins are needed to make $1? ____

6 Write down the **smallest number** of coins needed to buy: ____
$ 2.95   cake

7 Write down the **smallest number** of coins needed for change from $5 for: ____
$3.75

8 Peter and Robert each bought a pen for $2.95. Complete the grid, showing the **different coins** they used.

		$2	$1	50c	20c	10c	5c
a	Peter						
b	Robert						

9 Add the following items and state which **notes and coins** could be used to **pay for the total**:
* printer paper $5.25 ____
* blank CD-ROM $2.45 ____
* CD-ROM case 40c ____

Money — notes

1 **How many** of each note or coin are needed to make $100?
a ____   b ____
c ____   d ____
e ____   f ____

2 Write down the **smallest number** of notes or coins needed to buy items that cost the following amounts:
a $75 ____   b $93 ____   c $37 ____
d $108 ____   e $169 ____   f $199 ____

3 Write down the **smallest number** of notes or coins required for change from $100 for each amount:
a $97 ____   b $83 ____   c $28 ____
d $42 ____   e $55 ____   f $66 ____

4 Find the **total** amount of money each person has:
a Chris
____
b Jayne
c Steven ____
d Julie
____
e Jo
____
f Ajit ____

5 **How many** are needed to make $40? ____

6 Write down the **smallest number** of notes or coins needed to buy an item that costs $146. ____

7 Write down the **smallest number** of notes or coins needed for change of $38 from $100. ____

8 Find the **total** amount of money Fiona has:

____

9 Give **three different combinations of notes** that could be used to **pay** for clothes costing $60.

____ , ____

____

Money – addition and subtraction

1 **Add** the following amounts:

| a | $2.45
+ $1.35 | b | $3.45
+ $1.90 | c | $4.83
+ $3.26 |

| d | $4.93
+ $0.25 | e | $1.95
+ $3.50 | f | $2.76
+ $0.43 |

2 **Subtract** the following amounts:

| a | $7.45
− $3.32 | b | $6.73
− $3.45 | c | $5.39
− $0.98 |

| d | $6.90
− $3.75 | e | $5.50
− $0.15 | f | $4.45
− $2.95 |

3 Find the **total** cost of:

a   a $1.10 pie and a 85c sausage roll _____

b   a $1.95 sandwich and a $2.20 drink _____

c   a $1.75 slice of pizza and a $2.40 milk drink

    _____

d   a $2.25 salad roll and a 90c apple _____

e   a $2.15 slice of cake and a $2.35 coffee _____

f   a $2.20 bottle of water and a $1.55 muffin

    _____

4 Find the **change** from:

a $5.00 after spending $3.00 _____

b $4.50 after spending $4.10 _____

c $10.00 after spending $8.30 _____

d $5.00 after spending $0.95 _____

e $7.60 after spending $5.80 _____

f $6.90 after spending $4.50 _____

5 **Add:** $3.45
    + $0.35

6 **Subtract:** $9.25
    − $6.72

7 Find the **total** cost of a $2.95 fruit bar and a $2.30 orange juice. _____

8 Find the **change** from $2.00 after spending $0.65.

    _____

9 Find the amount I needed to **pay** if I bought a DVD at $24.95 and a CD at $21.65, and had a $30.00 gift voucher. _____

Money – multiplication and division

1 **Multiply** the following amounts:

a $5.00 × 2 _____

b $1.00 × 3 _____

c $3.00 × 2 _____

d   5c × 3 _____

e $5.00 × 4 _____

f   20c × 4 _____

2 **Divide** the following amounts:

a $4.00 ÷ 2 _____

b $6.00 ÷ 3 _____

c   40c ÷ 4 _____

d   50c ÷ 5 _____

e $20.00 ÷ 10 _____

f   90c ÷ 3 _____

3 Find the **total** cost of:

a   3 apples at 20c each _____

b   2 tins of dog food at $1.00 each _____

c   5 chocolate frogs at 10c each _____

d   3 loaves of bread at $2.00 each _____

e   2 tins of peaches at 40c each _____

f   2 kiwifruit at 30c each _____

4 **How many** of each item could I buy for $10?

a   caps at $5.00 each _____

b   drink bottles at $2.00 each _____

c   golf balls at $1.00 each _____

d   sunscreen at $4.00 each _____

e   basketballs at $10.00 each _____

f   scorecards at $1.00 each _____

5 **Multiply** $5.00 × 3. _____

6 **Divide** $8.00 ÷ 4. _____

7 Find the **total** cost of 3 cartons of milk at $2.00 each.

    _____

8 **How many** oranges could I buy for $5.00 if each one cost $1.00? _____

9 **Estimate and then calculate** what it would cost to buy 5 DVDs at a cost of $29.95 for each DVD.

    _____

Money – rounding

1 Circle the **best answer**:

a $1.95 is closest to $1.00 or $2.00 or $19.00?

b $5.25 is closest to $5.00 or $6.00 or $25.00?

c $10.85 is closest to $2.00 or $9.00 or $11.00?

d $11.95 is closest to $10.00 or $11.00 or $12.00?

e $8.15 is closest to $8.00 or $9.00 or $15.00?

f $19.10 is closest to $18.00 or $19.00 or $20.00?

2 Round the following amounts to the **nearest dollar**:

a $6.05 _____   b $5.95 _____

c $9.75 _____   d $3.15 _____

e $10.98 _____   f $18.89 _____

3 Round the following to the **nearest 10 cents**:

a 92c _____   b 57c _____

c 26c _____   d 43c _____

e 89c _____   f 64c _____

4 Round the following amounts to the **nearest dollar** and then add:

a $4.65   b $2.95
   + $3.98   + $8.65
   _____   _____

c $7.35   d $10.95
   + $4.67   + $5.29
   _____   _____

e $12.42   f $8.97
   + $8.31   + $6.65
   _____   _____

5 Circle the **best answer**:

$3.45 is closest to $3.00 or $4.00 or $5.00?

6 Round $8.95 to the **nearest dollar**. _____

7 Round 76c to the **nearest 10 cents**. _____

8 Round $3.75 to the **nearest dollar** and then add:
      + $10.10
      _____

9 Add the following and $6.98
round to the **nearest** $3.25
10 cents.   + $1.56
_____

Money – estimating

1 **Estimate** the cost of the following by completing the spaces:

a 3 × $1.95   b 4 × $5.95
   ≃ 3 × $2.00   ≃ _____ × $6.00
   ≃ _____   ≃ _____

c 3 × $3.05   d 5 × $6.05
   ≃ _____ × $3.00   ≃ 5 × _____
   ≃ _____   ≃ _____

e 9 × $2.98   f 4 × $4.10
   ≃ 9 × _____   ≃ 4 × _____
   ≃ _____   ≃ _____

2 **Estimate the total cost** of each of the following:

a 3 × $2.95 _____   b 2 × $5.05 _____

c 6 × $1.95 _____   d 4 × $3.10 _____

e 7 × $0.98 _____   f 5 × $4.15 _____

3 **Estimate the change** for each of the following:

a $10.00 – $7.98   b $10.00 – $6.05
   ≃ $10.00 – $8.00   ≃ _____ – $6.00
   ≃ _____   ≃ _____

c $5.00 – $3.95   d $5.00 – $2.10
   ≃ $5.00 – _____   ≃ $5.00 – _____
   ≃ _____   ≃ _____

e $20.00 – $16.80   f $20.00 – $10.95
   ≃ _____ – $17.00   ≃ $20.00 – _____
   ≃ _____   ≃ _____

4 **Estimate the total cost** of:

a 4 bags of lollies, when 1 bag costs $2.95 _____

b 3 milk cartons, when 1 carton costs $3.05 _____

c 2 videos, when 1 video costs $7.95 _____

d 4 pencil sets, when 1 set costs $4.15 _____

e 3 chocolate bars, when 1 bar costs $2.95 _____

f 5 rulers, when 1 ruler costs $1.10 _____

5 **Estimate** by   4 × $1.90 ≃ 4 × _____
completing the spaces: ≃ _____

6 **Estimate the total cost** of: 3 × $4.05 _____

7 **Estimate the** $10.00 – $5.97 ≃ $10.00 – _____
change for: ≃ _____

8 **Estimate the total cost** of two jumpers when one jumper costs $9.95. _____

9 To paint my bedroom, estimate the **total cost**:
* 1 tin of paint is $34.95   * 1 roller is $7.15
* 1 paint tray is $3.98   * 1 drop sheet is $1.95

_____

UNIT 101

See START UPS page 7

Symmetry

1 Use a pencil and a ruler to draw a **line of symmetry** on each picture:

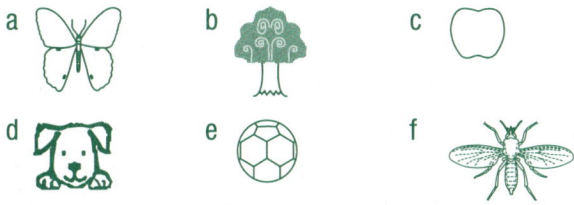

a b c

d e f

2 Use a pencil and a ruler to draw **two lines of symmetry** on each shape:

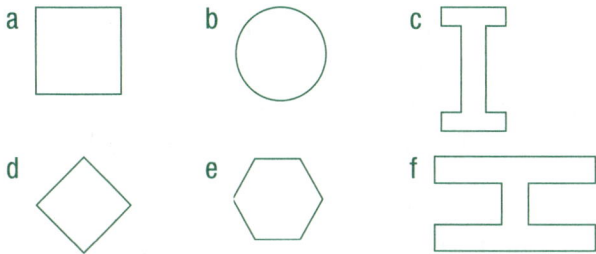

a b c

d e f

3 Which of the following shapes do not have a **line of symmetry**?

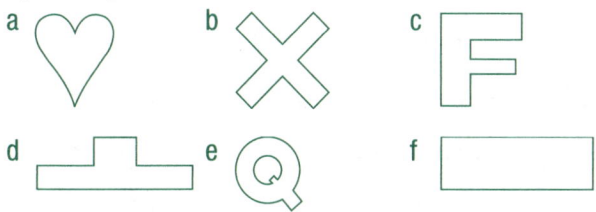

a b c

d e f

4 Complete each of the drawings so that they are **symmetrical**:

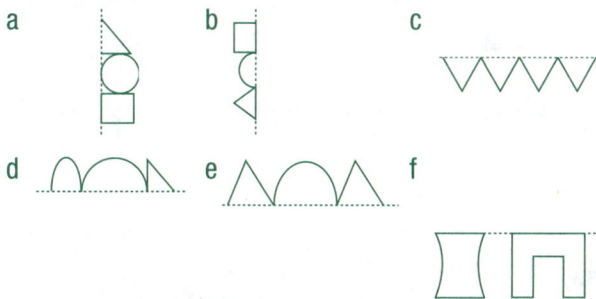

a b c

d e f

5 Use a pencil and a ruler to draw a **line of symmetry** on:

6 Use a pencil and a ruler to draw **two lines of symmetry** on:

7 Does the shape P have a **line of symmetry**?

8 Complete the drawing so that it is **symmetrical**.

9 Complete the drawing so that it is **symmetrical**.

UNIT 102

See START UPS page 7

2D shapes (1)

1 **Match** the name to the shape from the word list: circle, square, rectangle, triangle, rhombus, hexagon

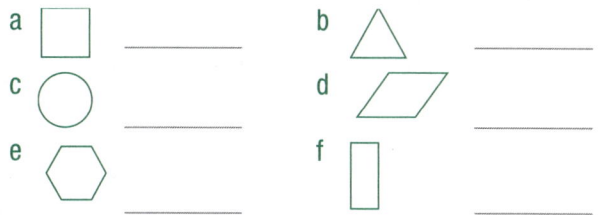

a _____ b _____

c _____ d _____

e _____ f _____

2 **Draw** a shape that has:

a 3 sides   b 4 equal sides

c six equal sides   d 2 opposite sides equal

e 5 equal sides   f no equal sides but is curved

3 Describe the following **shapes**:

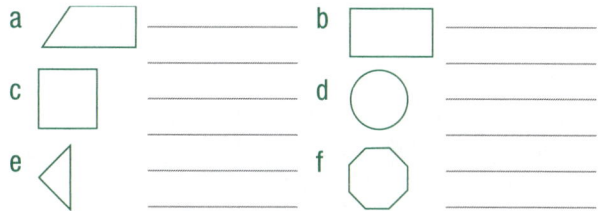

a _____ b _____

c _____ d _____

e _____ f _____

4 **Draw lines** inside each shape to show how it is constructed. Use the shaded blocks as a guide:

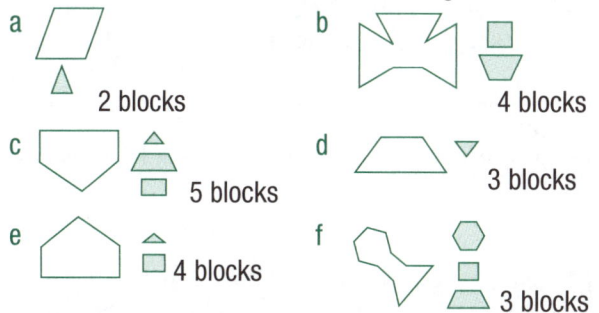

a 2 blocks   b 4 blocks

c 5 blocks   d 3 blocks

e 4 blocks   f 3 blocks

5 **Match** the name to the shape from the word list: circle, square, rectangle, triangle. _____

6 **Draw** a shape that has 8 equal sides.

7 Describe the **shape**: _____

8 **Draw lines** inside the shape to show how it is constructed. Use the shaded blocks as a guide.

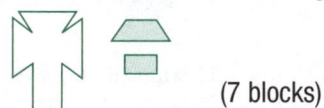

(7 blocks)

9 **Construct** your own shape using:
* 3 triangles   * 2 squares
* 1 rhombus   * 1 hexagon

2D shapes (2)

1 Circle the **shape** that does not belong:

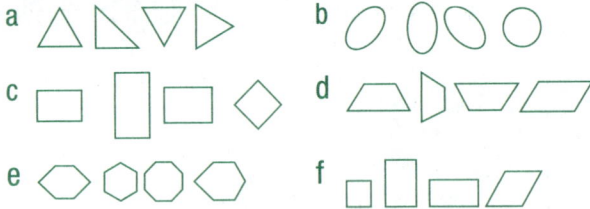

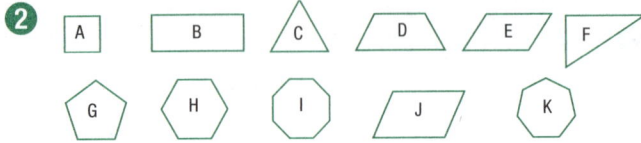

a △ △ ▽ ▷　　b ◯ ◯ ⬭ ◯

c ▢ ▯ ▢ ◇　　d ⬟ ⬠ ▱ ▱

e ⬡ ⬡ ◯ ⬡　　f ▢ ▯ ▱

2

A ▢　B ▭　C △　D ▱　E ▱　F ◥

G ⬠　H ⬡　I ⬡　J ▱　K ◯

Which of the above **shapes** have:

a　3 sides? _____　　b　4 sides? _____
c　equal sides? _____　　d　6 sides? _____
e　7 sides? _____　　f　5 sides? _____

3 How many **corners** does each of the following shapes have?

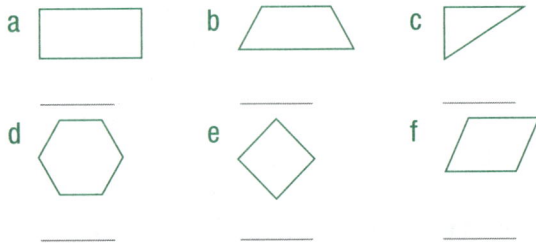

a ▭　　b ⬯　　c ◹

_____　　_____　　_____

d ⬡　　e ◇　　f ▱

_____　　_____　　_____

4 **Draw** the following shapes:

a　triangle　　b　rectangle　　c　trapezium

d　square　　e　rhombus　　f　parallelogram

5 Circle the **shape** that does not belong:

△　　◇　　⬡　　⬠

6 Which of the **shapes** have equal length sides?

A △　B ▢　C ▭　D ⬠ _____

7 How many **corners** does ◇ have? _____

8 **Draw** an octagon.

9 Find **how many** different sized **squares** of a can be drawn using these dots.

· · ·
· · ·
· · ·

2D shapes (3)

1 A▢ B▢ C△ D⬠ E▱ F▱ G⬡ H⬡

Give the letter for each **shape**:

a　rectangle _____　b　triangle _____　c　square _____
d　rhombus _____　e　octagon _____　f　pentagon _____

2 On the **Geoboard**:

a　Draw a triangle using 3 pegs.
b　How many sides does it have? _____
c　How many corners does it have? _____
d　Draw a square using 8 pegs.
e　How many sides does it have? _____
f　How many corners does it have? _____

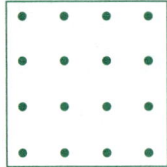

· · · ·
· · · ·
· · · ·
· · · ·

3 **Draw** each of the following shapes:

a　a shape with 4 equal sides　　b　a shape with 3 equal sides
c　a shape with 6 equal sides　　d　a shape with 4 sides, 2 of them equal
e　a pushed-over square　　f　a shape with 8 equal sides

4 **Name** the shapes from their descriptions:

a　I have 3 sides. All of my sides are the same length.

_____

b　I have 5 sides and all of my angles are the same.

_____

c　I am a regular closed shape that is made up of a curved line. _____
d　I have 4 sides. All of my sides are the same length and all of my angles are the same size.

_____

e　I am half a circle. I have one straight side and a curved side. _____
f　I have 4 sides. I have 2 sets of equal side lengths. All of my angles are the same size. _____

5 Give the letter for the **rhombus**:

A ▱　B △　C ◯　D ▢

_____

6 On the **Geoboard** draw a rectangle using 6 pegs.

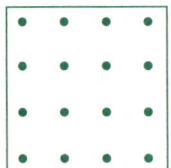

· · · ·
· · · ·
· · · ·
· · · ·

7 **Draw** a shape with 3 sides (none of them equal).

8 **Name** the shape: I have 6 sides. All of my angles are the same size and all of my sides are equal. _____

9 Write a 'who am I?' for a **rhombus**. _____

_____

Pentagons and octagons

1 Count and record the number of **sides and angles** on each of the following shapes:

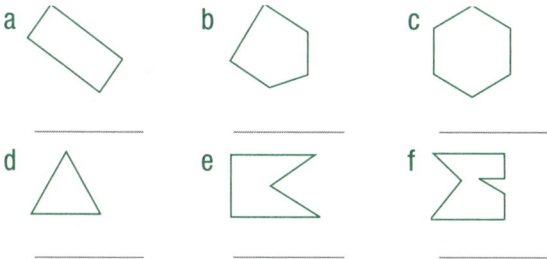

a　　　　b　　　　c

d　　　　e　　　　f

2 Name the following **shapes** which are:

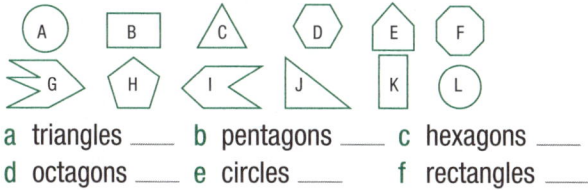

A　B　C　D　E　F
G　H　I　J　K　L

a triangles ___ b pentagons ___ c hexagons ___
d octagons ___ e circles ___ f rectangles ___

3 **Draw** each of the following shapes:

a irregular　b square　c triangle
pentagon

d octagon　e regular　f regular
hexagon　pentagon

4 **How many sides** are there on:

a 2 pentagons? ___　b 3 octagons? ___
c 2 pentagons and 2 octagons? ___
d 5 squares and 3 pentagons? ___
e 10 octagons? ___
f 1 rectangle, 1 square and 5 pentagons? ___

5 Count and record the number of **sides and angles** on:

_____

6 Name the **shapes** which are pentagons ___

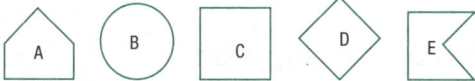

A　B　C　D　E

7 **Draw** an irregular octagon.

8 **How many sides** on 2 pentagons and 3 octagons? ___

9 **Join the dots** and **name** the shape.

4●　5●
3●
2●　●8　●6
1●　●7

_____

Trapeziums and parallelograms

1 **Match** the following names with the shapes: parallelogram, rectangle, oval, triangle, trapezium, hexagon.

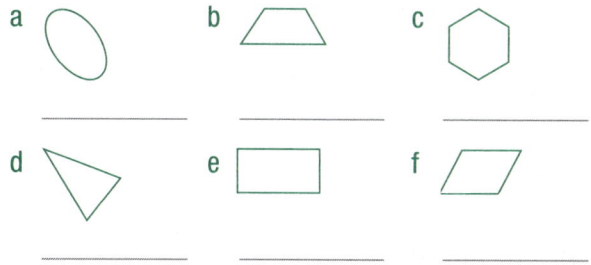

a　　　　b　　　　c

_____　_____　_____

d　　　　e　　　　f

_____　_____　_____

2 Write down the **number of sides** on each of the following shapes:

a square ___　b octagon ___
c triangle ___　d parallelogram ___
e pentagon ___　f trapezium ___

3 Which of the following shapes are **trapeziums**? ___

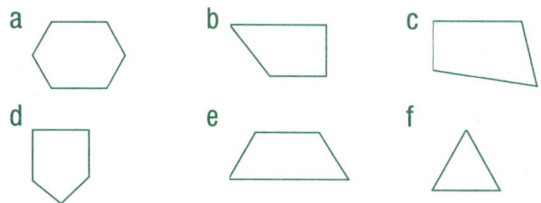

a　　　　b　　　　c

d　　　　e　　　　f

4 **Find how many angles** are there in:

a 2 trapeziums ___
b 5 parallelograms ___
c 3 trapeziums and 2 parallelograms ___
d 1 octagon, 1 pentagon and 2 trapeziums ___
e 1 parallelogram and 3 triangles ___
f 2 octagons and 2 trapeziums ___

5 **Match** the name to the shape: parallelogram, octagon, rectangle, square

6 Write down the **number of sides** on a hexagon. ___

7 Which of the following shapes are **trapeziums**? ___

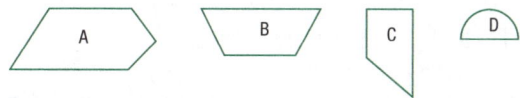

A　B　C　D

8 **Find how many angles** there are in 2 trapeziums and 4 parallelograms. _____

9 On the dot paper, draw 3 different **trapeziums**.

Rigidity

1 Name the following shapes:

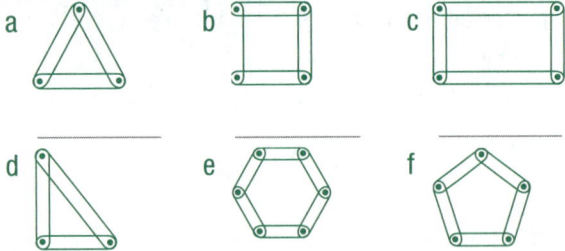

a   b   c

_____   _____   _____

d   e   f

_____   _____   _____

2 Indicate which of the following shapes are **rigid** or not rigid:

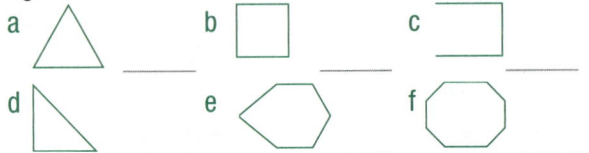

a _____   b _____   c _____

d _____   e _____   f _____

3 Which shapes in the following pictures make the objects **rigid**?

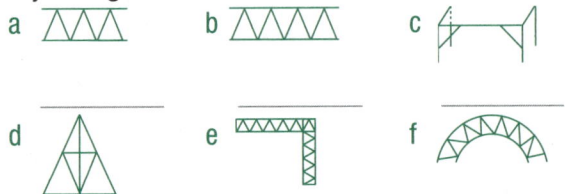

a _____   b _____   c

_____   _____

d _____   e _____   f

_____   _____

4 Shapes can be made more rigid by adding supports. Draw in the Geostrips to create **supports** for the following shapes.

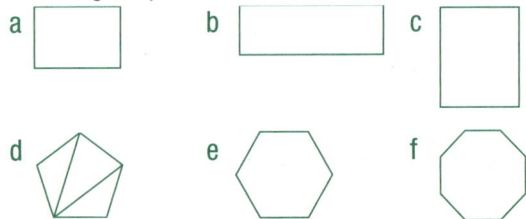

a   b   c

d   e   f

5 Name the shape: _____

6 Indicate if ◯ is a **rigid** shape. _____

7 Which shape in the picture makes the shelf **rigid**?

_____

8 Draw in the Geostrip to create **support** for:

9 **Design your own bridge** that uses triangles in its supports.

Regular and irregular shapes

1 **Join the dots** to complete the shape and then state if it is **regular** or irregular.

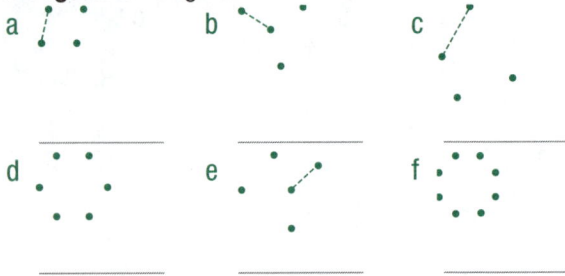

a   b   c

_____

d   e   f

_____

2 Name the following regular shapes:

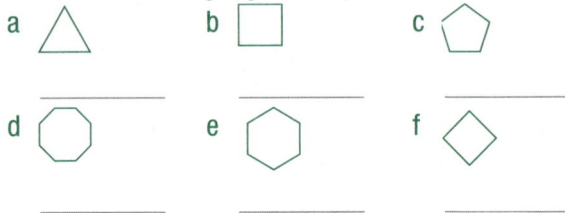

a   b   c

d   e   f

3 Name the following irregular shapes.

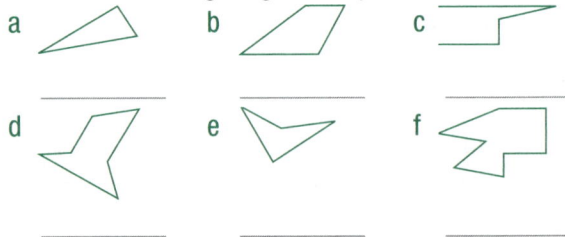

a   b   c

d   e   f

_____

4 Draw an irregular shape for each of the following:

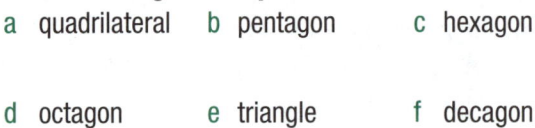

a   quadrilateral   b   pentagon   c   hexagon

d   octagon   e   triangle   f   decagon

5 **Join the dots** and state if the shape is **regular** or irregular. _____

6 Name the regular shape. _____

7 Name the irregular shape. _____

8 Draw an irregular quadrilateral (different to question 4).

9 Draw a house which has only regular shapes.

Angles in real life

1 Answer the following questions:

a Which is the **smallest** angle? ____
b Which is the **largest** angle? ____
c Which angle is a **right angle**? ____
d Is angle A **smaller** than angle D? _____
e Is angle C **smaller** than angle E? _____
f Is angle C **smaller** or larger than angle B? _____

2 For each of the following marked angles, state if it is **smaller or larger** than a right angle:

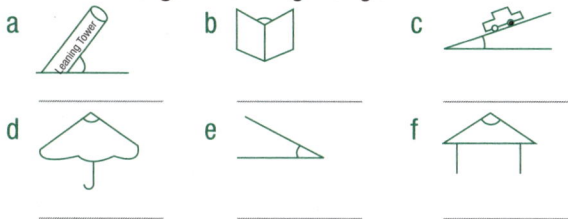

3 Answer the following questions:

a Which book forms the **smallest** angle? ____
b Which book forms the **largest** angle? ____
c Which book is closest to a **right angle**? ____
d Is the angle of book E **smaller** than book A? _____
e Is the angle of book D **larger** than book A? _____
f Which of the angles, A or E or D, is **smaller**? ____

4 Look at the clock faces and answer these questions:

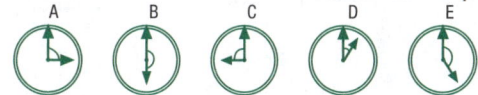

a Which clock hands have the **smallest angle**? ____
b Which clock hands have the **largest angle**? ____
c Which two clocks have the **same angle**? _____
d How many **minutes** is the angle of clock C? _____
e How many **minutes** is the angle of clock E? _____
f How many **minutes** is the largest angle? _____

5 Which angles in question 1 are **larger** than B? ____

6 Is the following marked angle **smaller or larger** than a right angle? _____

7 Which book forms the **largest** angle? ____

8 Which clock hands form the **smallest** angle? ____

9 Order the angles in question 1 from **smallest to largest**. ____

Angles

1 How many **angles** can be seen on each of the shapes?

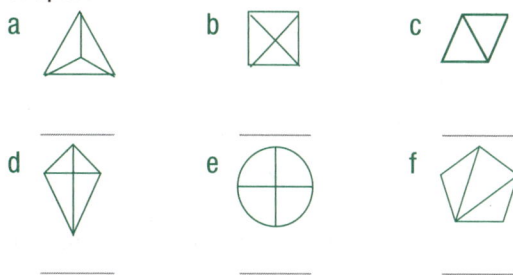

2 For each of the following angles, indicate if they are **smaller or larger** than a right angle:

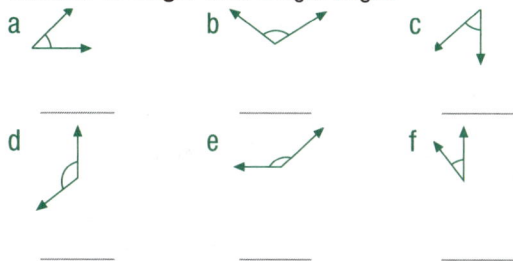

3 For each of the following angles, indicate if they are **smaller or larger** than angle *x*:

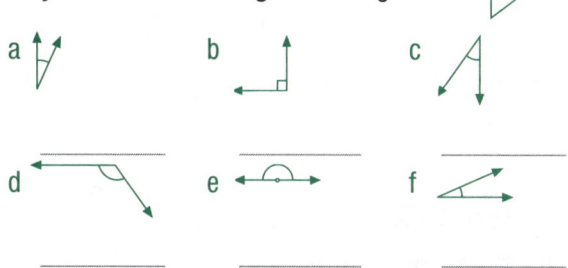

4 Order the following angles from the **smallest** (1) **to the largest** (6):

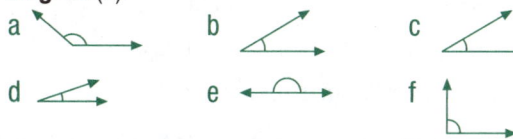

5 How many **angles** can be seen on the shape?

6 Is the angle ⌐ **smaller or larger** than a right angle? _____

7 Is the angle ∠ **smaller or larger** than ∠ ?

8 Order the three angles from **smallest** (1) **to largest** (3).

9 Draw a **picture of a house** that has at least ten angles.

Right angles

1 Circle the angles which are **smaller** than a right angle:

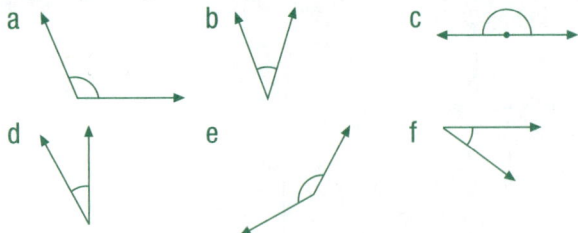

a   b   c

d   e   f

2 Circle the angles which are **larger** than a right angle:

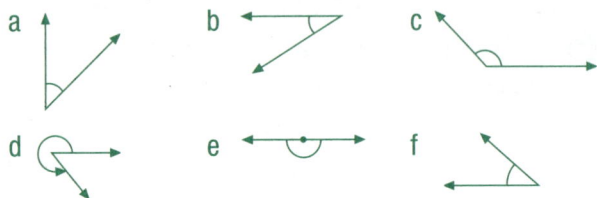

a   b   c

d   e   f

3 Circle the angles which are **right angles**:

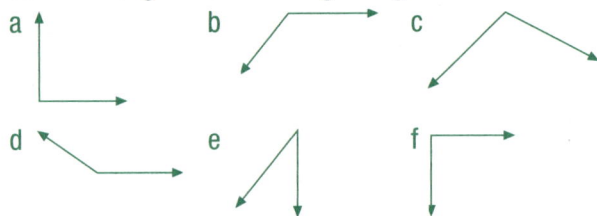

a   b   c

d   e   f

4 Using the diagram, answer the following questions:

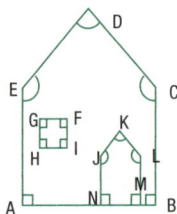

a   Name 4 **angles**. _____

b   Name 2 **right angles**. _____

c   Name 2 angles **larger than** 90°. _____

d   Name 2 angles **smaller than** 90°. _____

e   Name 2 **right angles** on the window. _____

f   Name 2 **right angles** on the door. _____

5 Is the angle   **smaller** than a right angle? _____

6 Is the angle   **larger** than a right angle? _____

7 Is the angle   a **right angle**? _____

8 In the diagram, name 2 **right angles**: _____

9 **Draw a picture** of a basketball/netball court and label the right angles.

Parallel lines

1 At **how many points** does each group of lines cross?

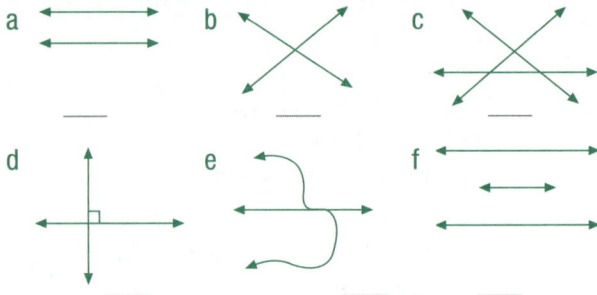

a   b   c

d   e   f

2 Circle the following which are **parallel lines**:

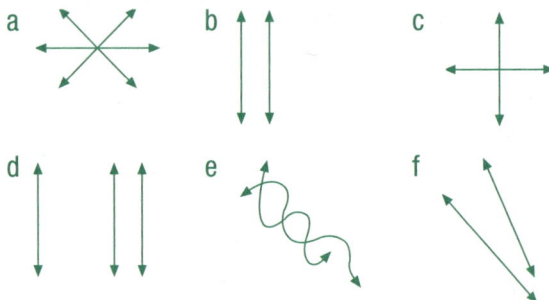

a   b   c

d   e   f

3 Indicate the **parallel lines** on the following letters:

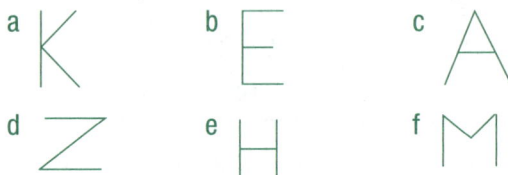

a   K   b   E   c   A

d   Z   e   H   f   M

4 Indicate on the following shapes the **parallel lines**:

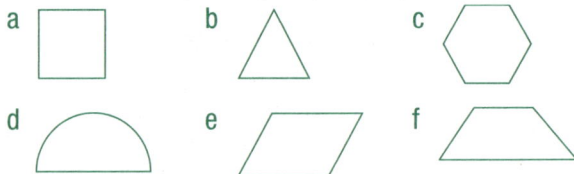

a   b   c

d   e   f

5 At **how many points** do the following lines cross? _____

6 Are   **parallel**? _____

7 Indicate the **parallel lines** on the letter F . _____

8 Does the shape   show **parallel lines**? _____

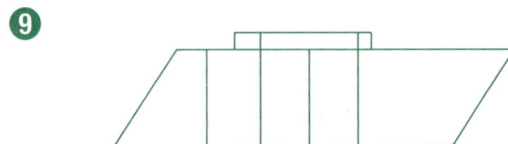

9

Label on the diagram all of the sets of **parallel lines**.

Perpendicular lines

1 At **how many points** does each group of lines cross?

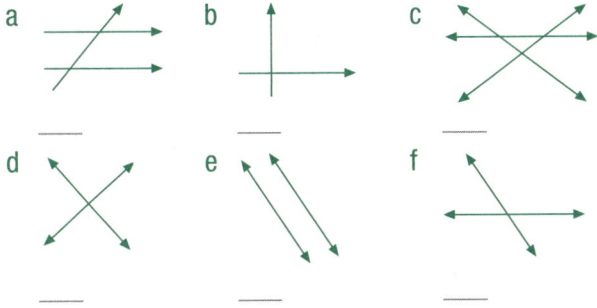

a ___   b ___   c ___

d ___   e ___   f ___

2 Indicate the sets of lines that are **perpendicular**:

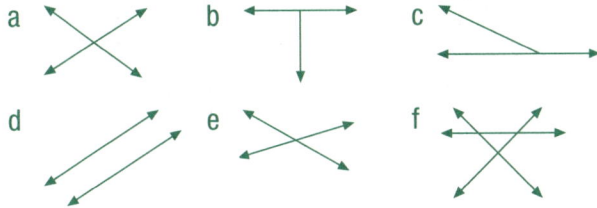

a   b   c

d   e   f

3 Indicate on the following shapes the **perpendicular** lines:

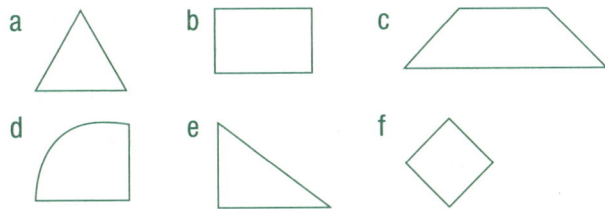

a   b   c

d   e   f

4 Mark on the following numbers any **perpendicular** lines:

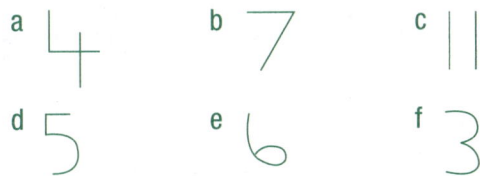

a 4   b 7   c ||

d 5   e 6   f 3

5 At **how many points** do the following lines cross? ___

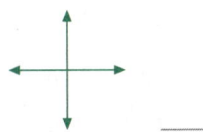

6 Are these lines **perpendicular**? ___

7 Does the shape show **perpendicular** lines? ___

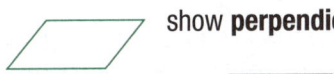

8 Indicate on the letter the **perpendicular** lines:

9 **Explain** why these lines are not perpendicular.

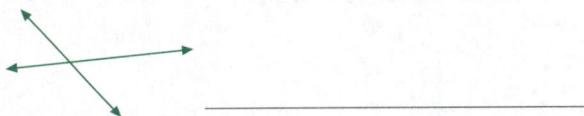

_____

3D objects (1)

1 A   B   C   D   E

F Cereals   G   H   I   J

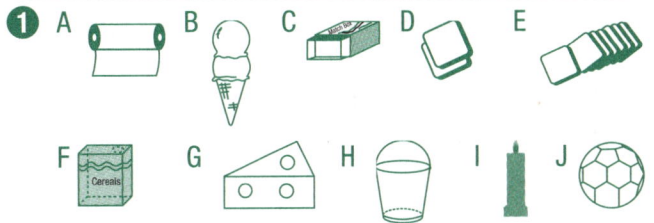

Which of the pictures:

a **look like** this ? ___

b **look like** this ? ___

c **look like** this ? ___

d show things that will **roll**? ___

e show things that only have **flat surfaces**? ___

f show things that have a **circle** on at least one of the surfaces? ___

2 **Name the shape** of each of the shaded faces:

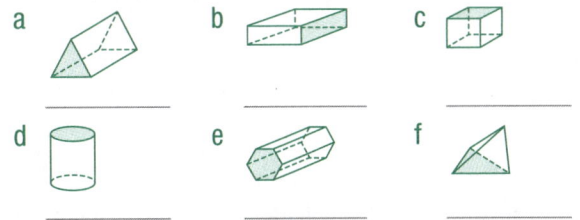

a   b   c

_____   _____   _____

d   e   f

_____   _____   _____

3 **Match** the 3D object with its name from the word list: cube, sphere, cylinder, cone, pyramid, triangular prism

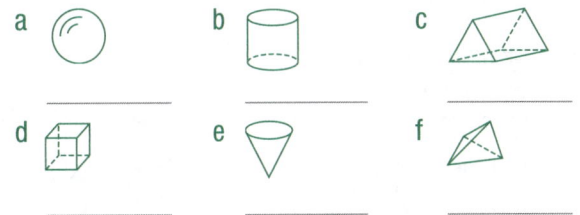

a   b   c

_____   _____   _____

d   e   f

_____   _____   _____

4 How many **surfaces** do each of the 3D objects have?

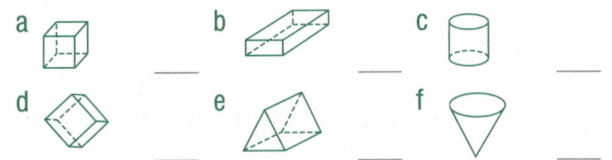

a   b   c

___   ___   ___

d   e   f

___   ___   ___

5 Which of the pictures in question 1 **looks like** ? ___

6 **Name the shape** of the shaded face: ___

7 **Match** the name of the 3D object to the picture: cone, cylinder, rectangular prism

8 How many **surfaces** does the shape have? ___

9 Who am I? I have one **curved surface**, and one **flat surface**, and this flat surface is a **circle**. I am a ___.

3D objects (2)

1 Draw a line **matching** each 3D object to its name:

a   sphere
b   pyramid
c   prism
d   cone
e   cylinder
f   cube

2 Name the **3D shapes** that fit together to make each of the following:

a   b

c   d

e   f

3 **Draw** each of the following shapes:

a cube   b rectangular prism   c triangular prism

d square pyramid   e triangular pyramid   f sphere

4 **How many** of each of the following objects can you see in the picture?

a   b   c

d   e   f

5 Draw a line **matching** each 3D object to its name:

rectangular prism
triangular prism

6 Name the **3D shapes** that fit together to make:

7 **Draw** a cylinder.

8 **How many** can you see in the picture from question 4?

9 **Design a dog house** that uses at least:
1 cone, 3 cylinders, 2 prisms.

Properties of 3D objects

1 List the different **flat surfaces** (faces) each solid has:

a   b   c

d   e   f

2 Which of the following **solids** has:

A   B   C   D   E

a 8 corners? _____   b 5 faces? _____
c 1 corner? _____   d 12 edges _____
e 9 edges? _____   f only curved surfaces? _____

3 What is the shape of the **cross-section** for each of the following solids?

a   b   c

d   e   f

4 For each solid below, draw what you would see if you looked at it from the **top** and from the **front**.

a   b   c

d   e   f

5 List the different **flat surfaces** (faces) for:

6 Which of the following solids have two **flat surfaces**?

A   B   C   D   E

7 What is the shape of the **cross-section**?

8 Draw what you would see if you looked at the solid from the **top** and from the **front**.

9 Study the solid, and then draw what it would look like from the **top**, **front** and **side**.

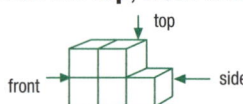

top
front   side

Prisms and cylinders

1 List the different shapes of the **faces** used in the construction of the following 3D shapes:

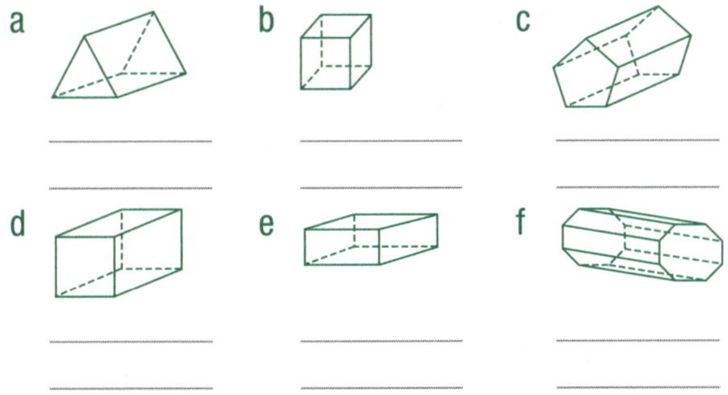

a _____   b _____   c _____

_____   _____   _____

d _____   e _____   f _____

_____   _____   _____

2 Label the following as a **prism**, **cylinder** or **neither**:

a   b   c Chocolate

d Spagetti   e   f Cereal

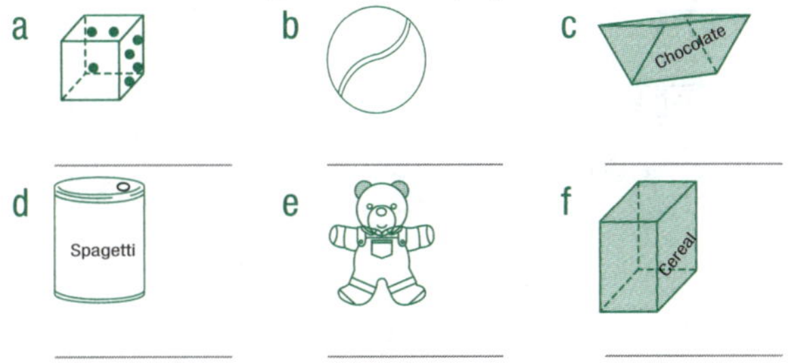

3 How many **faces** do each of the following have?

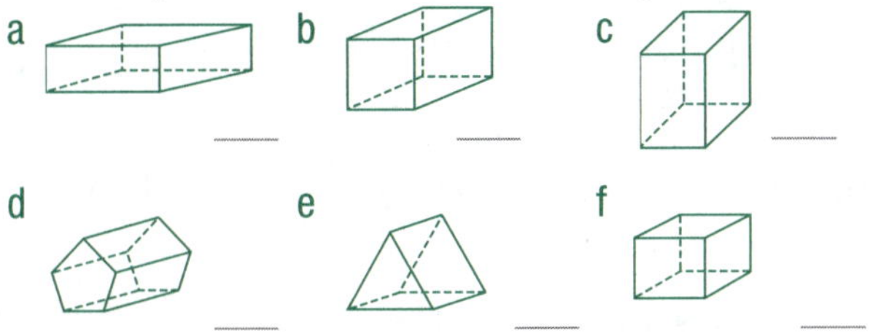

a ____   b ____   c ____

d ____   e ____   f ____

4 How many **edges** do each of the following have?

a ____   b ____   c ____

d ____   e ____   f ____

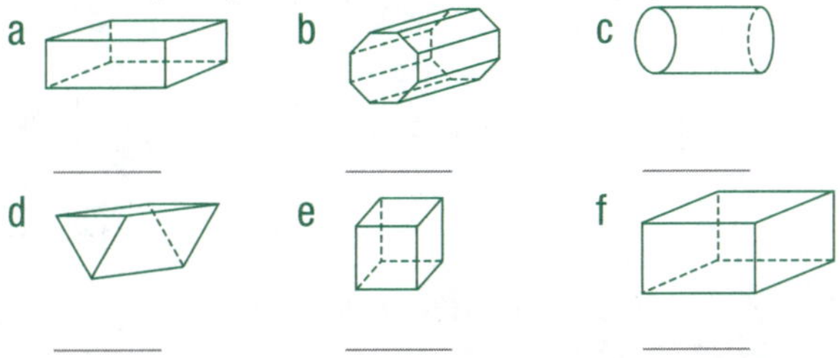

5 List the different shapes of the **faces** used in the construction of:

_____

6 Label 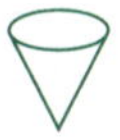 ▽ as **prism**, **cylinder** or **neither**.

_____

7 How many **faces** does ▱ have?

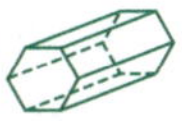

____

8 How many **edges** does ▱ have?

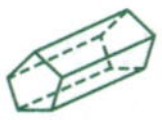

____

9 In the spaces, draw each **face** of the prism.

Prism	Shape of each face				
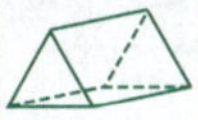					

Pyramids

1 Which of the following are **pyramids**? ____

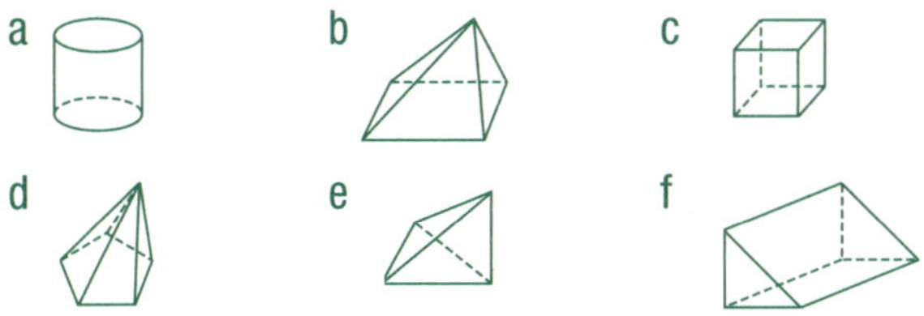

a   b   c

d   e   f

2 How many **faces** do each of the following have?

a ____   b ____   c ____

d ____   e ____   f ____

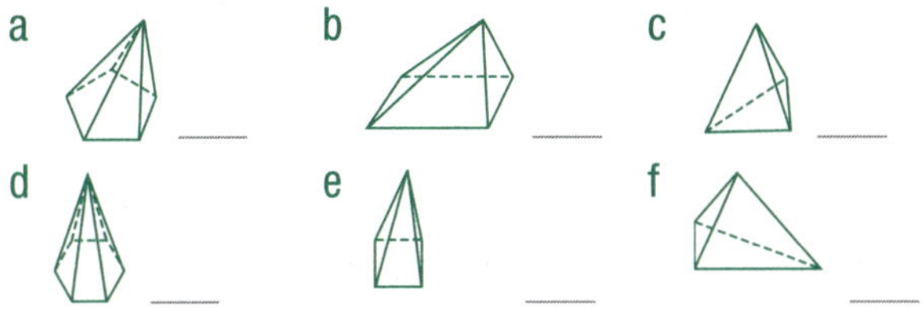

3 Draw the shapes of the **faces** for each pyramid:

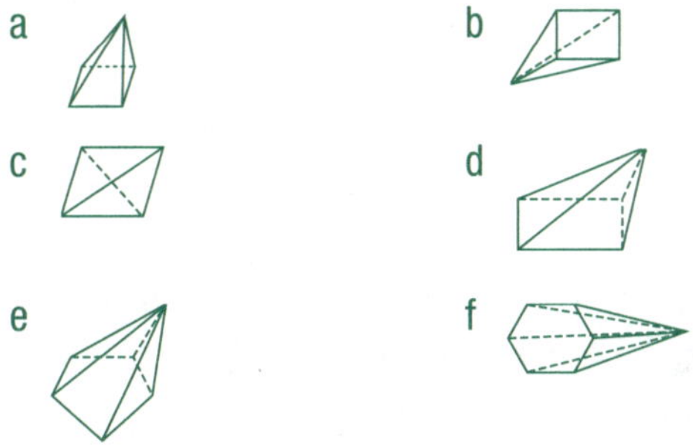

a   b

c   d

e   f

4 How many **edges** do each of the following have?

a   b   c

d ____   e ____   f ____

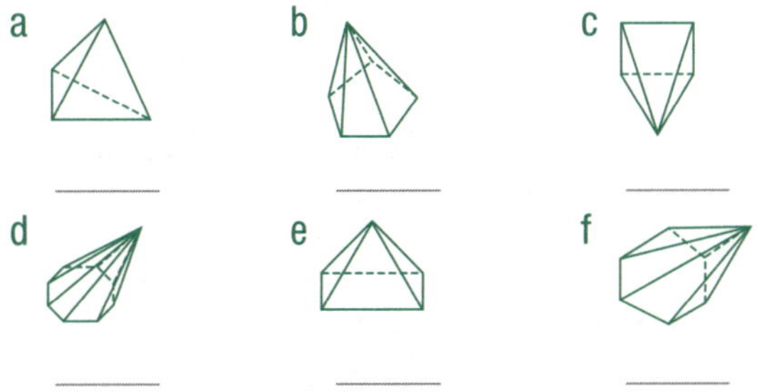

5 Is 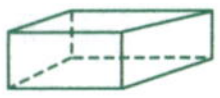 ▱ a **pyramid**? ____

6 How many **faces** does ◺ have?

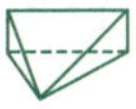

____

7 Draw the shapes of the **faces** for: ◺

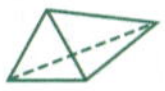

8 How many **edges** does 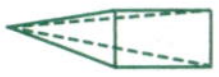 ◁ have?

____

9 Write a general description for this **pyramid**:

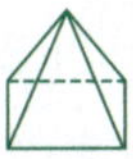

_____

_____

Nets and 3D objects

1 How many **faces** (flat surfaces) does each solid have?

a ___ b ___ c ___

d ___ e ___ f ___

2 Circle the following **nets** that would fold to make a cube?

a b c

d e f

3 **How many blocks** are used in the following constructions?

a ___ b ___ c ___

d ___ e ___ f ___

4 For each of the following solids, draw what you would see from the **top** and the **side**:

a b c

d e f

5 How many **faces** does [shape] have? ___

6 Indicate if the following **net** would fold to make a cube. ___

7 **How many blocks** were used in the following construction? ___

8 For the solid, draw what you would see from the **top** and the **side**.

9 The following rectangular box was cut open to reveal the **net**. Draw what this may look like.

Movement of shapes

1 Use the words **reflection** (flip), **translation** (slide) or **rotation** (turn) to describe the movement of the following shapes:

a b c

_____ _____ _____

d e f

_____ _____ _____

2 Complete the patterns by **reflecting** (flipping) the tiles to the right or down:

a b c

d e f

3 Do the following shapes **tessellate**?

a b c

d e f

4 Complete the patterns by **translating** (sliding) tiles to the right and/or down:

a b c

d e f

5 Use the words **reflection**, **translation** or **rotation** to describe: _____

6 Complete the pattern by **reflecting** tiles to the right.

7 Do these shapes **tessellate**? _____

8 Complete the pattern by **translating** the tiles to the right and/or down.

9 Complete the pattern by **rotating** (turning) the tiles.

Position – giving directions

1 The picture shows lunch boxes on shelves:

Tom	Morgan	Arthur
Jackson	Issac	Veronica
Eddy	Daisy	Tessa

Whose lunch box is:

  a on the bottom shelf on the **left**? _____

  b in the middle of the **top** shelf? _____

  c in the second row to the **right**? _____

Describe the **position** of:

  d Tom's lunch box _____

  e Daisy's lunch box _____

  f Isaac's lunch box _____

2 Use the map to give **directions** from:

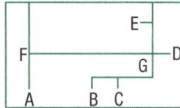

  a A to B _____

  b C to D _____

  c E to F _____

  d F to B _____

  e C to E _____

  f D to F _____

3 Use the **map** of the classroom to answer:

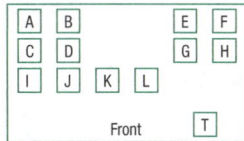

  a Alan is in A. He moves 1 right and 2 forwards. Where is he now? ____

  b Carly is in C. She moves 1 forward and 3 right. Where is she now? ____

  c Liam is in L. He moves 3 left, 1 back and 1 right. Where is he now? ____

  d If Ty is in G, describe how he can move to F. _____

  e If Fiona is in F, describe how she can move to L. ____

  f Describe how Jo can move from K to A. _____

4 Draw a **map** showing a:

  a school at the top right

  b hospital at the bottom left

  c roundabout in the **centre**

  d post office to the **left** of the roundabout

  e road **joining** the hospital and the post office

  f road **joining** the post office and the school, passing through the roundabout

5 Using the picture in question 1, whose lunch box is on the **top** shelf to the **right**? _____

6 Using the map from question 2, give **directions** from B to E. _____

7 Using the **map** of question 3, describe how Jackson in J can move to H. _____

8 Add to your **map** in question 4 a shop in the top left-hand corner and a road joining it to the school.

9 **Describe the path** from the front door to the back door.

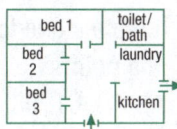

_____

Position

1 Draw which cake is:

  a in the **middle** of the bottom shelf.

  b on the **left** side of the top shelf.

  c on the **right** side of the middle shelf.

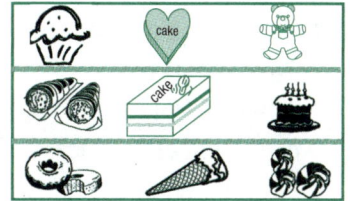

On the shelves, **where**

  d are the doughnuts? _____

  e is the cake roll? _____

  f is the heart cake? _____

2 In the cupboards, **where are the**

  a cups? _____

  b bottles? _____

  c pots? _____

What is kept in the cupboard:

  d 2nd from the **left** in the bottom row? _____

  e 3rd from the **right** in the top row? _____

  f 4th from the **left** in the bottom row? _____

3 Write the name of the toy the children chose.

  a Horacio, top row on the **right**. _____

  b Pauline, bottom row in the **middle**. _____

  c Mark, middle row 2nd from the **right**. _____

  d Bev, top row on the **left**. _____

  e William, middle row, 3rd from the **right**. _____

  f Keith, bottom row **left**. _____

4 Using the diagram from question 3, write the **position** of the:

  a car _____   b ball _____

  c die _____   d teddy _____

  e truck _____   f cups _____

5 Using the diagram from question 1, **where** on the shelves is the gingerbread man? _____

6 In the cupboards of question 2, **where** are the glasses kept? _____

7 From the toys in question 3, what is the toy that Jo selects from the **middle** of the **top** row? _____

8 What is the **position** of the cards on the table in question 3? _____

9 Write the **names** and **positions** of two toys that you would select from the table of question 3. _____

_____

Compass directions

1 The dog is standing in the yard.
What direction is:

a on the dog's **right**? ____

b in **front of** the dog? ____

c on the dog's **left**? ____

From the dog, what animal is to the:

d **south**? _____ e **west**? _____ f **east**? ____

2 What state is

a **north** of South
Australia? _____

b **south** of Victoria? _____

c to the **west** of the
Northern Territory? _____

d to the **north** of New South Wales? _____

e to the **east** of Western Australia? _____

f to the **east** of South Australia? _____

3 Which landmark is:

a **north** of School
House? _____

b **east** of Diary
Mountain? _____

c **south** of Ruler Pier? _____

Give the **direction** of:

d Eraser Beach from Diary Mountain. _____

e Calculator Cove from School House. _____

f Diary Mountain from Pencil Point. _____

4 Write the **directions**
for Sam to the:

a sharks ____

b dolphins ____

c island ____

Where is Sam from the:

d turtle? ____

e shark? ____

f island? ____

5 Look at the diagram in question 1. What is the
direction below the dog? ____

6 Look at the map of Australia in question 2. What state is
to the **south** of New South Wales? _____

7 Look at the map in question 3. Which landmark is **north**
of Calculator Cove? _____

8 Look at the diagram in question 4 and write the
direction of Sam in the boat from the dolphin. _____

9 Colour the **locations** using:

a blue is south of red.

b green is west of red.

c blue is east of yellow.   d pink is north of yellow.

Maps

1 Move the counter **along the shaded
path** and complete the answers in
order:

a move ____ right   b move ____ up

c move ____ left   d move ____ up

e move ____ left   f move ____ down

2 Follow the **directions** given
and colour the path of the
mouse. Move:

a 7 right   b 5 up

c 6 left   d 3 down

e 4 right   f 1 up

3 On the map, who lives on:

a Learn St? _____

b House Rd? _____

c Book Rd? _____

d Golf St? _____

e Where is the shop? ____

f Who lives closest to the pool? _____

4

Look at the **map** and answer the questions:

a Which town can you drive from to Ocean Hill?

_____

b What is the name of the river? _____

c Describe how to travel from Boat Town to Seaweed
Forest. _____

d Can you drive to Sea Lake? _____

e How do you travel between the two towns? _____

f Can you drive to Seagull River? _____

5 Using the grid from question 1, to **complete the path**,
move the counter ____ right.

6 Add the **direction**, 2 left, to complete the diagram in
question 2.

7 Using the map in question 3, **describe** how to go from
the oval to the school. _____

8 Using the map in question 4, **describe** how to travel
from Beach Town to Seagull River. _____

9 Create a grid to show
the **points**:
A2, C3, C1, D3, A4 and B1.

Coordinates

1 Follow the butterfly's path and **give the letter** at the point where she **crosses**. (She begins at the start each time.)

a 3 up, 1 left, 3 right and 3 up ___

b 3 up, 4 right and 3 up ___

c 4 up, 2 right and 2 up ___

d 3 up, 4 right, 2 down, 1 left and 5 up ___

e 3 right and 6 up ___

f 1 left, 2 up, 2 right and 4 up ___

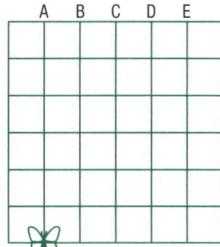

2 Use directions like those in question 1 to describe a **path** from:

a A to Y _____

b B to Z _____

c C to V _____

d D to X _____

e E to W _____

f C to Z _____

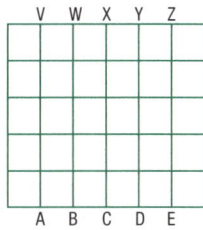

3 Using the grid, find the **symbols** from the grid reference. Remember to read across and then up.

a A3 ___   b F5 ___   c B4 ___

d E2 ___   e C5 ___   f D5 ___

4 Using the grid from question 3, give the **grid reference** for the following symbols:

a ÷ ___   b ★ ___   c × ___

d ■ ___   e ♥ ___   f + ___

5 Using the grid from question 1, follow the butterfly's path and **give the letter** at the point where it **crosses** if it goes 1 left, 4 up, 5 right and 2 up. ___

6 Using the grid from question 2, use directions to describe a **path** from E to X. _____

7 Using the grid from question 3, find the **symbol** at A4. ___

8 Using the grid from question 3, give the **grid reference** for @. ___

9 Using the grid from question 3, **describe** how you could move from point B1 to F5, by not passing through any blank squares. _____

Analog time (1)

1 Write the **time** shown on each of the following clock faces:

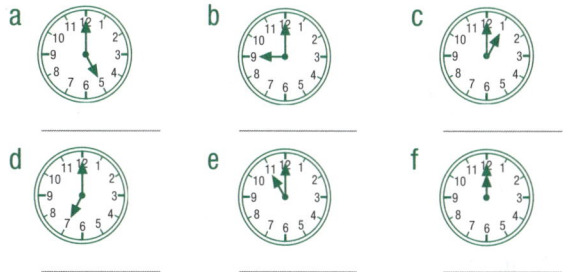

a ___   b ___   c ___

d ___   e ___   f ___

2 On each clock face, **draw** the time given:

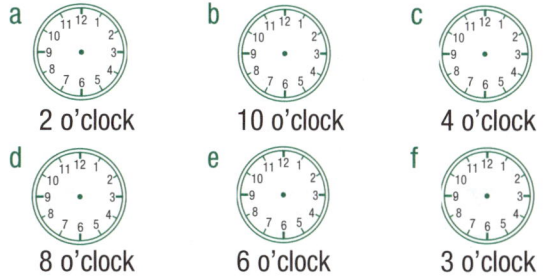

a 2 o'clock   b 10 o'clock   c 4 o'clock

d 8 o'clock   e 6 o'clock   f 3 o'clock

3 Write the **time** shown on each of the clock faces:

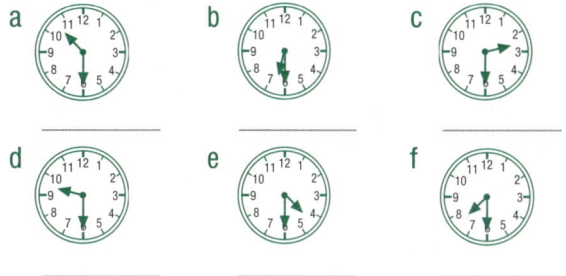

a ___   b ___   c ___

d ___   e ___   f ___

4 On each clock face, **draw** the time given:

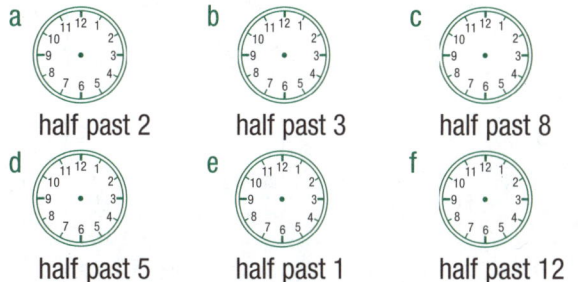

a half past 2   b half past 3   c half past 8

d half past 5   e half past 1   f half past 12

5 Write the **time** shown: ___

6 **Draw** the time 1 o'clock.

7 Write the **time** shown: ___

8 **Draw** the time half past 6.

9 How many **minutes** does it take the hour hand to move from one number to the next? ___

Analog time (2)

1 On each clock face, **draw** the time given:

a  b  c

quarter past 6   quarter to 5   quarter past 3

d  e  f

quarter to 10   quarter past 7   quarter to 1

2 Write the time shown on each clock face using **quarter to** or **quarter past**:

a  b  c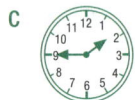

_____   _____   _____

d  e  f

_____   _____   _____

3 On each clock face **draw** the time given:

a  b  c

quarter to 4   5 o'clock   quarter past 2

d  e  f

half past 9   quarter to 11   quarter past 10

4 Write the **time** shown on each clock face:

a  b  c

_____   _____   _____

d  e  f

_____   _____   _____

5 Draw the time quarter to 6 on the clock face.

6 Write the time on the clock face using **quarter to** or **quarter past**. _____

7 Draw the time, 1 o'clock on the clock face.

8 Write the **time** on the clock face. _____

9 If Chi finishes school at quarter past 3, but soccer practice doesn't start until 5 o'clock, **how long** does he have to wait? _____

Analog time in minutes

1 Write how many **minutes** it takes for the minute hand to move from:

a 12 to 1 _____ b 12 to 5 _____ c 12 to 9 _____
d 12 to 11 _____ e 12 to 6 _____ f 12 to 10 _____

2 Find how many **minutes** it takes for the minute hand to move from:

a 2 to 4 _____ b 3 to 7 _____ c 4 to 6 _____
d 8 to 12 _____ e 7 to 9 _____ f 3 to 11 _____

3 Write the **time** shown on each clock face by completing the boxes:

a b c

☐ past ☐   ☐ past ☐   ☐ past ☐

d e f

☐ past ☐   ☐ past ☐   ☐ past ☐

4 **Draw** the hands on the following watches to show the time:

a b c

5 past 7   25 past 4   10 past 2

d e f

5 past 3   20 past 8   10 past 12

5 How many **minutes** does it take for the minute hand to move from 12 to 3? _____

6 How many **minutes** does it take for the minute hand to move from 1 to 5? _____

7 Write the **time** by completing the boxes.

☐ past ☐

8 **Draw** the hands on the following watch to show the time 25 past 1.

9 Write the **time** shown on the two different clock faces by completing the boxes:

☐ past ☐   ☐ past ☐
☐ to ☐   ☐ to ☐

Digital time (1)

❶   Write the following digital times as **numbers**:

a   six sixteen _____

b   nine twenty-two _____

c   ten fifty-five _____

d   two thirty-five _____

e   four oh three _____

f   twelve forty-five _____

❷   **Match** the following digital times with the words:

9:25   11:14 7:36   8:42   12:03   4:00

a   seven thirty-six _____

b   three minutes past twelve _____

c   four o'clock _____

d   fourteen minutes past eleven _____

e   eight forty-two _____

f   twenty-five minutes past nine _____

❸   Write what the following times mean in **words**:

a   6:18 _____

b   3:21 _____

c   8:59 _____

d   1:32 _____

e   5:06 _____

f   12:45 _____

❹   Look at the following watches and complete the **labels**:

a   8:05   b   3:09

_____ past _____   _____ past _____

c   2:04   d   5:05

_____ past _____   _____ past _____

e   10:01   f   12:07

_____ past _____   _____ past _____

❺   Write the digital time eight forty-three as **numbers**.

_____

❻   **Match** the correct digital time with the words:

5:31   5:29   5:20   5:19

twenty-nine minutes past five _____

❼   Write what the time 11:49 means in **words**.

_____

❽   Look at the watch   6:07   and complete the **label**:

_____ past _____.

❾   Sophie's different subjects are at the following times. Write them in **order**.

Maths   9:15
Reading   1:30
Science   11:20
Art   10:25 _____

Digital time (2)

❶   Look at the watch face and complete the **labels**:

a   2:36   b   9:21

_____ past 2   _____ past 9

c   1:15   d   4:30

_____ past 1   _____ past 4

e   10:06   f   6:55

_____ past 10   _____ past 6

❷   Write **digital times** for the times given in **words**:

a   36 minutes past 3 _____

b   five forty-two _____

c   seven fifty-six _____

d   27 minutes past 8 _____

e   thirteen minutes past 11 _____

f   6 minutes past 12 _____

❸   Write what the following times mean in **words**:

a   2:49 _____

b   9:58 _____

c   4:23 _____

d   10:16 _____

e   7:06 _____

f   11:34 _____

❹   Look at the following digital times and write what the **time will be** in 5 minutes:

a   1:13 _____   b   3:23 _____

c   5:35 _____   d   6:51 _____

e   8:04 _____   f   12:46 _____

❺   Look at the watch face   8:29   and complete the **label**:

_____ past 8.

❻   Write the **digital time** for the time in words:
nineteen minutes past one. _____

❼   Write what the time 6:32 means in **words**.

_____

❽   Look at the digital time 9:26 and write down what the **time will be** in 5 minutes. _____

❾   If school finishes at 3:15 and the time is now 2:52, **how long** is it before the end of the school day?

_____

Digital and analog time

1 Read the times and write them on the **digital clocks**:

a 10 past 2
`[ : ]`

b 25 past 5
`[ : ]`

c 5 past 12
`[ : ]`

d 20 past 8
`[ : ]`

e 15 past 10
`[ : ]`

f 40 past 4
`[ : ]`

2 Look at the **clock faces** and complete:

a
____ past 9
`[ : ]`

b
____ past 7
`[ : ]`

c
____ past 1
`[ : ]`

d
____ past 11
`[ : ]`

e
____ past 3
`[ : ]`

f
____ past 6
`[ : ]`

3 **Draw** the times on each analog clock:

a
half past 11

b
quarter to 5

c
quarter past 3

d
10 minutes past 10

e
7 o'clock

f
20 minutes past 1

4 Write the times in **words**:

a `11:45`
_____

b `9:30`
_____

c `2:00`
_____

d `8:36`
_____

e `6:09`
_____

f `4:55`
_____

5 Read the time and write it on the **digital clock**:
20 past 6 `[ : ]`

6 Look at the **clock face** and complete:
_____ past 11
`[ : ]`

7 **Draw** half past 2 on the analog clock.

8 Write the time `6:00` in **words**. _____

9 The clock shows: `7:00`
How many **minutes** will it take for the clock to display a quarter to 8? _____

Calendars

1 **How many days** are there in:

a one week? _____
b a fortnight? _____
c January? _____
d September? _____
e December? _____
f June? _____

2 On **which day** of the week are the following dates?

a 18 April? _____
b 30 April? _____
c 7 April? _____
d 26 April? _____
e 3 April? _____
f 15 April? _____

April						
S	M	T	W	Th	F	S
					1	2
3	4	5	6	7	8	9
10	11	12	13	14	15	16
17	18	19	20	21	22	23
24	25	26	27	28	29	30

3 Calculate the **number of days** (using the calendar from question 2, and include the first and last days) from:

a Friday 1 April to Wednesday 6 April _____
b Monday 11 April to Friday 15 April _____
c Wednesday 20 April to Saturday 23 April _____
d Monday 25 April to Saturday 30 April _____
e Friday 8 April to Sunday 10 April _____
f Saturday 16 April to Saturday 23 April _____

4 Look at the calendar of December and answer the following questions:

December						
S	M	T	W	Th	F	S
				1	2	3
4	5	6	7	8	9	10
11	12	13	14	15	16	17
18	19	20	21	22	23	24
25	26	27	28	29	30	31

a **How many days** are there in December? _____
b **On what day** of the week is 1 December? _____
c **On what day** of the week is 25 December? _____
d Write the **date** of the first Sunday. _____
e Write the **date** of the last Thursday. _____
f **How many** Wednesdays are there in December? _____

5 **How many days** are in November? _____

6 Looking at the month of April in question 2, on **which day** is the 21 April? _____

7 Looking at the month of April in question 2, calculate the **number of days** from Monday 18 April to Tuesday 26 April, including the first and last days. _____

8 Looking at the month of December in question 4, on **what day** of the week does December end?
_____

9 If January starts on a Sunday this year, **what day** of the week will it begin on next year? _____

Timelines and timetables

1 Give the time you would **arrive** at the pool:

Train timetable			
Station Rd	9:00	9:30	10:00
Long Rd	9:06	9:36	10:06
Short Street	9:12	9:42	10:12
Middle Plaza	9:15	9:45	10:15
Beral Lane	9:22	9:52	10:22
Round Rd	9:27	9:57	10:27
Swimming pool	9:30	10:00	10:30

a on the 9:00 train from the Station Rd _____

b on the 9:42 train from Short St _____

c on the 10:15 train from Middle Plaza _____

How long does it take the train to travel from:

d Station Rd to the pool? _____

e Short Street to the pool? _____

f Station Rd to Middle Plaza? _____

2 Using the timetable from question 1, complete the **timeline**:

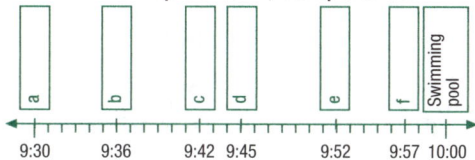

a b c d e f Swimming pool
9:30 9:36 9:42 9:45 9:52 9:57 10:00

3 Here is Veronica's morning.

7:00 wake up
7:15 breakfast
7:30 get dressed
7:35 clean teeth
7:40 feed dogs
7:50 pack bag
8:00 leave for school
8:30 arrive at school
9:00 start school
10:15 morning break
10:45 end break

a **What time** is breakfast? _____

b **How many minutes** does it take Veronica to brush her teeth? _____

c **How long** does Veronica have to play at school before classes start? _____

d Does Veronica have any **pets**? _____

e **How long** is morning break? _____

f What **time** does Veronica wake up? _____

4 Use the timetable from question 3 to complete the **timeline**:

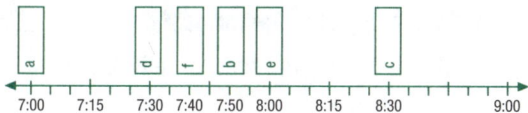

a d f b e c
7:00 7:15 7:30 7:40 7:50 8:00 8:15 8:30 9:00

5 **How long** does it take for the train in question 1 to travel from Middle Plaza to the pool? _____

6 Complete the **timeline** using the information from question 1:

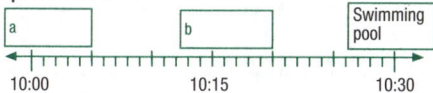

a b Swimming pool
10:00 10:15 10:30

7 Using the information from question 3, at **what time** does morning break finish? _____

8 Complete the **timeline** using the information from question 3:

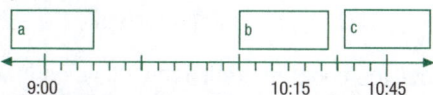

a b c
9:00 10:15 10:45

9 What is Veronica doing at each of the following **times**?

a _____   b 10:45 _____

Length in centimetres

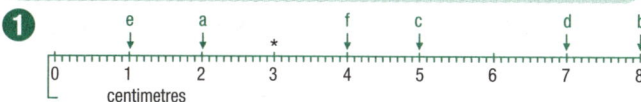

1

e a * f c d b
0 1 2 3 4 5 6 7 8
centimetres

Give the length in **centimetres** to each letter above the ruler:

a _____ cm   b _____ cm   c _____ cm

d _____ cm   e _____ cm   f _____ cm

2 Estimate the **length** of each crayon:

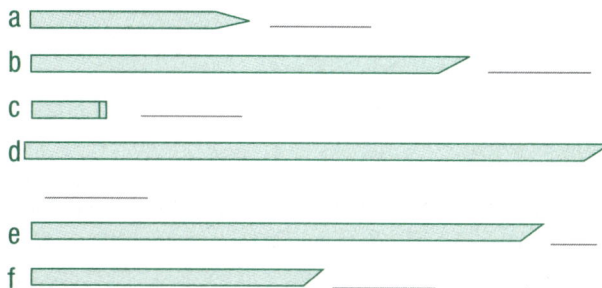

a _____
b _____
c _____
d _____
e _____
f _____

3 Measure the **length** of each crayon:

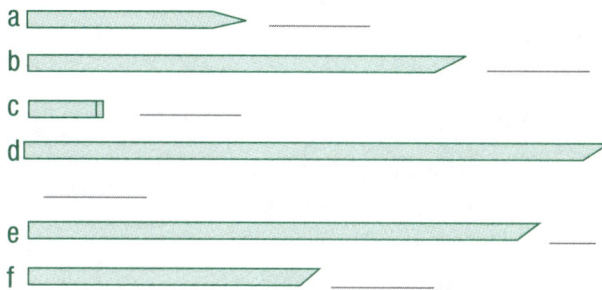

a _____
b _____
c _____
d _____
e _____
f _____

4 Use a ruler to **draw lines** of the following lengths:

a 2 cm

b 5 cm

c 7 cm

d 3 cm

e 6 cm

f 4 cm

5 Give the length in **centimetres** for the length marked with a star on the ruler in question 1. _____

6 Estimate the **length** of the crayon:

_____

7 Measure the **length** of the crayon:

_____

8 Use a ruler to **draw a line** 1 centimetre long.

9 **Estimate** and then **measure** the length of each side of the rectangle.

Estimate: _____ _____ _____

Measure: _____ _____ _____

Length (1)

1 **Estimate** and then **measure** the length of each side of the following shapes:

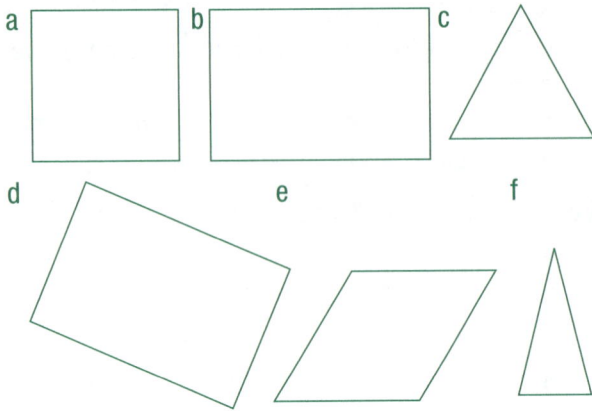

a   b   c

d   e   f

2 Use the 1 cm dot paper to **draw** each of the following lines:

a 5 cm
b 6 cm
c 3 cm
d 1 cm
e 7 cm
f 4 cm

3 Use the **short form** to write:

a 1 metre 15 centimetres = _____ m _____ cm
b 7 metres 2 centimetres = _____ m _____ cm
c 15 metres 50 centimetres = _____ m _____ cm
d 2 metres 30 centimetres = _____ m _____ cm
e 5 metres 89 centimetres = _____ m _____ cm
f 10 metres 90 centimetres = _____ m _____ cm

4 Would you use **metres or centimetres** to measure:

a a pencil? _____
b your hand? _____
c a basketball court? _____
d a tissue box? _____
e your shoe? _____
f your classroom? _____

5 **Estimate** and then **measure** the length of each side of:

_____

6 Use the 1 cm dot paper to **draw** a line 2 cm long.

7 Use the **short form** to write:

3 metres 29 centimetres = _____ m _____ cm

8 Would you use **metres or centimetres** to measure the height of your desk? _____

9 If you measured the **length** 10 cm, what might the object be? Give three suggestions.

_____ _____ _____

Length (2)

1 Write these in **centimetres**:

a 1 m 15 cm _____   b 1 m 82 cm _____
c 2 m 50 cm _____   d 3 m 95 cm _____
e 2 m 11 cm _____   f 1 m 7 cm _____

2 Write these as **metres and centimetres**:

a 135 cm _____   b 290 cm _____
c 305 cm _____   d 236 cm _____
e 142 cm _____   f 336 cm _____

3 Give the **unit**, metres, centimetres or both, you would use to measure the following:

a the length of a car _____
b the length of a football field _____
c the length of a pair of scissors _____
d the length of a piece of A4 paper _____
e the length of your house _____
f the length of a plate _____

4

scissors

paperclip

pen

Games counter

highlighter

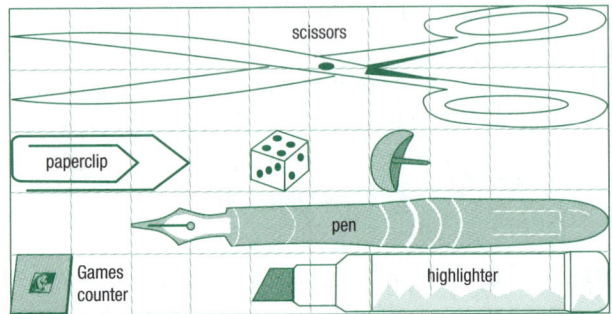

a Which object is the **longest**? _____
b Which objects are the **same length**?

_____

c **How long** is the highlighter? _____
d Which is **shorter**: the scissors or the pen? _____
e The paper clip is ___ cm **longer** than the die. ___
f The counter is ___ cm **shorter** than the pen. ___

5 Write 2 m 19 cm in **centimetres**. _____

6 Write 172 cm as **metres and centimetres**. _____

7 Give the **unit**, metres, centimetres or both, you would use to measure the length of a dog? _____

8 In the picture, which object is the **shortest**? _____

9 Describe how you could **measure** the following line:

Length in millimetres

1 Use the rulers to measure the lines in **millimetres**:

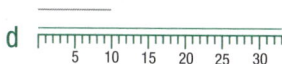

a
b

c
d

e
f

2 Write these in **millimetres**:

a   1 cm 2 mm _____

b   2 cm 8 mm _____

c   3 cm 5 mm _____

d   8 cm 3 mm _____

e   3 cm 9 mm _____

f   4 cm 7 mm _____

3 Write these as **centimetres and millimetres**:

a   14 mm _____

b   26 mm _____

c   39 mm _____

d   19 mm _____

e   42 mm _____

f   51 mm _____

4 **Draw lines** of these lengths using the 1 cm dot paper:

a   50 mm

b   25 mm

c   10 mm

d   35 mm

e   20 mm

f   40 mm

5 Use the ruler to measure the line in **millimetres**:

6 Write 2 cm 3 mm in **millimetres**. _____

7 Write 52 mm in **centimetres and millimetres**.

_____

8 Use the 1 cm dot paper to **draw a line** 30 mm long.

9 a   How many **millimetres** in a centimetre? _____

b   How many **centimetres** in a metre? _____

Length with decimals

1 Rewrite these as **metres and centimetres**:

a   1.23 m _____

b   1.69 m _____

c   3.72 m _____

d   1.78 m _____

e   2.56 m _____

f   3.14 m _____

2 Use **decimal** form to write:

a   2 m 6 cm _____

b   3 m 42 cm _____

c   6 m 72 cm _____

d   1 m 58 cm _____

e   2 m 97 cm _____

f   3 m 25 cm _____

3 Write these as **centimetres**:

a   27 mm _____

b   2 m 40 cm _____

c   49 mm _____

d   1 m 25 cm _____

e   85 mm _____

f   3 m 75 cm _____

4 Measure the **length** of each of the lines in centimetres, using one decimal place:

a

b

c

d

e

f

5 Rewrite 1.06 m as **metres and centimetres**.

_____

6 Use **decimal** form to write 3 m 75 cm. _____

7 Write 1 m 19 cm as **centimetres**. _____

8 Measure the **length** of the line in centimetres, using one decimal place.

9 **Which unit** (m, cm or mm) has been left off the following?

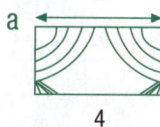

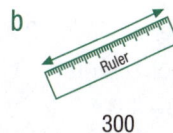

a   b   c

4   300   6

Perimeter (1)

1 **Estimate the perimeter** of each shape in centimetres:

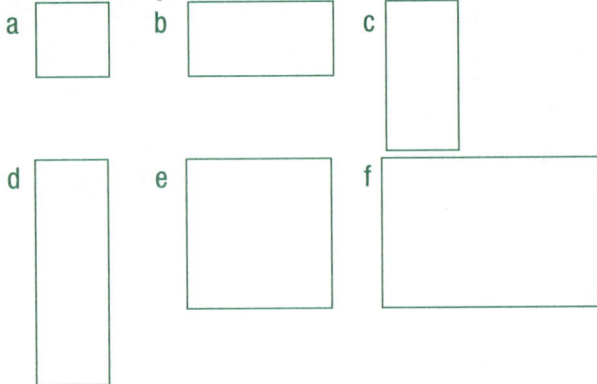

a ☐   b ☐   c ☐

d ☐   e ☐   f ☐

2 **Measure the perimeter** of each shape in question 1 in centimetres:

a _____   b _____   c _____
d _____   e _____   f _____

3 **Measure the perimeter** of each shape in centimetres:

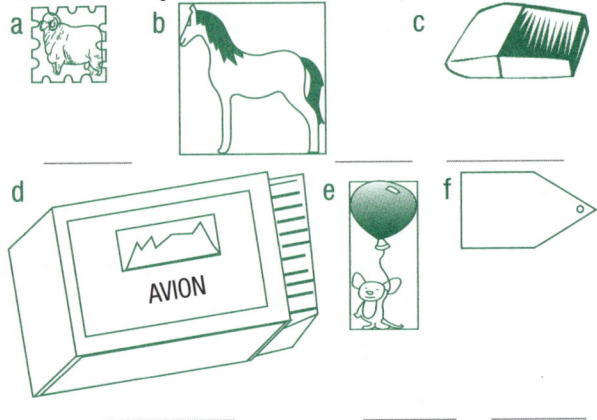

a [stamp with horse]   b [horse picture]   c [eraser]

d [matchbox AVION]   e [balloon]   f [tag]

4 **Draw** on dot paper on page 12 the following shapes:

a   a square with perimeter of 4 cm
b   a rectangle with perimeter of 6 cm
c   a rectangle with perimeter of 10 cm
d   a square with perimeter of 8 cm
e   a rectangle with perimeter of 8 cm
f   a square with perimeter of 12 cm

5 **Estimate the perimeter** of the rectangle: _____

6 **Measure the perimeter** of the rectangle in question 5:
_____

7 **Measure the perimeter** of the shape in centimetres. [barcode]
_____

8 **Draw** on dot paper on page 12 a rectangle with a perimeter of 10 cm.

9 Find the **perimeter** of:

[L-shaped figure: 2 cm, 1 cm, 3 cm, 3 cm, 2 cm, 5 cm]

Perimeter (2)

1 Find the **perimeter** of the following shapes by adding:

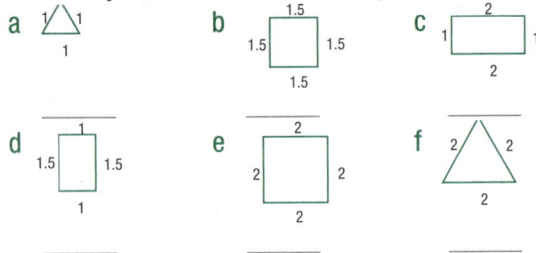

a [triangle 1, 1, 1]   b [triangle 1.5, 1.5, 1.5, 1.5]   c [rectangle 2, 1, 1, 2]

_____

d [rectangle 1, 1.5, 1.5, 1]   e [square 2, 2, 2, 2]   f [triangle 2, 2, 2]

_____

2 Find the **perimeter** of each shape:

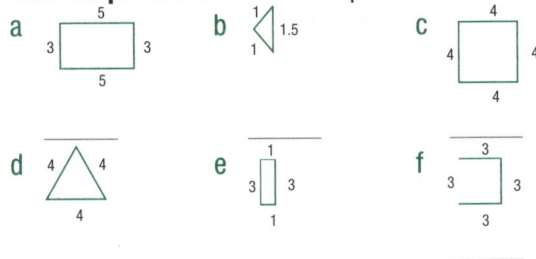

a [rectangle 5, 3, 3, 5]   b [triangle 1, 1, 1.5]   c [square 4, 4, 4, 4]

d [triangle 4, 4, 4]   e [rectangle 1, 3, 3, 1]   f [rectangle 3, 3, 3, 3]

3 Find the **perimeter** of each shape:

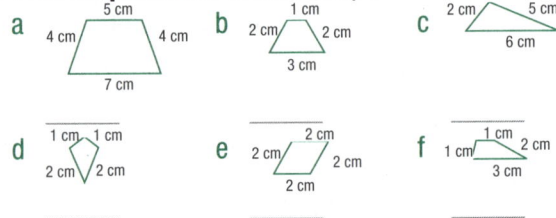

a [trapezium 5 cm, 4 cm, 4 cm, 7 cm]   b [trapezium 1 cm, 2 cm, 2 cm, 3 cm]   c [triangle 2 cm, 5 cm, 6 cm]

d [kite 1 cm, 1 cm, 2 cm, 2 cm]   e [parallelogram 2 cm, 2 cm, 2 cm, 2 cm]   f [trapezium 1 cm, 1 cm, 2 cm, 3 cm]

4 **Draw** each of the following shapes:

a a square with sides lengths 2 cm
b a 3-sided shape with side lengths 1 cm, 2 cm and 1 cm
c a 4-sided shape with side lengths 2 cm, 2 cm, 3 cm and 4 cm
d a parallelogram with side lengths 2 cm, 3 cm, 2 cm and 3 cm
e a trapezium with side lengths 1 cm, 2 cm, 2 cm and 3 cm
f a 4-sided irregular shape with side lengths 1 cm, 2 cm, 1 cm and 3 cm

5 Find the **perimeter** by adding: [square 3, 3, 3, 3]
_____

6 Find the **perimeter** of: _____ [triangle 3, 3, 3]

7 Find the **perimeter** of: _____ [parallelogram 2 cm, 1 cm, 1 cm, 2 cm]

8 **Draw** a rectangle with side lengths 2 cm, 3 cm, 2 cm and 3 cm.

9 Find the **perimeter** of: [shape 5, 3, 3, 5]

❶

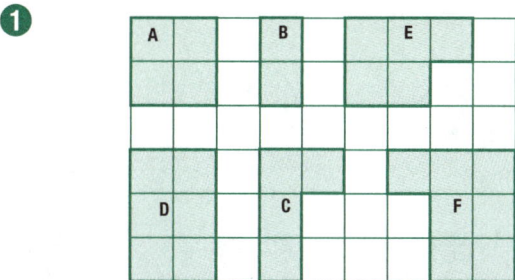

Estimate the area of each of the above shapes in squares:

a　A = ＿＿ squares　　b　B = ＿＿ squares

c　C = ＿＿ squares　　d　D = ＿＿ squares

e　E = ＿＿ squares　　f　F = ＿＿ squares

❷ **Count** the number of squares for each of the above shapes:

a　A = ＿＿ squares　　b　B = ＿＿ squares

c　C = ＿＿ squares　　d　D = ＿＿ squares

e　E = ＿＿ squares　　f　F = ＿＿ squares

❸ Answer the following questions, using the diagram from question 1:

a　Which shape has the **smallest** area? ＿＿

b　Which shape has the **larger** area? ＿＿

c　Which two shapes have the **same area**? ＿＿

d　Is shape A **larger or smaller** than shape D? ＿＿＿

e　Is shape E **larger or smaller** than shape F? ＿＿＿

f　**How many squares** do you need to add to shape B to make it the same area as shape C? ＿＿

❹ Circle which would have the **larger** area of the following pairs:

a　book or crayon　　b　football field or table

c　T-shirt or tent　　d　pizza or doughnut

e　5c coin or 50c coin　　f　poster or credit card

❺ **Estimate the area** of: ＿＿ squares

❻ **Count** the number of squares of: ＿＿ squares

❼ Is the shape in question 5 **larger** than the shape in question 6? ＿＿＿

❽ Circle which has the **larger** area:
a pillowcase or a blanket.

❾ **Draw** two different shapes that have an area of three squares.

---

❶ Find the **area** of each of the following shapes:

a 　　b

＿＿＿＿＿＿＿＿　　＿＿＿＿＿＿＿＿

c 　　d

＿＿＿＿＿＿＿＿　　＿＿＿＿＿＿＿＿

e 　　f

＿＿＿＿＿＿＿＿　　＿＿＿＿＿＿＿＿

❷ Circle the following objects that are **smaller** than one square metre:

a　a calculator　　b　a sports oval

c　a schoolyard　　d　a basketball court

e　a pancake　　f　a mobile phone

❸ Use the **short form** to write:

a　three square metres ＿＿＿＿＿＿

b　five square metres ＿＿＿＿＿＿

c　nine square metres ＿＿＿＿＿＿

d　sixteen square metres ＿＿＿＿＿＿

e　one hundred square metres ＿＿＿＿＿＿

f　fifty square metres ＿＿＿＿＿＿

❹ Which **unit** of measurement (cm^2 or m^2) would you use to find the area of:

a　a tennis court ＿＿＿＿＿＿

b　the top of a matchbox ＿＿＿＿＿＿

c　a kitchen floor ＿＿＿＿＿＿

d　a CD cover ＿＿＿＿＿＿

e　a $5 note ＿＿＿＿＿＿

f　a road ＿＿＿＿＿＿

❺ Find the **area** of: ＿＿＿＿＿＿

❻ Is a slice of cheese **smaller** than one square metre? ＿＿＿＿＿＿

❼ Use the **short form** to write twenty square metres. ＿＿＿＿＿＿

❽ Which **unit** of measurement (cm^2 or m^2) would you use to find the area of the top of a swimming pool? ＿＿＿＿＿＿

❾ List five objects that are **smaller** than one square metre and five objects that are **larger** than one square metre. ＿＿＿＿＿＿＿＿＿＿＿＿＿＿＿＿＿＿＿

Mass in kg (1)

1 Indicate if each of the following is **heavier or lighter** than one kilogram:

a a feather _____   b 10 large books _____

c a pencil case _____   d a television _____

e a football _____   f 5 bricks _____

2 Complete the following sentences:

a The pumpkin **weighs** _____ than 1 kg.

b The apple **weighs** _____ than 1 kg.

c The bananas **weigh** _____ than 1 kg.

d The strawberries **weigh** _____ than 1 kg.

e The biscuits **weigh** _____ than 1 kg.

f The sugar **weighs** _____ than 1 kg.

3 Circle which of the following items you estimate to have a mass of **less than** 1 kg:

a a pair of scissors   b a chair

c a car tyre   d a mushroom

e a bag of potatoes   f a dog

4 Circle the items that would be measured in **kilograms**.

a Jam   b Washing powder   c Chips

d Flour   e Potatoes   f Sweets

5 Is a glue stick **heavier or lighter** than one kilogram?

_____

6 The oranges **weigh** _____ than 1 kg.

7 Does a pear have a mass **less than** 1 kilogram?

_____

8 Would the watermelons be measured in **kilograms**?

_____

9 List five items/objects that are weighed in **kilograms**.

_____

Mass in kg (2)

1 Record the **mass** of each object:

a _____   b _____   c _____

d _____   e _____   f _____

2 Use the **short form** to write:

a 5 kilograms _____   b 9 kilograms _____

c 16 kilograms _____   d two kilograms _____

e eighteen kilograms _____   f ten kilograms _____

3 Look at the following items and answer the following questions:

What is the **total mass** of:

a chocolate and dog food? _____

b cereal and vegemite? _____

c meat and onions? _____

d dog food and meat? _____

e vegemite and onions? _____

f cereal and chocolate? _____

Chocolate 1 kg   meat 7 kg   VEGEMITE Concentrated yeast extract 2 kg   Cereal 1 kg   10 kg   Dog food 15 kg

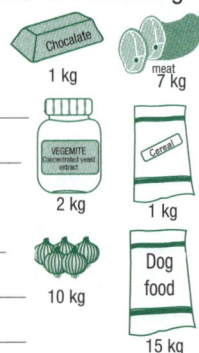

4 **How many** of each item could be packed in a bag that holds 12 kg?

a Sugar 7 kg   b Soap powder 3 kg   c Rice 4 kg

d Dog food 6 kg   e Toffee 1 kg   f Bird seed 10 kg

5 Record the **mass** of the DVDs: _____

6 Use the **short form** to write thirteen kilograms. _____

7 Look at the items from question 3. What is the **total mass** of the onions and chocolate? _____

8 **How many** tins of Chocolate powder can be packed in a bag that holds 8 kg? Chocolate powder 2 kg

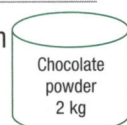

9 Find the **total mass** of all of the items in question 3. _____

UNIT 145
See START UPS page 10

Mass in grams

1 Use the **short form** to write:

a sixty grams _____

b forty-five grams _____

c three hundred grams _____

d one hundred and fifty grams _____

e ten grams _____

f two hundred grams _____

2 Circle the following items that are **heavier** than 10 grams:

a a feather   b a large bird

c a grain of rice   d a truck

e a basketball   f a ball of cotton wool

3 Look at the items and answer each of the following questions:

500 g   20 g   300 g   200 g   100 g

50 g

What is the **total mass** of:

a cheese and chocolate? _____

b egg and noodles? _____

c jam and a pear? _____

d cheese and an egg? _____

e jam and noodles? _____

f a pear and chocolate? _____

4 Order the following items from **lightest to heaviest**:

a 50 g, 200 g, 100 g _____

b 200 g, 750 g, 500 g _____

c 600 g, 300 g, 750 g _____

d 200 g, 50 g, 2 kg _____

e 10 kg, 5 kg, 2 kg _____

f 300 g, 450 g, 400 g _____

5 Use the **short form** to write twenty-five grams. _____

6 Are 5 golf balls **heavier** than 10 grams? _____

7 Look at the items from question 3. What is the **total mass** of jam and chocolate? _____

8 Order the items from **lightest to heaviest**:

1 kg, 3 kg, 500 g _____

9 What is the **total mass** of the following objects?

500 g + 200 g + 200 g + 50 g + 100 g

= _____

UNIT 146
See START UPS page 10

Capacity – informal

1 Match the following containers which would be the most suitable to **measure** the capacity of each of the objects:

A   B   C

a   b   c   d   e   f

2 Daisy used a cup to fill different containers with water:

Containers	Number of cups needed
A	🍵🍵
B	🍵🍵🍵🍵🍵
C	🍵🍵🍵🍵
D	🍵🍵🍵🍵🍵🍵
E	🍵🍵🍵
F	🍵🍵🍵

a Which container holds the **most** water? ____

b Which container holds the **least** water? ____

c **How many** cups did container B hold? _____

d Which 2 containers hold the **same** amount? ____

e Which container holds **3 cups** of water? ____

f Which container holds **2 cups** of water? ____

3 Tom used a different cup to fill the containers in question 2. He needed 2 cups to fill container E.

a Is Tom's cup **bigger or smaller** than Daisy's? ____

b **How many** of Tom's cups will fill container A? ____

c Which container will Tom **fill** with 3 cups? ____

d Of Tom's cup and Daisy's cup, whose will be used the **least** to fill container B? _____

e Which container held the **most water** with Tom's cup? _____

f Which container held the **least** with Tom's cup? ____

4 **True or false?**

a A dose of medicine is 5 L. _____

b A dog drank 10 L of water. _____

c A car holds 40 L of petrol. _____

d Tom drank 1 L of juice today. _____

e There is 5 L of water in the ocean. _____

f I can buy a 1 L container of milk. _____

5 Which of the containers in question 1 would be used to **measure**: _____

6 Using the information from question 2, is container C **smaller** than container D? _____

7 Which of the containers in question 2 is **smaller** than container F? ____

8 **True or false?** A swimming pool will only hold 1 L of water. ____

9 Name four things that could be measured in **litres**.

_____

Units

Capacity in litres

1 Use the **short form** to write:

a 3 litres _____   b 10 litres _____

c 15 litres _____   d 24 litres _____

e 8 litres _____   f 13 litres _____

2

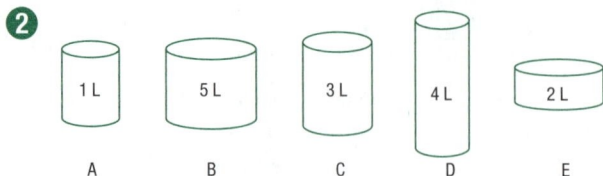

| 1 L | 5 L | 3 L | 4 L | 2 L |
| A | B | C | D | E |

a Which containers hold the **most** water? ____

b Which containers hold the **least** water? ____

c Which container holds **more** water than C but less than B? ____

d Which containers hold **more** water than E? ____

e Which containers hold **less** water than C? ____

f **How much** water would be needed to fill both C and E? _____

3 Circle the following objects that would hold **more than** one litre:

a a bucket   b a medicine container

c a sink   d a teaspoon

e a pool   f a small teacup

4

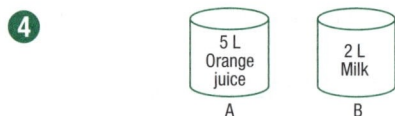

5 L Orange juice (A)   2 L Milk (B)

a What is the **capacity** of A? _____

b What is the **capacity** of B? _____

c Which container holds **more**? ____

d **How much more** does it hold? _____

e Which container holds **least**? ____

f What is the **total held** by the two containers? _____

5 Use the **short form** to write three litres. _____

6 Which of the containers:

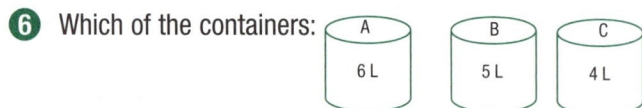

A 6 L   B 5 L   C 4 L

holds **more than** 5 L? ____

7 Does an oil drum hold **more than** one litre? _____

8 What is the **capacity** of container A? _____

2 L Orange juice (A)   3 L Milk (B)

9 List four things that hold **less than** one litre.

_____

Capacity in millilitres

1 Use the **short form** to write:

a 6 litres _____

b 11 litres _____

c 19 litres _____

d 250 millilitres _____

e 400 millilitres _____

f 700 millilitres _____

2 Find how many **millilitres** there are in:

a 1 litre _____

b 2 litres _____

c 3 litres _____

d 5 litres _____

e 7 litres _____

f 4 litres _____

3 These containers measure **millilitres**.

| A | B | C | D |
| 400 | 200 | 800 | 300 |

a How much water is in container C? _____

b How much water is in container D? _____

c How much more water is in container A than B? _____

d How much more water is in container A than D? _____

e How much water needs to be added to container C to make one litre? _____

f How much water needs to be added to container B to make one litre? _____

4 Circle the following objects which would hold **less than** one litre:

a an eggcup   b a swimming pool

c a small jam jar   d a bath

e a medicine cup   f a water tank

5 Use the **short form** to write 80 millilitres. _____

6 How many **millilitres** are there in 9 litres? _____

7 How much water is in the container in **millilitres**?

450 _____

8 Does a large bucket hold **less than** one litre? _____

9 Dave put 50 L of petrol in his car and 36 L in Cassandra's car. How many litres of petrol in **total**?

_____

Cubic centimetres

1 How many **cubes** are there in each model?

a   b   c

_____   _____   _____

d   e   f

_____   _____   _____

2 Complete the **label** for each model:

a   ___ layers of ___ cubes

b   ___ layers of ___ cubes

c   ___ layers of ___ cubes

d   ___ layers of ___ cubes

e 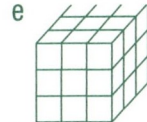   ___ layers of ___ cubes

f   ___ layers of ___cubes

3 Use the **short form** to write:

a 3 cubic centimetres ____ b 25 cubic centimetres ____
c 13 cubic centimetres ____ d 40 cubic centimetres ____
e 7 cubic centimetres ____ f 1 cubic centimetre ____

4 What is the **volume** of each of the models if each cube is 1 cm³?

a   b   c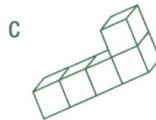

_____   _____   _____

c 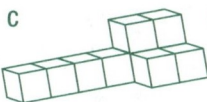 d   e

_____   _____   _____

5 How many **cubes** are there? _____

6 Complete the **label**:
___ layer of ___ cubes.

7 Use the **short form** to write 17 cubic centimetres.

_____

8 What is the **volume**?

_____

9 **Draw** two different models that use five cubic centimetres. (Note: it may be easier to build with Centicubes first.)

Volume

1 Record the volumes by **counting** the number of cubes used in each of the constructions:

a   b   c

d   e   f

_____   _____   _____

2 Of the constructions in question 1:
a Which object has the **largest** volume? ___
b Which object has the **smallest** volume? ___
c Which 2 objects have the **same** volume? ___
d Which object has a **volume** of 5 cm³? ___
e Which object has a volume of **more than** 7 cm³? ___
f Which object has a volume of **less than** 3 cm³? ___

3 Use the **short form** to write:

a 4 cubic centimetres ____ b 10 cubic centimetres ____
c 1 cubic centimetre ____ d 3 cubic centimetres ____
e 7 cubic centimetres ____ f 9 cubic centimetres ____

4 If the following objects are made from cubes, find the **volume**:

	Length	Breadth	Height	Volume
a	4	1	1	
b	3	1	2	
c	2	2	2	
d	3	2	3	
e	3	3	3	
f	5	1	2	

5 Record the volume by **counting** the number of cubes used in the construction.

_____

6 Of the constructions in question 1, which object has a **volume** of 4 cm³? ___

7 Use the **short form** to write 12 cubic centimetres.

_____

8 Find the **volume** of an object that has a length of 1 cube, a breadth of 2 cubes and a height of 5 cubes.

_____

9 **Draw** an object that has a length of 4 cubes, a height of 3 cubes, and a breadth of 2 cubes.

Arrangements

1 **How many different ways** can you arrange each of the following in a row?

a □ △ ○ _____　　b • •• _____　　c ☆☆☽ _____

d ○ ◁ ○ ◠ _____　　e ①①②② _____　　f □ ◇ △ _____

2 4 pink iced doughnuts, 2 brown iced doughnuts and 3 yellow iced doughnuts are placed in a bag.
Which colour is:

a **most likely** to be selected first? _____

b **least likely** to be selected first? _____

c **most likely** to be selected last? _____

If a pink doughnut is selected, could the **next one** selected be:

d pink? _____　　e yellow? _____　　f green? _____

3 7 blocks are placed in a box. 3 are red, 3 are yellow and 1 is green. One block is selected at random.

a Which colour is **least likely** to be selected? _____

b Could a yellow block be selected **first**? _____

c Could a red block be selected **first**? _____

If a red block is selected first, could the **next one** be:

d yellow? _____　　e green? _____　　f blue? _____

4 Here is the menu at a school canteen.

Lunch　Salad roll　Sausage roll　Hotdog Vegemite sandwich
Drinks　Orange juice　Milk　Water

a **How many** different lunches are there? _____

b **How many** different drinks are there? _____

c Scarlett had a salad roll. **How many** different drinks could she have with it? _____

d Jackson had water. **How many** different lunches could he have with it? _____

e If Emily had a sausage roll but wanted another different lunch item, **how many** did she have to select from? _____

f If Amy wanted a hot lunch, **how many** items could she choose from? _____

5 **How many different ways** can you arrange ☺ ☹ ☺ in a row? _____

6 There are 5 circles, 4 squares and 8 triangles in a bag. If one shape is selected at random, which shape is **most likely** to be chosen? _____

7 4 strawberry, 3 peppermint and 5 chocolate frogs are in a packet. If one is selected at random, which flavour is **least likely** to be chosen? _____

8 In the menu in question 4, Adam did not like water. **How many** other drinks did he have to select from? _____

9 For the menu in question 4, **list six** different lunches, e.g. salad roll and water.

Chance (1)

1 Write one of the words from the list to **match** the statements:
certain, likely, unlikely, impossible

a It will snow today. _____

b I will fly to the moon tomorrow. _____

c I will finish school on Monday. _____

d I will watch television tonight. _____

e I will have school holidays this year. _____

f I will become Prime Minister. _____

2 Write an **example** for each of the following words:

a never _____

b unlikely _____

c certain _____

d likely _____

e impossible _____

f equal chance _____

3 Look at the following dice.

a How many **faces** are there on 1 die? _____

If 1 die is rolled:

b What **numbers** could be on top? _____

c What is the **chance** that a 5 could be on top? _____

d What is the **chance** that a 3 could be on top? _____

e Is there any **chance** 7 dots could be rolled? _____

f Is there any **chance** 7 could be rolled with 2 dice? _____

4 The teacher put 20 Easter eggs in a bag.
How many of the Easter eggs are:

a red? _____

b green? _____

c blue? _____

d purple? _____

A student chose one egg without looking.

e What is the **most likely** colour of the egg? _____

f What is the **least likely** colour of the egg? _____

5 Write one of the words from the list to **match** the statement: certain, likely, unlikely, impossible.
The sun will rise tomorrow. _____

6 Write an **example** for the word: maybe _____

7 What is the **chance** of rolling a 6 on one die? _____

8 From the Easter eggs in question 4, is it **more likely** a green egg will be selected than a purple one? _____

9 Mum mixed up the socks in the washing and these are all the odd ones.
Draw all of the possible pairs of socks. _____

Red　Blue　Green　Yellow

Chance (2)

1 For the spinner:

a How many **different** outcomes are possible? _____

b Do all of the outcomes have the **same chance** of being selected? _____

c Which outcome is the **most likely** to be selected? _____

d Which outcome is the **least likely** to be selected? _____

e Is the * **more likely** to be selected than the ⁝? _____

f What is **more likely** to be selected than * ? _____

2 For the spinner, answer true or false:

a Orange is the **most likely** colour to be spun. _____

b Pink is the **least likely** colour to be spun. _____

c There is **no chance** of spinning yellow. _____

d It is **more likely** to spin brown than orange. _____

e It is **less likely** to spin brown than pink. _____

f There is **equal chance** of spinning purple and all of the other colours combined. _____

3 For the spinner, colour as for the following statements.

a Yellow has **2 chances** of being spun.

b Purple has **1 chance** of being spun.

c There is **no chance** of spinning black.

d Blue has an **equal chance** as purple of being spun.

e There are **3 chances** of spinning red.

f There is only **1 chance** of spinning green.

4 For the spinner, colour as for the following statements. The area that has:

a the **least chance** of being spun, green.

b the **greatest chance** of being spun, stars.

c the 2nd **most likely** to be spun, dots.

d the 2nd **least likely** to be spun, triangles.

e Put stripes in the **remaining** area.

f Name two areas that are **equal**. _____

5 For the spinner in question 1, are the stripes **more likely** to be selected than the dots? _____

6 For the spinner in question 2, answer true or false: there is on **equal chance** of spinning either orange or brown and pink together? _____

7 Colour the area of the spinner:

* which has the **least chance**, blue

* which has the **greatest chance**, yellow

* which has a **greater than blue but less chance than yellow** of being spun, green

8 For the spinner, place:

* stars in the area of **least chance**

* dots in the area **greatest chance**

* stripes in the area that has a chance **less than** the dots

9 **Draw** a spinner that has 5 different colours/shapes and 4 different outcomes.

Picture graphs

1 Adam made this graph using cut-out pictures of animals he saw at the farm.

a What animal did Adam see the **most**? _____

b What animal did Adam see the **least**? _____

c **How many** goats did he see? _____

d **How many** cows did he see? _____

e **How many more** sheep than cows did he see? _____

f How many animals did Adam see **altogether**? _____

2 The number of toys sold is shown on the graph.

Monday	
Tuesday	
Wednesday	
Thursday	
Friday	

a **How many** toys were sold on Wednesday? _____

b On which day were the **most** toys sold? _____

c On which day were the **least** toys sold? _____

d How many toys were sold **altogether**? _____

e **How many more** toys were sold on Monday than Tuesday? _____

f If there were 20 toys to be sold, how many toys were **not sold** at the end of the week? _____

3 This is a graph of students' favourite fruit.

a What is the **most popular** fruit? _____

b What is the **least popular** fruit? _____

c **How many** students liked oranges the best? _____

d How many **more** students liked apples more than oranges? _____

e How many **more** students liked bananas more than oranges? _____

f What was the **total** number of students who liked apples and bananas the best? _____

4 Albert collected information about different coloured eyes. Use the information to create a **picture graph**.

blue	ЦН
brown	ЦН II
green	III
grey	ЦН
other	ЦН

a blue　b brown　c green　d grey　e other

5 Using the information from question 1, what was the **total** number of cows and horses that Adam saw? _____

6 Using the information from question 2, what was the **total** number of toys sold on Monday and Friday? _____

7 In question 3, what was the **total** number of students asked about their favourite fruit? _____

8 Using the information from question 4, what was the **most common** eye colour? _____

9 Here is some information about the number of children in families. **Write two questions** you could ask about the information.

1	III
2	ЦН
3	ЦН
4	II
5	I

_____ , _____

Tally marks

1 Here is the tick sheet of students' favourite drink.

milk	✓✓✓✓
water	✓✓✓✓✓✓✓✓
orange juice	✓✓✓✓✓
soft drink	✓✓✓✓✓✓✓

a What was the **most popular** drink? _____

b What was the **least popular** drink? _____

How many children:

c preferred a soft drink? _____

d preferred orange juice? _____

e preferred orange juice to milk? _____

f What was the **total** number of children who preferred water or milk? _____

2 Here is a tally sheet of musical instruments played.

drums	ЖІ І
violin	ЖІ ІІІ
trumpet	ІІІІ
flute	ІІ

What was:

a the **most** common instrument played? _____

b the **least** common instrument played? _____

c the **total** number of people asked? _____

d **How many** people played the trumpet? ____

e **How many** people played the drums? ____

f How many **more** people played the drums than the flute? ____

3 A coin was tossed and here are the results. **Complete** the table.

H, T, T, H, T, T, H, H, T, T, H, T, H, T, H, T, H

	Tally	Total
Heads	a	b
Tails	c	d
Total	e	f

4 Here is a tally sheet that records how many televisions there are in homes.

0	ІІІ
1	ІІІІ
2	ЖІ ЖІ І
3	ЖІ ІІІ
4	ІІІІ

a What is the **most** common number of televisions? ____

b What was the **least** common number of televisions? ____

c **How many** homes had 4 televisions? ____

d **How many** homes had 2 or 3 televisions? ____

e **How many** homes had 0 or 1 televisions? ____

f Which numbers of televisions had the same result? ____

5 Using the information from question 1, **how many** children were asked about their favourite drink? _____

6 Using the information from question 2, what was the **total** number of people who played the violin or trumpet? _____

7 Using the information from question 3, **how many more** times did tails appear than heads? _____

8 Using the information from question 4, **how many** people were asked about televisions? _____

9 Here is a collection of data. Create a **tally sheet** of the information.

△□○○□△○○△□□
○△□○△△□○○

Reading tables

1 Meryl sorted all of the pencils into different coloured groups and recorded the information in a table:

Red	Blue	Green	Yellow	Brown	Pink	Black
3	6	5	9	15	12	4

a What was the **most** common colour? _____

b What was the **least** common colour? _____

c Which colour is there **3 times more of** than green? ____

d What is the **total** number of black and brown pencils? _____

e What colours have **less than** 7 pencils? _____

f **How many more** pink pencils are there than red? ____

2 Here is a table of the number of cards different children have of the Xeon or Alpha collections.

	No. of Xeon cards	No. of Alpha cards
Alfred	29	36
Betty	32	19
Conrad	50	25
David	16	48
Erin	45	27

How many Xeon cards have been collected by:

a Alfred? _____   b David? _____   c Erin? _____

How many Alpha cards have been collected by:

d Betty? _____   e Conrad? _____   f Erin? _____

3 What **month** was:

Name	Birth month
Fred	June
Gerri	March
Jack	September
Lisa	May
Hilda	April
Isaac	October
Kelly	January
Mike	November

a Isaac born? _____

b Lisa born? _____

c Kelly born? _____

Who was born in:

d June? _____

e November? _____

f September? _____

4 Here is some information about insects collected in the backyard.

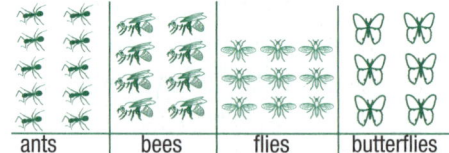

ants   bees   flies   butterflies

Use the information to complete the following table:

Insects	Tally	Number
ants	a	e
bees	b	8
flies	c	f
butterflies	d	6

5 Using the information from question 1, what was the **total** number of pencils? _____

6 Using the information from question 2, what was the **total** number of cards collected by Betty? _____

7 Using the information from question 3, **who** was born in March? _____

8 Using the information from question 4, what was the **total** number of insects found? _____

9 Use the graph to draw a **table**.

Column graphs

1 Interpret the following graph about different foods.

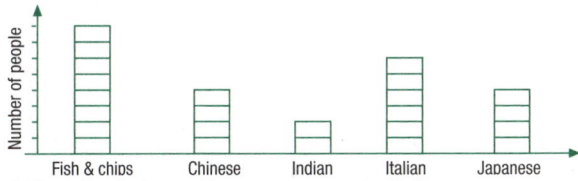

Number of people

Fish & chips Chinese Indian Italian Japanese

a What foods have the **same** popularity? _____

How many:

b **more** people like Italian than Japanese? ____

c **more** people like Italian than Indian? ____

d people liked the two most popular foods? _____

e people **in total** like Chinese and Japanese? _____

f **more** people like Italian, than Chinese? _____

2 Simone surveyed a car park with different coloured cars. The cars are marked with the first letter of the colours. Complete the following **tally sheet**.

W	R	R	W	W	G	Y	Y
G	W	Y	B	W	G	R	W
R	W	W	R	Y	R	R	R
B	Y	W	P	B	B

Colour	Tally
a white	
b red	
c yellow	
d green	
e blue	
f pink	

3 From the tally sheet in question 2, create a **column graph**:

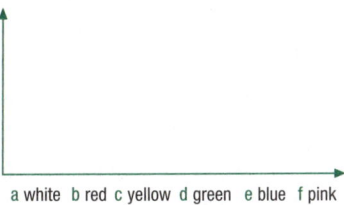

a white b red c yellow d green e blue f pink

4 Answer the following questions using the information in questions 2 and 3.

a What is the **most** common coloured car? _____

b What is the **least** common coloured car? _____

c Which coloured car had a **tally** of 3? _____

How many:

d green cars are in the car park? _____

e yellow and blue cars are in the car park? _____

f more red cars would need to be added to the car park to make 10? ____

5 For the graph in question 1, how many people were asked **in total**? _____

6 Three more cars pulled into the car park and they were all pink. Add them to your **tally** in question 2 in a different colour.

7 Now add the three pink cars to the **graph** in question 3.

8 If there were 40 car parking spaces in the car park, **how many** are now empty? _____

9 The following dice numbers were thrown. Create a **column graph** of the information.

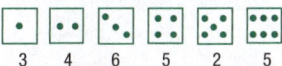

3   4   6   5   2   5

Two-way tables

1 Emily asked her friends who likes swimming and who likes running.

	Like to run	Don't like to run
Like to swim	Arthur Veronica	Daisy Erin
Don't like to swim	Caitlin	Jill Dante Tom

a **How many** friends did Emily ask? ____

How many of Emily's friends:

b like running but not swimming? ____

c like running and swimming? ____

d like swimming but not running? ____

e do not like running or swimming? ____

f like running? ____

2 Hannah asked people who owned bikes and who owned skateboards.

	Own skateboard	Don't own skateboard
Own bike	ЖІ ІІ	ІІІІ
Don't own bike	ЖІ	ІІ

How many people owned:

a both bikes and skateboards? ____

b skateboards but not bikes? ____

c bikes but not skateboards? ____

d neither skateboards nor bikes? ____

e bikes? ____   f skateboards? ____

3 Here is some information:

	Like cherries	Don't like cherries
Like apples	6	3
Don't like apples	7	5

How many people:

a like both apples and cherries? ____

b don't like either apples or cherries? ____

c like apples but not cherries? ____

d like cherries but not apples? ____

e like cherries? ____   f don't like cherries? ____

4 Here is some information:

	Have a cat	Don't have a cat
Have a dog	3	3
Don't have a dog	2	4

How many people have:

a a dog? ____   b a cat? ____

c a cat and a dog? ____   d neither cat nor dog? ____

e no dog? ____   f no cat? ____

5 Of Emily's friends in question 1, **how many** of them like swimming? ____

6 Of the people Hannah asked in question 2, **how many** people did not own a bike? ____

7 In question 3, **how many** people were asked? _____

8 In question 4, **how many** people have a cat but don't have a dog? ____

9 Make a **two-way table** showing people who:

* like pizza and burgers: 6

* don't like pizza but like burgers: 4

* don't like burgers but like pizza: 5

* don't like burgers or pizza: 3

Guided problem solving

1 On the farm, there were 25 parrots in 1 cage and 49 canaries in another. How many birds **altogether**?

a What is the question asking you to find? _____
How many:

b parrots? _____   c canaries? _____

d Name the process that needs to be used.

e Write a number sentence _____

f Write the answer. _____

2 Lisa had 85 apples. She gave 17 to Megan, 25 to Elisa and 14 to Jo. How many apples did she have **left**?

a What is the question asking you to find? _____

b How many apples were there to start with? _____

c How many apples were given away? _____

d Add the total number of apples given away. _____

e Write a number sentence _____

f Write the answer. _____

3 Greg planted flowers in rows of 7. He planted 8 full rows and had 6 flowers left. How many plants were there **altogether**?

a What is the question asking you to find? _____

b How many rows were there? _____

c How many plants were there in each row? _____

d Name the process that needs to be used. _____

e Find the answer. _____

f Add these flowers to find the total number. _____

4 **How many rows** of blocks could you make if you had 48 blocks and put 6 is each row?

a What is the question asking you to find? _____

b How many blocks in total? _____

c How many blocks in each row? _____

d Name the process that needs to be used. _____

e Write a number sentence. _____

f Write the answer. _____

5 There are 20 exercise books in the cupboard and the teacher added another 13. What process would be used to find the **total** number of exercise books? _____

6 The school bus had 35 students on it. 11 students were let off at the 1st stop and another 16 students at the 2nd stop. What process would be used to find the number of students **left** on the bus? _____

7 There are 6 cans in a packet and the canteen has 9 packets. What process would be used to find the **total** number of cans? _____

8 Six workers shared 24 biscuits. How would you find the **number** of biscuits each worker received? _____

9 Terry had 18 boxes to arrange on display. **Draw** at least three different ways Terry could arrange his display.

Problem solving

1 **Complete** the boxes:

a
```
   4 7
 +  □□
   6 3
```

b
```
   9 5
 -  □□
   4 2
```

c
```
  □ 7
   )35
```

d
```
     9
  ×  □
   4 5
```

e
```
   2 1 5
 + □ 4 □
   7 □ 1
```

f
```
   2 4 3
 - 1 □□
   1 2 7
```

2 a The zoo has 9 lions and 17 tigers. How many big cats are there **altogether**? _____

b In an aviary, there are 26 parrots and 18 quail. How many birds are there **altogether**? _____

c There are 59 public drink taps at the zoo and 12 for the staff. How many drink taps **altogether**? _____

d On Monday there were 32 frogs and on Friday there were 67 frogs in total. How many frogs had been **added** during the week? _____

e On Wednesday there were 19 chicks and by Thursday there were 26 chicks. **How many** chicks had hatched overnight? _____

f Initially there were 92 butterflies on display. The keeper removed 37. How many **left**? _____

3 How many were there **altogether**?

a There were 5 cows in each of 6 paddocks. _____

b There were 4 sheep in each of 7 paddocks. _____

c There were 4 pigs in each of 8 pens. _____

How many are there in each pen?

d 10 chickens to be placed evenly in 2 pens. _____

e 18 ducks to be placed evenly in 3 pens. _____

f 27 horses to be placed evenly in 3 pens. _____

4 a If I had $5.00, $16.25 and $14.30, how much money do I have in **total**? _____

b If I had $100 and spent $8, how much **left**? _____

c If there were five $5 notes and six $2 coins, how much money would there be **altogether**? _____

d If $15.00 had to be divided evenly between 3 people, how much would **each** person receive? _____

e I bought a $1.75 fruit bar and a 50c banana. How much did I spend **altogether**? _____

f I had $5 and bought a $2.90 loaf of bread. How much **change** did I receive? _____

5 **Complete**: $2 \times \boxed{} = 18$

6 The zoo has 68 keepers and 25 office staff. How many employees are there **altogether**? _____

7 There were 5 emus in each of 4 paddocks. How many emus were there **altogether**? _____

8 I bought a magazine for $5.90. If I paid $7.00, how much **change** did I receive? _____

9 **Write a question** for this: _____ = 29 aliens

Tables practice (1)

1 Complete:

a 6 groups of 3 = _____   b 8 groups of 7 = _____

c 10 groups of 4 = _____   d 5 groups of 2 = _____

e 2 groups of 9 = _____   f 7 groups of 5 = _____

2 Complete:

a 2 × 3 = _____   b 9 × 6 = _____

c 4 × 7 = _____   d 10 × 10 = _____

e 8 × 9 = _____   f 2 × 0 = _____

3 Complete:

a 4 × ___ = 20   b 7 × ___ = 28

c ___ × 10 = 60   d 8 × ___ = 64

e ___ × 9 = 27   f 9 × ___ = 27

4 **Draw arrays** to illustrate the following tables and then solve:

a 3 × 10 = _____   b 3 × 7 = _____

c 9 × 2 = _____   d 7 × 4 = _____

e 4 × 8 = _____   f 9 × 9 = _____

5 Complete: 6 groups of 9 = _____

6 Complete: 5 × 3 = _____

7 Complete: _____ × 7 = 70

8 **Draw an array** to illustrate the following table and then solve: 5 × 6 = _____

9 For Mother's Day, mum received 3 boxes of chocolates. Each box contained 6 rows of 2 chocolates. How many chocolates did mum receive **altogether**?

_____

Tables practice (2)

1 Find the **product** of:

a 5 and 7 _____   b 6 and 2 _____

c 7 and 8 _____   d 10 and 9 _____

e 1 and 4 _____   f 2 and 0 _____

2 Complete:

a	7	b	9	c	7
	× 7		× 3		× 9

d	6	e	9	f	10
	× 5		× 7		× 2

3 **Complete** the spaces:

a 1 × 6 = ___ = 3 × ___

b 8 × 5 = _____ = 4 × _____

c 3 × ___ = 12 = 2 × ___

d 5 × ___ = 20 = 2 × _____

e ___ × 6 = 36 = 4 × _____

f 5 × ___ = 30 = 10 × ___

4 Complete the **tables**:

a
×	6	7	8	9
3				

b
×	9	10	8	7
9				

c
×	8	9	10	7
5				

d
×	9	10	8	7
8				

e
×	4	6	8	9
4				

f
×	2	4	6	9
7				

5 Find the **product** of 7 and 6. _____

6 Complete:
```
    9
  × 6
  ___
```

7 **Complete** the spaces: 6 × ___ = 24 = 3 × ___

8 Complete:

×	4	7	8	9
6				

9 In the piggy bank there were ten 10c coins, eight 5c coins, six $2 coins, and five $5 notes. How much money was there in **total**? _____

Addition practice

1 Use the **jump strategy** to find the answer:

a 39 + 17 = _____   b 45 + 26 = _____

c 62 + 35 = _____   d 58 + 24 = _____

e 47 + 44 = _____   f 59 + 36 = _____

2 **Complete** the following:

a 2 8   b 5 4   c 2 6
  + 4 9   + 2 8   + 1 9

d 3 6   e 6 3 6   f 7 3 5
   2 5   + 1 2 3   + 1 2 8
  + 1 7

3 Write **number sentences** and find the answers to:

a fifty-six and twenty-nine _____

b eighty-three plus nine _____

c add fifty-seven to thirty-eight _____

d the total of twenty-seven and fifty

_____

e find the sum of eighteen, twenty-five and thirty-two

_____

f add seventeen, thirty-four and eleven_____

4 Find how many **altogether** if:

a There were 27 cows in one paddock and 36 sheep in another. _____

b Chris needed 43 nails and 58 tacks. _____

c There were 34 bricks in one pile and 28 bricks in another. _____

d Jake had collected 19 ants, 12 butterflies and 16 beetles for his science project. _____

e There were 52 pieces of paper in one pile and 117 in another pile. _____

f The farmer collected 28 eggs on Saturday, 22 eggs on Sunday and 30 eggs on Monday. _____

5 Use the **jump strategy** to find the answer of:

63 + 19 = _____

6 **Complete**:   2 6
                1 3
              + 4 5

7 Write a **number sentence** and solve: the sum of fifteen, sixteen and seventeen. _____

8 There were 14 biscuits in one packet and 37 biscuits in a box. How many biscuits **altogether**? _____

9 **Complete**:

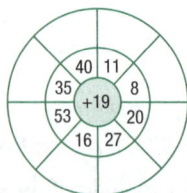

Subtraction practice

1 **Complete**:

a 15 − 11 = _____   b 26 − 14 = _____

c 79 − 35 = _____   d 28 − 16 = _____

e 56 − 31 = _____   f 66 − 33 = _____

2 Complete:

a thirty-six **take away** twenty-two _____

b forty-seven **minus** fifteen _____

c the **difference** between sixty-two and forty-two

_____

d **subtract** thirty-one from forty _____

e fifty-five **take away** thirty-four _____

f sixty-nine **minus** twenty-seven _____

3 **Complete**:

a	T	U		b	T	U		c	T	U
	2	9			5	6			6	6
−	1	8		−	3	0		−	2	5

d	T	U		e	H	T	U		f	H	T	U
	9	6			5	9	9			8	5	6
−	6	4		−	3	4	2		−	3	2	1

4 **Complete** the following:

a	T	U		b	T	U		c	T	U
	4	5			5	5			7	3
−	3	8		−	3	6		−	4	5

d	T	U		e	T	U		f	T	U
	9	4			9	1			6	0
−	6	6		−	4	6		−	3	4

5 **Complete**: 86 − 63 = _____

6 Find the **difference** between fifty-eight and thirty-six.

_____

7 **Complete**:

H	T	U
4	8	9
− 2	6	1

8 **Complete**:

T	U
7	2
− 3	8

9 856 students entered a colouring competition. Certificates were awarded to 64 students. **How many** students did not receive a certificate? _____

Multiplication practice

1 **Complete** the following:

a 5 rows of 3 = _____　　b 5 rows of 9 = _____

c 9 rows of 6 = _____　　d 4 lots of 3 = _____

e 10 lots of 8 = _____　　f 7 lots of 5 = _____

2 Complete the following:

a 3 **groups of** 10 fish _____

b 2 **groups of** 9 eggs _____

c 8 **groups of** 7 children _____

d 1 **group of** 7 monkeys _____

e 8 **groups of** 7 days _____

f 9 **groups of** 10 pencils _____

3 Answer **true or false**:

a 6×5 equals 5×6 _____

b 4×7 equals $7 + 7 + 7 + 7$ _____

c 9×8 equals 8×9 _____

d 5×4 equals 1×10 _____

e 3×4 equals $3 + 3 + 3$ _____

f 10×6 equals $10 + 10 + 10 + 10 + 10 + 10$

_____

4 **Complete**:

a $\begin{array}{r} 10 \\ \times\ 9 \\ \hline \end{array}$　　b $\begin{array}{r} 9 \\ \times\ 9 \\ \hline \end{array}$　　c $\begin{array}{r} 8 \\ \times\ 6 \\ \hline \end{array}$

d $\begin{array}{r} 4 \\ \times\ 8 \\ \hline \end{array}$　　e $\begin{array}{r} 8 \\ \times\ 7 \\ \hline \end{array}$　　f $\begin{array}{r} 6 \\ \times\ 7 \\ \hline \end{array}$

5 **Complete**: 4 lots of 7 = _____

6 Complete: 9 **groups of** 8 insects _____

7 Answer **true or false**:
6×3 equals $6 + 6 + 6$ _____

8 **Complete**:

$\begin{array}{r} 9 \\ \times\ 5 \\ \hline \end{array}$

9 There are 8 packets of textas with 9 textas in each packet. **Are there enough** textas for 70 children to have one texta each? _____

Division practice

1 **Complete**:

a 20 shared among 4 = ___

b 18 shared among 6 = ___

c 40 shared among 10 = ___

d 36 shared among 4 = ___

e 5 shared among 5 = ___

f 24 shared among 4 = ___

2 **Complete**:

a $70 \div 7$ = _____　　b $42 \div 6$ = _____

c $81 \div 9$ = _____　　d $100 \div 10$ = _____

e $72 \div 8$ = _____　　f $28 \div 4$ = _____

3 Use the multiplication table to answer the **division** equations:

a $9 \times 3 = 27$　　　　b $6 \times 8 = 48$

$3\overline{)27}$　　　　　　$6\overline{)48}$

c $9 \times 5 = 45$　　　　d $6 \times 8 = 48$

$9\overline{)45}$　　　　　　$8\overline{)48}$

e $8 \times 4 = 32$　　　　f $4 \times 2 = 8$

$4\overline{)32}$　　　　　　$2\overline{)8}$

4 Find the following **answers with remainders**:

a How many groups of 8 rulers in 20? _____

b How many groups of 5 pens in 12? _____

c How many groups of 3 biros in 25? _____

d How many groups of 8 pencils in 50? _____

e How many groups of 4 books in 30? _____

f How many groups of 6 cards in 40? _____

5 **Complete**: 21 shared among 7 = ___

6 **Complete** $60 \div 6$ = ___

7 Use the multiplication table to answer the **division** equation:　　$6 \times 9 = 54$

$6\overline{)54}$

8 Find the **answer with a remainder**:
How many groups of 8 whiteboard markers are there in 35? _____

9 There are 80 pears. **How many boxes** are needed if 9 pears are put in each box? _____
How many pears are **left over**? ___

Fractions practice

1 Complete:

a $\frac{1}{3}$ is ___ **out of** ___ equal parts.

b $\frac{3}{4}$ is ___ **out of** ___ equal parts.

c $\frac{2}{5}$ is ___ **out of** ___ equal parts.

d $\frac{7}{10}$ is ___ **out of** ___ equal parts.

e $\frac{3}{8}$ is ___ **out of** ___ equal parts.

f $\frac{2}{2}$ is ___ **out of** ___ equal parts.

2 **What part** of each of the following has been shaded?

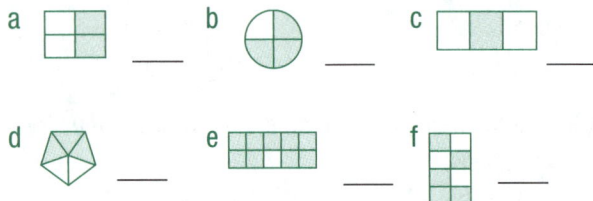

a ___   b ___   c ___

d ___   e ___   f ___

3 **Colour** part of each group to match the given fraction

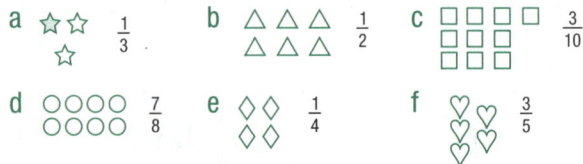

a $\frac{1}{3}$ b $\frac{1}{2}$ c $\frac{3}{10}$

d $\frac{7}{8}$ e $\frac{1}{4}$ f $\frac{3}{5}$

4 Order the following sets of fractions from **smallest to largest**.

a $\frac{3}{4}, \frac{1}{4}, \frac{4}{4}, \frac{2}{4}$ _____

b $\frac{2}{5}, \frac{4}{5}, \frac{3}{5}, \frac{1}{5}$ _____

c $\frac{1}{7}, \frac{4}{7}, \frac{3}{7}, \frac{6}{7}$ _____

d $\frac{3}{6}, \frac{4}{6}, \frac{2}{6}, \frac{5}{6}$ _____

e $\frac{3}{8}, \frac{5}{8}, \frac{2}{8}, \frac{4}{8}$ _____

f $\frac{8}{9}, \frac{7}{9}, \frac{3}{9}, \frac{5}{9}$ _____

5 Complete: $\frac{4}{10}$ is ___ **out of** ___ equal parts.

6 **What part** of ▦ has been shaded? ___

7 **Colour** $\frac{2}{5}$ of: ○ ○ ○ ○ ○

8 Order the set of fractions from **smallest to largest**.

$\frac{5}{10}, \frac{7}{10}, \frac{4}{10}, \frac{2}{10}$ _____

9 **Draw** a picture to show the fractions

$\frac{1}{3}$ and $\frac{1}{4}$ and circle the **larger** fraction.

Decimals practice

1 Write as a **decimal**:

a 4 tenths _____

b 7 tenths _____

c 1 tenth _____

d 36 hundredths _____

e 89 hundredths _____

f 12 hundredths _____

2 Write as a **decimal**:

a $\frac{9}{10}$ _____   b $\frac{3}{10}$ _____

c $\frac{49}{100}$ _____   d $\frac{72}{100}$ _____

e $1\frac{6}{10}$ _____   f $2\frac{93}{100}$ _____

3 **Add** the following decimals:

a $\begin{array}{r} 0.4 \\ + 0.3 \\ \hline \end{array}$ b $\begin{array}{r} 4.6 \\ + 1.3 \\ \hline \end{array}$ c $\begin{array}{r} 2.5 \\ + 1.3 \\ \hline \end{array}$

d $\begin{array}{r} 1.06 \\ + 3.11 \\ \hline \end{array}$ e $\begin{array}{r} 8.42 \\ + 1.57 \\ \hline \end{array}$ f $\begin{array}{r} 3.72 \\ + 1.46 \\ \hline \end{array}$

4 **Subtract** the following decimals:

a $\begin{array}{r} 0.9 \\ - 0.7 \\ \hline \end{array}$ b $\begin{array}{r} 2.9 \\ - 1.6 \\ \hline \end{array}$ c $\begin{array}{r} 5.6 \\ - 1.3 \\ \hline \end{array}$

d $\begin{array}{r} 2.89 \\ - 1.46 \\ \hline \end{array}$ e $\begin{array}{r} 3.76 \\ - 2.15 \\ \hline \end{array}$ f $\begin{array}{r} 6.34 \\ - 5.17 \\ \hline \end{array}$

5 Write 25 hundredths as a **decimal**. _____

6 Write $1\frac{2}{10}$ as a **decimal**. _____

7 **Add**: $\begin{array}{r} 4.52 \\ + 3.16 \\ \hline \end{array}$

8 **Subtract**: $\begin{array}{r} 4.76 \\ - 2.53 \\ \hline \end{array}$

9 Find the **total** of: 6.49 and 2.36 _____

Money practice

1 **Add** the following amounts:

a $2.35   b $1.95   c $2.80
  + $1.60   + $2.50   + $1.55

d $1.76   e $4.95   f $3.98
  + $2.23   + $1.30   + $1.50

2 Find the following **change** from:

a $5.00 after spending $2.60 _____

b $3.00 after spending $1.10 _____

c $10.00 after spending $7.90 _____

d $4.00 after spending $3.60 _____

e $6.00 after spending $5.80 _____

f $7.00 after spending $6.20 _____

3 **Round** the following amounts to the **nearest 10c**.

a 42c _____   b 38c _____

c 78c _____   d 51c _____

e 63c _____   f 75c _____

4 **Estimate**, to the nearest dollar, the **total** cost of:

a 3 × $1.95 _____   b 4 × $2.10 _____

c 8 × $4.99 _____   d 6 × $0.95 _____

e 5 × $5.02 _____   f 7 × $4.05 _____

5 **Add**: $8.62
          + $1.56

6 Find the **change** from $9.10 after spending $8.05.

_____

7 **Round** 22c to the **nearest 10c**. _____

8 **Estimate**, to the nearest dollar, the **total** cost of:
2 × $8.95 _____

9 To make a costume for the school play, **estimate** the total cost, to the **nearest dollar**:

2 × material $1.95 each
1 × hat $3.05
1 × mask $2.95
1 × wig $4.95
3 × balloons $0.90 each

_____

Time practice

1 Write **digital times** for each of the times given:

a twenty-five minutes past six _____

b three fifteen _____

c eight minutes past one _____

d nine fifty-two _____

e half past five _____

f forty-seven minutes past ten _____

2 On each **clock face**, draw the time given:

a 11 o'clock   b half past 2   c quarter to 6

d quarter past 4   e 25 past 3   f 5 past 1

3 **Complete**:

a 8:12   b 6:59   c 2:33
  ___ past ___   ___ past ___   ___ past ___

d 7:27   e 10:10   f 11:41
  ___ past ___   ___ past ___   ___ past ___

4 Look at the clock faces and **complete**:

a   b   c
  ___ past ___   ___ past ___   ___ past ___
  _____ : _____   _____ : _____   _____ : _____

d   e   f
  ___ past ___   ___ past ___   ___ past ___
  _____ : _____   _____ : _____   _____ : _____

5 Write a **digital time** for eleven forty-three. _____

6 On the **clock face** draw a quarter to 3:

7 **Complete**: ___ past ___   4:06

8 **Complete**:

  _____ past ___
  _____ : _____

9 If a clock shows 9:50 , **what will the time be** in 1 hour and 45 minutes? _____

1 The **number** shown by the Base ten blocks is:
UNIT 1 Q1 2 Q1 3 Q1

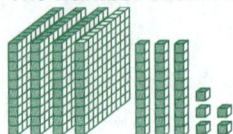

A 534   B 543   C 435   D 453

2 The **number** shown on the abacus is:
1 Q2 2 Q1 3 Q1

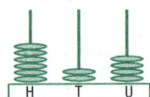

A 426   B 624   C 462   D 246

3 True or false?
2 Q4
The next number after 3860 is 3862. _____

4 True or false?
2 Q2
The value of the 5 in 305 is 5 units. _____

5 How many **digits** are in the number 1039? _____ *3 Q2*

6 Circle the **larger** number of 491 or 419. *2 Q3*

7 Write the numeral for two thousand and sixty-five. *1 Q4 3 Q3*
_____

8 Write the **next three** numbers: *4 Q4*
125, 126, 127, _____, _____, _____

9 Order the following numbers from **smallest to largest**: *4 Q3 4 Q4*
two hundred and three,
four hundred and twenty-five,
one hundred and fifty-six,
eight hundred and fifteen.

_____, _____, _____, _____

10 What is the **value** in the tens position? _____ *4 Q1*

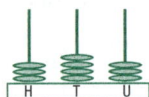

11 Write the **value** of the hundreds column *1 Q3 3 Q4*
in words of the number 8426. _____

12 Cross out the number which does not belong in *4 Q2*
the following number **pattern**:
1943, 1933, 1930, 1923, 1913, 1903, 1893

Score = _____ **/12**

---

1 The **total** number of pencils is: *UNIT 5 Q1*

A 11   B 55   C 56   D 65

2 The **largest** possible number that can be written *8 Q3*
with the digits 4, 3, 0, 7 is: _____
A 7430   B 0347   C 3470   D 7034

3 True or false?   498 < 489 _____ *8 Q4*

4 True or false? _____ *5 Q2 5 Q4 6 Q2 6 Q3*
The missing number in the pattern is 140.

150, _____, 130, 120

5 Arrange the numbers from **smallest to largest**: *8 Q1*
51, 81, 31, 101, 121, 21

_____

6 Continue the **pattern**: *10 Q1*

7 Start at 26 and make a pattern by *9 Q1 10 Q4*
going **forwards** by 6, five times:
_____

8 Complete the **pattern** and describe it in **words**: *5 Q3 6 Q3 10 Q2 10 Q3*
600, 590, 580, 570, _____, _____, _____

_____

9 Complete the **table**: *6 Q1 7 Q1 7 Q2 7 Q3 7 Q4*

100 less	100 less	Number	100 more	100 more	100 more
		892			

10 Complete and use **words** to describe the pattern: *7 Q4 10 Q3*
915, _____, 715, _____, 515

_____

11 Select the correct **numbers** to write in the spaces: *5 Q3 6 Q4*
599, 579, 539, 619, 569, 609,
589, _____, _____, 559, 549, _____

12 Complete the **trail**: *9 Q1 9 Q2 9 Q3 9 Q4*

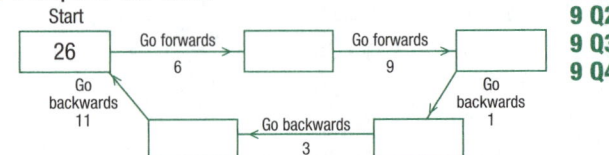

Start
26   Go forwards 6   Go forwards 9
Go backwards 11   Go backwards 3   Go backwards 1

Score = _____ **/12**

1 The **numeral** for 600 + 80 + 2 is: *UNIT 11 Q3 / 12 Q2*
A 862   B 682   C 286   D 628

2 The **value** of the underlined digit in 34$\underline{1}$9 is: *11 Q4 / 12 Q4*
A 1 hundred   B 1 thousand
C 1 unit   D 1 ten

3 **True or false**?   *15 Q2*
61 is an even number? _____

4 **True or false**?   *13 Q4 / 14 Q2*
9201 is the largest number possible from
the digits 1, 0, 9, 2. _____

5 **Expand** 9152.   *11 Q2 / 12 Q3 / 13 Q1*
_____

6 Complete the counting pattern, counting   *15 Q3*
by **twos**:
78, 80, 82, _____, _____, _____.

7 Write the **number** on the abacus in the numeral   *11 Q1 / 12 Q1*
expander.

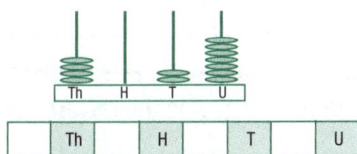

8 Write the numbers in **words** before and after.   *13 Q2*
_____ six hundred and nineteen _____

9 Write the two **smallest** numbers possible with the   *14 Q3*
digits 6, 0, 1, 2: _____, _____

10 Circle the **largest** number of: *14 Q4*
481, 841, 491, 852

11 Circle the **odd** numbers: 45, 60, 89, 107, 126   *15 Q1*

12 a Order the following numbers from **smallest to   *13 Q3 / 14 Q1*
largest**: 482, 369, 582, 495, 691
_____

b Now order the numbers from **largest to
smallest.** _____

c What do you notice about the **two lists**?
_____

---

1 The correct number **sentence** for: *UNIT 17 Q1 / 18 Q1 / 19 Q1*

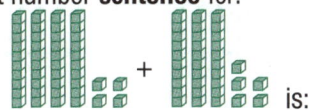

[+] is:
A 45 + 35 = 80   B 70 + 8 = 78
C 40 + 30 = 70   D 44 + 35 = 79

2 The **answer** to 41 + 37 is: *17 Q2 / 18 Q2 / 18 Q3 / 19 Q3 / 19 Q4 / 20 Q3*
A 5   B 78
C 87   D 77

3 **True or false**?   6 tens and 5 units   *20 Q1*
+ 3 tens and 1 unit
9 tens and 6 units _____

4 **True or false**?   _____   *17 Q3 / 21 Q1*
Twenty-five plus thirteen equals thirty-nine.

5 **Complete**:   *19 Q2 / 20 Q2 / 21 Q2*

T	U
1	9
+4	0

6 Write and solve the number sentence for: there   *20 Q4*
are 37 pens and 42 pencils. How many writing
items are there **altogether**? _____

7 Look for combinations when **adding**:   *16 Q1 / 16 Q2 / 16 Q3*
2 6
1 7
+ 2 4

8 **Solve**: $ 5 6   *19 Q2 / 20 Q2 / 21 Q3*
+ $ 2 3

9 Find the **missing** number: 4 0   *18 Q4 / 21 Q4*
+ [ ]
9 3

10 Complete the **table**:   *16 Q1 / 16 Q2 / 16 Q3 / 17 Q2 / 17 Q4 / 18 Q2 / 19 Q3 / 20 Q3*

+	14
6	
12	
35	
43	

11 Tony has three piggy banks. He counts the coins in   *16 Q1 / 16 Q2 / 18 Q3 / 20 Q4*
each and finds that he has $7, $9 and $3. What is
the **total** amount of money Tony has? _____

12 Write a vertical equation to   *21 Q4*
find the **missing** numbers of:
3___ + ___6 = 57

Score = ( ) /12   Score = ( ) /12

REVIEW TESTS: Units 22 – 32

1 The best **estimate** to 49 + 22 is: **UNIT 22 Q2**
  A 65   B 70   C 80   D 75

2 The **answer** to 35 + 47 is: **22 Q4 / 23 Q2 / 27 Q4**
  A 85   B 53   C 82   D 80

3 True or false?   **22 Q1 / 23 Q1**
  The number sentence for the pencils and bundles is 44 + 29 = 73. _____

4 True or false?   **25 Q1 / 25 Q2**
  The answer to 27 + 15 is 41

  _____

5 Complete: 7 0 9   **26 Q1 / 26 Q2**
             + 2 5 6

6 Complete the **magic square**:   **25 Q4**

8		11
	9	
	10	

7 Using the **jump strategy**, complete the number line and the spaces.   **22 Q3**
  66 + 16 = 66 + ____ + ____ = ____

  60   70   80   90

8 Write an **equation** and solve it for: **23 Q2 / 23 Q4 / 24 Q1**
  sixty-six plus twenty-nine _____

9 Complete: 3 7 9   **26 Q3**
               4 3 5

10 Complete: 1 7 chickens   **24 Q3 / 25 Q3**
             + 4 5 geese
             _____ birds

11 Solve by **looking for tens**:   1 9   **25 Q2 / 27 Q2**
                    2 3
                    4 1
                  + 1 7

12 Find the **total** number of insects: _____   **25 Q3 / 26 Q4**

Score = __/12__

---

1 Which number is 296 **closest** to?   **UNIT 28 Q1**
  A 350   B 250   C 200   D 300

2 38 – 26 =   **31 Q3 / 32 Q3**
  A 22   B 12   C 64   D 15

3 True or false?   **28 Q2 / 28 Q4**
  1479 rounded to the nearest hundred is 1500.

  _____

4 True or false?   **29 Q1**
  The difference between 40 and 12 is 8.

  _____

5 Complete: **31 Q4 / 32 Q1**

T	U
5	8
– 2	7

6 Write a **number sentence** and solve it for: **29 Q3**

  _____

7 Sean makes 87 runs in a game of cricket. Belinda made 36 runs. What was the **difference** in their scores? _____   **29 Q4 / 32 Q4**

8 Round five hundred and twelve to the **nearest ten**. _____   **28 Q3**

9 Draw a **number line** to show the answer to: **29 Q2 / 31 Q2**
  19 – 12 = _____

10 Complete: 9 – 2 = ____   **30 Q1 / 30 Q4**
            ____ – 20 = 70
            900 – ____ = 700

11 Complete: **30 Q2 / 30 Q4 / 31 Q1**
  24 + 8 = _____   8 + 24 = _____
  32 – _____ = 24   32 – _____ = 8

12 Complete: **31 Q1 / 32 Q3**

–	16	24	39	48	53
13					

Score = __/12__

1	2	3	4	5	6	7	8	9	10
11	12	13	14	15	16	17	18	19	20
21	22	23	24	25	26	27	28	29	30
31	32	33	34	35	36	37	38	39	40
41	42	43	44	45	46	47	48	49	50
51	52	53	54	55	56	57	58	59	60
61	62	63	64	65	66	67	68	69	70
71	72	73	74	75	76	77	78	79	80
81	82	83	84	85	86	87	88	89	90
91	92	93	94	95	96	97	98	99	100

UNIT

1 Use the chart to find the number **8 less than** 31: **37 Q1**
   A 23   B 24   C 22   D 39

2 Use the chart to find the number **6 less than** 73: **37 Q2**
   A 63   B 66   C 67   D 70

3 **True or false?** $50 - 26 = 34$ _____   **33 Q3 / 34 Q3**

4 **True or false?**   The missing numbers are 9, 5 and 5 in the equation.   **34 Q4 / 36 Q2**

$$\begin{array}{r} \square\ 8\ 6 \\ -\ 7\ \square\ \square \\ \hline 2\ 3\ 1 \end{array}$$ _____

5 **Complete:**   **33 Q2 / 34 Q2 / 35 Q2 / 38 Q2**

$$\begin{array}{r} 5\ 2 \\ -\ 3\ 6 \\ \hline \end{array}$$

6 Complete the **pattern:**   **33 Q1 / 34 Q1 / 35 Q1 / 37 Q4**
   $12 - 8 = $ _____
   $22 - $ _____ $ = 14$
   _____ $ - 8 = 24$
   $42 - 8 = $ _____

7 Write an **addition** equation to check the answer.   **35 Q3 / 38 Q1**

$$\begin{array}{r} \$82 \\ -\ \$65 \\ \hline \$17 \end{array}$$

8 Use the equation $\begin{array}{r}42\\+\ 39\\\hline 81\end{array}$ to **complete:** $\begin{array}{r}8\ 1\\-\ \square\ 9\\\hline 4\ \square\end{array}$ **33 Q4**

9 Find the **difference** between 74 and 59. ____   **35 Q4 / 38 Q4**

10 Annie had saved $159 towards a $325 stereo. **How much more** did she need to save? ____   **36 Q3 / 36 Q4**

11 The lady had 72 counters but she needed 100 for the game. By **counting on**, find how many more counters she needed. _____   **37 Q3**

12 **Complete:**   **36 Q1 / 36 Q2**

926	−6		−20		−155	

1 381 rounded off to the **nearest hundred** is: **UNIT 40 Q1**
   A 400   B 300   C 390   D 380

2 **5 rows of** 4 =   **42 Q2**
   A 16   B 10   C 25   D 20

3 **True or false?**   407 rounded off to the nearest ten is 410. _____   **40 Q3 / 40 Q4**

4 **True or false?** $4 \times 3 = 3 + 3 + 3$ _____   **42 Q4**

5 Find the best **estimate** for the equation from those given: 120 or 160 or 200   **39 Q1 / 39 Q2 / 39 Q3**
   $41 + 41 + 41 + 41 = $ _____

6 Complete the **number sentence** for: **42 Q1**
   □ □ □ □
   □ □ □ □ ____ rows of ____ = _____

7 **Estimate** the answer to: **39 Q4**
   $150 - 8 - 8 - 8 - 8 - 8 - 8 = $ _____

8 Circle the number which is 1091 rounded to the **nearest hundred.** 1000 or 1100 or 1010 or 1110   **40 Q2**

9 Rose bought 61 apples and 48 bananas for the school canteen. **Estimate** how many pieces of fruit she had. _____   **41 Q2**

10 There are four teams of softballers playing round robin games. If there are 10 players in each team, how many softball players are there in **total?** _____   **42 Q3**

11 Joe needed 30 counters to play a game. If he started with 102 counters and gave away 68, **estimate** if he had enough counters.   **41 Q3**
   _____

12 Dad was building a planter box in the garden, as in the diagram. He estimated that he needed 30 m of wood. **How short** was dad in his estimate?   **41 Q4**

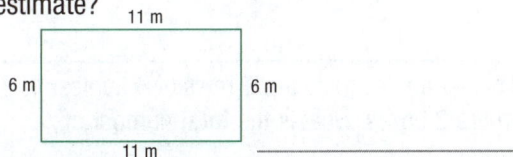

11 m
6 m   6 m
11 m   _____

Score = ___ **/12**   Score = ___ **/12**

REVIEW TESTS: Units 43 – 52

1 The correct **number sentence** for
<small>UNIT 43 Q1 45 Q1</small>

| x x | x x | x x |
| x x | x x | x x |

is: A 4×4 B 3×4 C 1×4 D 3×3

2 A possible **diagram** for 6×3 is:
<small>43 Q4 44 Q3</small>

A   B   C   D

3 **True or false**?
<small>45 Q2</small>
$10 \times 0 = 10$ _____

4 **True or false**?
<small>46 Q3</small>
There are 18 points on 6 triangles. _____

5 **Complete** the spaces: $4 \times$ ____ $= 40 = 5 \times$ ____
<small>46 Q2 47 Q4</small>

6 Use the diagram to complete:
<small>46 Q1</small>
____ **groups of** $10 =$ _____

7 Write the **equation** for the answer 54 from the 6 times table. _____
<small>47 Q3</small>

8 Describe the **pattern** in the answers:
<small>47 Q2</small>
$10 - 1 = 9$
$20 - 2 = 18$
$30 - 3 = 27$
$40 - 4 = 36$
$50 - 5 = 45$ _____

9 Draw an **array** that would help answer the following tables:
<small>43 Q2 43 Q3</small>
$3 \times 2, 5 \times 2, 6 \times 2, 10 \times 2, 9 \times 2, 2 \times 1$

10 Write two **multiplication table equations** that equal 40. _____
<small>45 Q4 47 Q4</small>

11 Complete:
<small>44 Q4 45 Q3</small>

×	5
3	
4	
7	
9	

12 In a box of apples there are 5 rows of 4 apples. If there are 2 boxes, what is the **total** number of apples? _____
<small>44 Q2</small>

Score = ____ /12

---

1 0 **groups of** 8 is:
<small>UNIT 49 Q2 51 Q2</small>
A 80   B 16   C 8   D 0

2
<small>48 Q3 49 Q4 51 Q4 52 Q4</small>
$\begin{array}{r} 4 \\ \times\, 7 \\ \hline \end{array}$

A 26   B 24   C 28   D 32

3 **True or false**?
<small>48 Q2 51 Q2</small>
The product of 7 and 9 is 72. _____

4 **True or false**?
<small>52 Q2</small>
$10 \times 9 = 90$ _____

5
<small>49 Q1</small>

How many legs are there on 5 spiders? _____

6 **Complete** the spaces:
<small>49 Q4 50 Q4</small>
$10 \times$ ____ $= 40 = 8 \times$ ____

7 Draw an **array** to solve: $6 \times 3 =$ ____
<small>48 Q1 50 Q1</small>

8 Complete the space:
<small>48 Q3 50 Q3</small>
two **multiplied by** _____ equals twelve.

9 Complete:
<small>52 Q3</small>

×	2	5	9	7
5				

10 If there are approximately 4 weeks in a month, how many **weeks** would there be in 3 months?
<small>50 Q1</small>
_____

11 What is the **total** number of hot cross buns, if there are 5 packets with 9 buns in each packet?
<small>48 Q2 50 Q2</small>
_____

12 Fill in the **missing** numbers:
<small>52 Q3</small>

Score = ____ /12

1 21 **shared** among 7 is: **UNIT 55 Q2**
A 4   B 3   C 7   D 6

2 $20 \div 2 =$ **56 Q4**
A 5   B 20   C 2   D 10

3 **True or false?**   **53 Q4**
66 is a squared number. _____

4 **True or false?**   **55 Q1**
6 shared by 2 is 3.

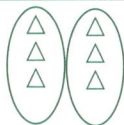

_____

5 Draw a square on the side.   **53 Q2**
Area = _____ squares

6 List the first 10 **multiples** of 4:   **54 Q3**

4									

7 Draw a **picture** for   **53 Q1**
$4^2 =$ _____ $\times$ _____ $=$ _____   **53 Q3**

8 Circle the **multiples** of 5.   **54 Q1**
   54 Q2

1	2	3	4	5	6	7	8	9	10
11	12	13	14	15	16	17	18	19	20

9 Draw a picture to show 20 lollipops **shared** among 3 children.   **55 Q3**
   55 Q4

10 Does 14 shared among 2 = 2 **groups of** 7?   **56 Q1**

11 Write an equation and solve it for: **56 Q2**
30 **divided** by 10.   **56 Q3**

_____

12 Shade the **multiples** of 2.   **54 Q4**

2   31   50   100   6   10
19   15   12   4   7   55

---

1 **How many** 6s are there in 42?   **UNIT 58 Q4**
A 7   B 6   C 8   D 9

2 **How many times** can I take three coins from 30   **57 Q3**
coins?
A 10   B 3   C 9   D 6

3 **True or false?**   **57 Q1**
6 groups of 2 could be made from

_____

4 **True or false?**   **60 Q3**
John could buy 6 stamps for 60c if he bought 10c stamps. _____

5 Use the **number line** to find $15 \div 5 =$ ____   **59 Q2**
   59 Q3
   59 Q4

0   10   20

6 Use the table $9 \times 4 = 36$ to **answer:**   **60 Q1**

9⌐36

7 There are 72 stickers in a box. If a line of 9 students took the same number of stickers, **how many** stickers did each student receive?   **57 Q2**

_____

8 Draw an **array** to model and solve the equation: **58 Q2**
$36 \div 4$

9 Draw a **number line** to solve: $27 \div 3$ **59 Q1**
   59 Q2
   59 Q3
   59 Q4

10 Make 3 **shares:**   **57 Q1**
   58 Q1
_____

11 **Divide** by 4.   **58 Q3**
   60 Q4

Divide by 4					
40	32	8	16	24	4

12 Amy bought 8 stamps and paid $0.80. **How much** did she pay for each stamp?   **60 Q2**
   60 Q3

_____

Score = _____ **/12**   Score = _____ **/12**

1 $42 \div 6 =$ **UNIT 63 Q2**
A 5   B 8   C 6   D 7

2 $26 \div 4 =$ **61 Q4 / 62 Q4 / 63 Q4**
A 6   B 6 r 2   C 4 r 2   D 4

3 True or false?   **63 Q1**
$$10\overline{)100} \quad \frac{10}{}$$ _____

4 True or false?   **62 Q3**
There are 3 groups of 2 and 1 remainder in 5 hats. _____

5 Use the first number sentence to **fill in** the other two.   **64 Q2**
$12 \times 4 = 48$
$48 \div 4 = $ _____
$48 \div 12 = $ _____

6 How many **groups of** 3 are there?   **61 Q2 / 61 Q3**
_____

7 Divide the stars into **groups of** 4. ★★★★★ ★★★★★ ★★★★★   **61 Q1 / 62 Q1**

8 Draw a picture to show 19 frogs **placed in** 5 buckets.   **62 Q3**

9 Complete the **spaces**:   **64 Q2 / 64 Q3**
$72 \div 9 = $ _____ $72 \div $ _____ $ = 9$
$9 \times $ _____ $ = 72$ $8 \times $ _____ $ = 72$

10 Anton had 15 golf balls. If he divided them into **groups of** 4, how many golf balls did he and his friends receive? _____   **62 Q2 / 62 Q3 / 63 Q1**

11 Agit had 49 sweets. If he **divided** them evenly between 7 party bags, how many sweets are in each bag? _____   **64 Q1**

12 This is the **top view** of a box of chocolates. Write two **division** facts and two **multiplication** facts about the chocolates.   **64 Q4**

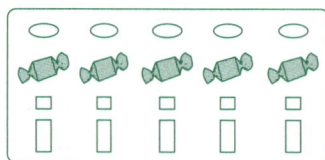

_____
_____

1 The **missing** number from the space in
$35 - $ _____ $ = 12$ is: **UNIT 69 Q1**
A 13   B 23   C 12   D 22

2 The **next** number in the pattern
30, 38, 46, 54, _____ is: **70 Q1 / 71 Q1**
A 64   B 58   C 60   D 62

3 True or false?   **69 Q4**
The missing symbol to make 19 _____ $6 = 12$ true is $-$ _____

4 True or false?   **70 Q3**
The tenth number of the pattern 100, 99, 98, 97, … is 90. _____

5 Write the **rule** for: 11, 22, 33, 44,   **71 Q3**
_____

6 Write a **division** fact from: $3 \times 9 = 27$ _____   **66 Q3**

7 Draw a **number line** to solve: $32 + 29 =$ **65 Q1**

8 Starting at 20, **add** 9, five times.   **71 Q2**
_____

9 Complete the **table**:   **70 Q4**

−	101	91	81	71	61
7					

10 Write an equation to describe the **number line**:   **65 Q3**

(number line 0 5 10 15 20)

_____

11 Complete the **spaces**:   **66 Q4 / 67 Q3 / 69 Q2 / 69 Q3**
$6 \times 9 = $ _____ $9 \times $ _____ $ = 54$
_____ $\div 6 = 9$ _____ $\div 9 = 6$
$9 + 9 + 9 + $ _____ $+$ _____ $= 54$

12 Mark off the **numbers** to find the winning card, A, B or C: **68 Q1 / 68 Q2 / 68 Q3 / 68 Q4**

11	26	60
10	24	100
28	3	110

2	9	0
10	16	13
5	6	1

12	35	17
46	8	7
4	36	49

A	B	C	
$15 - 4$	$49 \div 7$	$72 \div 8$	8×2
$100 + 10$	4×6	$6 + 6$	$21 + 15$
$15 + 2$	$9 - 8$	$36 - 8$	$20 - 12$
$20 \div 10$	$25 \div 5$	$20 \div 2$	5×12
8×0	2×2	$9 + 37$	$20 + 15$
$17 + 9$	$100 - 87$	$60 - 11$	$8 - 5$

Score = _____ /12

Score = _____ /12

1 The **answer** to 1469 + 1281 is: **UNIT 73 Q1**
A 2750　　　　　　B 2777
C 2687　　　　　　D 1427

2 The answer to 9 **multiplied** by 67 is: **74 Q3**
A 585　　　B 536　　　C 603　　　D 469

3 **True or false?** **72 Q3**
The calculator sentence you could use to
change 597 to 97 is: 597 – 500 _____

4 **True or false?** **74 Q2**
The answer to 115 ÷ 5 is 575. _____

5 Write the **calculator sentence** you would use to **72 Q4**
change 325 to 6325.
_____

6 Find the answer to 569 **plus** 325. **73 Q3**
_____

7 Dave had 3 bags of sweets. There were 365 **73 Q4**
in one bag, 272 in the second bag and 299 in the
third. How many sweets did Dave have
altogether?
_____

8 Lin wrote the calculator sentence 196 + 100 for **72 Q4**
changing 196 to 1196. What was her
mistake? _____

9 Find the **difference** between nine hundred and **73 Q2**
eight and three hundred and eighty. **73 Q3**
_____

10 Find the **product** of 21 and 16. **74 Q1**
_____

11 Albert had to find how many **groups of** 7 were in **74 Q4**
238 using his calculator. Explain what he did.
_____

12 Sam calculated the equation 21 × 39 on her **73 Q4**
calculator and got the answer 819. How could **74 Q4**
she check her answer using **estimation**?
_____

1 $\frac{3}{4}$ written in **words** is: **UNIT 75 Q3**

A one third　　　　B two thirds
C three quarters　　D four thirds

2 The shaded **part** of the shape is: **76 Q3 77 Q1**

A $\frac{8}{3}$　　　B $\frac{3}{8}$　　　C $\frac{4}{8}$　　　D $\frac{1}{2}$

3 **True or false?** **75 Q1**

$\frac{6}{10}$ is 6 out of 10 equal parts. _____

4 **True or false?** **76 Q4**

$\frac{2}{6}$ of the group has been shaded. _____

5 Write five eighths in **digits**. ___ **75 Q2**

6 Complete the label: **76 Q1**
___ **out of** ___

7 Complete the **picture** to show $\frac{1}{6}$: **75 Q4**

8 Colour one **half** of the group. **77 Q3**

9 What **fraction** of this shape is not coloured? ___ **76 Q3 77 Q1**

10 What **fraction** of this shape is coloured? **76 Q1 76 Q2**
___ ninths

11 Shade part of the group to **match** seven tenths. **77 Q3 77 Q4**

12 Is this shape **cut** into halves or quarters? **75 Q4**
_____

Score = /12

Score = /12

1 The **fraction** shaded of the rectangle is: **UNIT 78 Q1**

A $\frac{3}{8}$ B $\frac{1}{2}$ C $\frac{5}{8}$ D $\frac{1}{4}$

2 Another **name** for the shaded part other than $\frac{4}{4}$ is: **78 Q3**

A 1   B 2   C $\frac{2}{4}$ D $\frac{1}{4}$

3 True or false? $\frac{1}{2} = \frac{3}{5}$ _____ **81 Q4**

4 True or false? $\frac{3}{5}$ is larger than $\frac{4}{5}$ _____ **81 Q2**

5 Colour part of the group to show $\frac{3}{5}$. **78 Q4**

6 Colour the **larger** fraction $\frac{5}{8}$ or $\frac{4}{8}$ for the group: **79 Q2**

7 Draw a **picture** to show $\frac{1}{4}$ of 12 slices of bread. **80 Q2**

8 Only $\frac{1}{2}$ of 10 cakes are cooked. **How many** cakes still need to be cooked? _____ **80 Q4**

9 Order the fractions from **smallest to largest**. $\frac{4}{10}, \frac{8}{10}, \frac{7}{10}, \frac{2}{10}, \frac{5}{10}, \frac{1}{10}$ **79 Q3**

_____

10 Circle the **smaller** fraction: three fifths or one fifth **79 Q4**

11 Demi had a collection of 20 teddy bears. If $\frac{1}{4}$ of her bears are white, **how many** of the bears are not white? _____ **80 Q4**

12 **78 Q1**

a What **fraction** of the grid is shaded? _____
b What **fraction** of the grid has dots? _____

1 Three tenths written as a **decimal** is: **UNIT 84 Q4 / 85 Q1**

A 0.2   B 0.1   C 0.6   D 0.3

2 0.7 written as a **fraction** is: **85 Q4**

A $\frac{7}{10}$ B $\frac{3}{10}$ C $\frac{5}{10}$ D $\frac{4}{10}$

3 **True or false?** Is the shaded part equal to 42 out of 100. _____ **82 Q1 / 82 Q3 / 83 Q1**

4 **True or false?** $\frac{4}{10}$ written as a decimal is 0.4 _____ **85 Q2**

5 What **fraction** of the hundredths square has been coloured? _____ **82 Q2 / 83 Q1**

6 Record the shaded fraction as a **decimal**. _____ **84 Q2 / 84 Q3**

7 Circle the **smaller** fraction: $\frac{92}{100}$ or $\frac{9}{100}$ **83 Q3**

8 Complete the **table**: **83 Q4**

0.1		0.3				0.7	0.8

9 How many **hundredths** are there in: _____ **82 Q1**

10 Circle the **larger** decimal: 0.6 or 0.8 **83 Q3**

11 **Complete:** one **tenth**, three tenths, _____ , seven tenths **83 Q4**

12 **Match** the decimals with the correct fraction: **85 Q3**

one tenth $2\frac{6}{10}$

one and three tenths $\frac{5}{10}$

five tenths $\frac{1}{10}$

two and six tenths $1\frac{3}{10}$

Score = ____ /12

Score = ____ /12

Excel Start Up Maths Year 3

☞ Answers on page 146

❶ The **decimal** form of $\frac{67}{100}$ is: **UNIT 88 Q1 / 89 Q3**

A 0.67   B 0.6   C 0.7   D 0.76

❷ The **fraction** form of 8 tenths is: **89 Q1**

A $\frac{8}{100}$ B $\frac{9}{10}$ C $\frac{8}{10}$ D $\frac{10}{8}$

❸ **True or false**? _____ | 0 | tenths | 5 | hundredths | **87 Q3**
0.05 is on the number expander.

❹ **True or false**? 5.8 rounded to the nearest whole   **90 Q3**
number is 5. _____

❺ Start at 0.1 and count forwards 0.6, now   **86 Q1 / 86 Q2 / 86 Q3 / 86 Q4**
backwards 0.2. What is the **final** number?

❻ What **decimal** is shown on the   **87 Q1**
hundredths square?

_____

❼ Write the **fraction** for: 0.91 ____   **89 Q1 / 89 Q2 / 89 Q2**

❽ Arrange in order from   **89 Q4**
largest to smallest: 0.1, 0.8, 0.7

_____

❾ Use the correct sign, **< or >**, to make the   **90 Q2 / 90 Q4**
statement true: 5 tenths ____ 3 tenths

❿ Draw a **number line** to show: starting at 0.9,   **86 Q1 / 86 Q2 / 86 Q3 / 86 Q4**
go backwards 0.7 and then go forwards 0.3

⓫ Write $\frac{31}{100}$ in **words**. _____   **88 Q3 / 89 Q1 / 89 Q2**

⓬ Complete the **table**:   **88 Q1 / 88 Q2 / 88 Q3 / 89 Q1 / 89 Q2**

In words	Decimal	Fraction
five tenths		
	0.9	
		$\frac{61}{100}$
	0.34	
three hundredths		

Score = ⬭ **/12**

---

❶ 25% written in **words** is: **UNIT 94 Q3**
A twenty percent   B five percent
C twenty-five percent   D fifty percent

❷ 0.3 + 0.4 =   **91 Q1**
A 4.3   B 0.7   C 3.4   D 0.9

❸ **True or false**?   **92 Q3**
0.9 − 0.2 = 0.7 _____

❹ **True or false**?   **94 Q4**
30% > 40% _____

❺ Find: **91 Q2 / 91 Q3 / 93 Q1 / 93 Q3**
$$\begin{array}{r} 5.31 \\ +\ 2.86 \\ \hline \end{array}$$

❻ Write ninety percent in **short form**.   **94 Q2**

_____

❼ Find the **sum** of one point six two and three point   **91 Q4**
five nine.

_____

❽ Bert had a piece of string 1.65 m in length and   **93 Q4**
Sophie had a piece 1.97 m in length. What was
the **difference** in length between the two pieces
of string?

_____

❾ Find: **92 Q2 / 92 Q3 / 93 Q2**

3.85 − 2.68 _____

❿ Find the **total cost** of: **91 Q4 / 93 Q4**

+ _____

$0.92 $1.75

⓫ Circle the **largest** percentage: **94 Q4**

20% or sixty percent or $\frac{40}{100}$

⓬ Find: **91 Q3 / 92 Q3 / 93 Q3**

4.69 + 3.50 = _____

Score = ⬭ **/12**

REVIEW TESTS: Units 95 – 104

1 **How many** 50c coins are needed to make $1? **UNIT 95 Q1**
A 20   B 1   C 10   D 2

2 $3.00 × 2 = **98 Q1**
A $6.50   B $6.00
C $7.00   D $5.00

3 **True or false**? **99 Q3**
73c rounded to the nearest 10c is 70c.
_____

4 **True or false**? **98 Q4**
I could buy 3 basketball cards for $10 if each
card cost $3.
_____

5 Write down the **smallest number** of coins **95 Q3**
needed for change from $10.00 if $7.35 was
spent. _____

6 Write down the **smallest number** of notes or **95 Q2**
coins needed to buy a pair of jeans costing **95 Q4**
$87.50 _____ **96 Q2**

7 Find the **total** of $2.50 and $3.60 _____ **97 Q1**

8 Find the **change** from [note] after spending **97 Q4**
[coins $5, $2, $1, 20c, 10c, 5c]
_____

9 Round each amount to the **nearest dollar** and **99 Q4**
then add: $2.92, $1.85 and $3.14.
_____

10 **Estimate** 2 × $4.95 by first rounding to the **100 Q1**
nearest dollar.
_____

11 Estimate the **change** from $70.00 after buying **100 Q3**
2 DVDs at a cost of $24.95 each.
_____

12 Find the **change** from $20.00 after spending **97 Q1**
$4.75, $6.25 and $1.98. Round your answer **97 Q3**
to the **nearest 10c**. **97 Q4**
_____ **99 Q3**

Score = [ ] **/12**

1 The **name** of [rhombus shape] is: **UNIT 102 Q1 103 Q4 104 Q1**
A rectangle   B square
C trapezium   D rhombus

2 Which of the following shapes does not have a **101 Q3**
line of symmetry?
A ?   B [arc shape]
C [triangle]   D [square]

3 **True or false**? **103 Q2**
[parallelogram] has 4 sides. _____

4 **True or false**? **103 Q1**
[square] [rectangle] [circle]
The circle does not belong. _____

5 Does this shape have **four **104 Q4**
equal angles**? [rectangle]
_____

6 Draw two **lines of symmetry** on: [octagon] **101 Q2**

7 Circle the following letters which are **101 Q3**
symmetrical: A B C D E F G

8 Draw a **shape** that has 4 sides, 2 sets of sides **102 Q2**
of equal length and 2 sets of equal angles. **104 Q4**

9 Colour in the **pentagon**: **102 Q1**
[square] [circle] [triangle] [rectangle] [pentagon arrow] **104 Q1**

10 Give the name of the **shapes** needed to make **102 Q4**
the picture: [pencil shape]
_____

11 How many **lines of symmetry** does this shape **101 Q1**
have? [diamond] **101 Q2**
_____

12 Use three lines to make **102 Q4**
this shape into one **square**
and three **triangles**. [triangle]

Score = [ ] **/12**

REVIEW TESTS: Units 105 – 113

1 The number of **sides** on a parallelogram is: **UNIT 106 Q2**
A 3   B 4   C 5   D 6

2 The **name** of ⬡ is: **106 Q1 106 Q3 107 Q1**
A trapezium   B parallelogram
C pentagon   D rhombus

3 **True or false?**   **108 Q1 108 Q2 108 Q3**
is a **regular** shape. _____

4 **True or false?**   **107 Q2**
is a **rigid** shape. _____

5 Draw a regular **pentagon**.   **105 Q3**

6 Draw in the Geostrips to create **supports** on: **107 Q4**

7 Cross out the shape that is **regular**.   **108 Q2 108 Q3**

8 How many **sides** on a quadrilateral? ____   **105 Q1**

9 Draw a shape that has **five sides** of different lengths.   **108 Q4**

10 What is the total number of **angles** in the following three shapes?   **106 Q4**

11 What is the **difference** between a regular and irregular shape?   **108 Q1**
_____

12 **Complete** the table: **105 Q1 105 Q2 105 Q3 106 Q2 108 Q2 108 Q3**

Shape	Picture	Number of sides	Number of angles
triangle			
quadrilateral			
pentagon			
hexagon			
octagon			

1 Which of the following are **parallel** lines?   **UNIT 112 Q2**
A   B   C   D

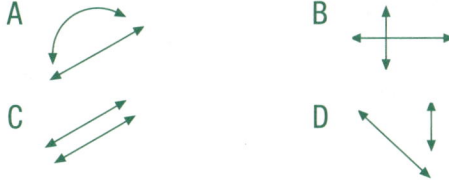

2 How many **angles** can be seen on the star?   **110 Q1**
A 5   B 10   C 4   D 9

3 **True or false?**   **111 Q1**
is smaller than a right angle. _____

4 **True or false?**   **110 Q3**
is larger than _____

5 Label on the shape any **perpendicular** lines: **113 Q3**

6 Which of A, B or C is a **right angle**?   **111 Q3**
A   B   C   ____

7 Draw a shape that has **parallel** lines.   **112 Q4**

8 What **angle** is shown on the clock face?   **109 Q4**
_____

9 Is the angle indicated in the picture larger or smaller than a **right angle**?   **109 Q2**
____

10 Cross out the shape that has no **angles**.   **110 Q1 111 Q4**

11 Which angle is **smaller**, A or B?   **110 Q4**
A   B   ____

12 Cross out any triangles that are not **right angled**.   **111 Q3**

Score = ____ /12   Score = ____ /12

REVIEW TESTS: Units 114 – 125

1 The name of the shaded **face** is: — **UNIT 114 Q2**
A square B rectangle
C triangle D rhombus

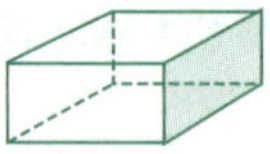

2 How many **corners** does 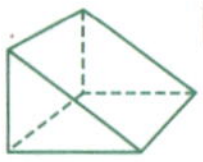 ___ have? — **116 Q2**
A 5 B 4
C 6 D 8

3 **True or false?** ___ is a pyramid. — **118 Q1**

4 **True or false?** ___ is a rectangular prism. ___ — **114 Q3**

5 Draw a **cylinder**. — **115 Q3**

6 How many **blocks** are used in this construction? — **119 Q3**
___

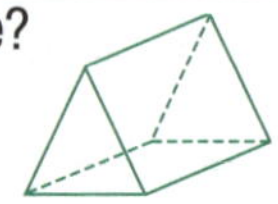

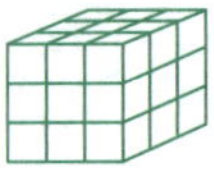

7 Draw a solid that has only one **point**. — **116 Q2**

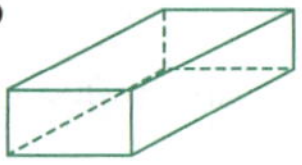

8 Draw the line of cross-section for the cone which will produce a **circle**. — **116 Q3**

9 Draw a set of **faces** for: — **116 Q1 / 117 Q1 / 118 Q3**

10 Circle the objects that have **circular surfaces**. — **114 Q1**

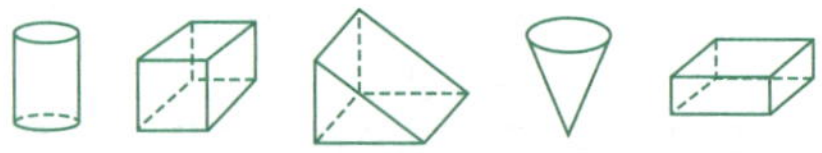

11 Which picture shows a **prism**? — **117 Q2**
bucket chocolate flower vase 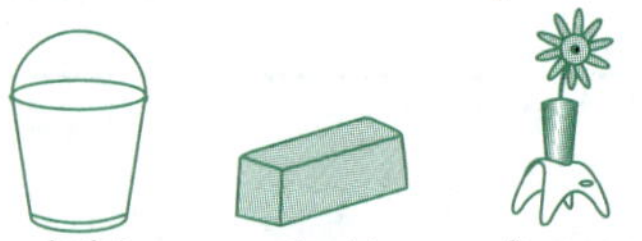

12 **Match** the information with the correct solid name. — **117 Q1 / 118 Q3**

pyramid	6 rectangles
rectangular prism	6 squares
cube	4 triangles, 1 square

Score = ___ /12

---

1 A word to describe the **movement** is: — **UNIT 120 Q1**
A translation B rotation
C slide D reflection

2 What **direction** is the circle from the square? — **123 Q1 / 123 Q2 / 123 Q3**
A east B west
C north D south

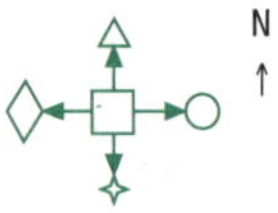

3 **True or false?** The cards are on the bottom shelf on the left. ___ — **121 Q1 / 122 Q1 / 122 Q2 / 122 Q3 / 122 Q4**

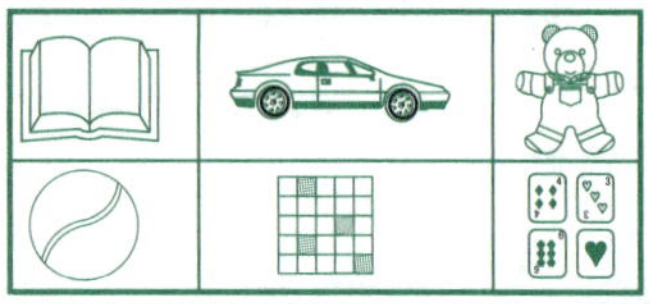

4 **True or false?** Using the picture from question 3, in the middle of the top shelf is the car. ___ — **121 Q1 / 122 Q1 / 122 Q2 / 122 Q3 / 122 Q4**

5 Colour on the grid: **move** the counter 3 spaces to the right and then 2 spaces up. — **124 Q1 / 124 Q2**

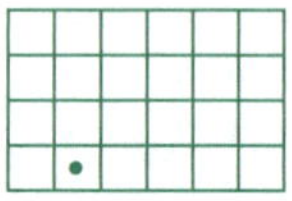

6 If the mouse starts at B, give where it **stops** if it moves 2 up, 3 right and 1 up. ___ — **125 Q1**

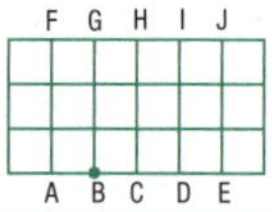

7 Using the grid from question 6, describe a **path** from E to G. ___ — **125 Q2**

8 **Tessellate:** — **120 Q3**

9 **Rotate** the triangle clockwise about the dot. — **120 Q2 / 120 Q4**

10 On the game board, describe how you could **move** from square A to square L. — **121 Q2 / 121 Q3**
___
___

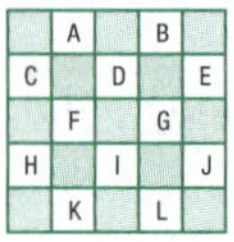

11 Draw a **map** of a room which includes a: — **121 Q4**
* door in the bottom left corner
* TV in the top right corner
* chair in the top left corner
* shelf opposite the TV
* circular rug in the middle of the room.

12 Give the **coordinates** for: — **125 Q3**
a ★ ___ b @ ___
c $ ___
Find what is at:
d D1 ___ e A4 ___
f C2 ___

	A	B	C	D
4	c	+	★	×
3	σ	●	☆	△
2	$	○	□	÷
1	◇	@	■	○

Score = ___ /12

REVIEW TESTS: Units 126 – 133

1 The **time** shown on the clock is:
A 25 to 8   B 12 o'clock
C 7 o'clock   D $\frac{1}{2}$ past 7

UNIT 126 Q1 126 Q3

2 25 **minutes past** 4 can be written as:
A 4:20   B 4:25   C 3:25   D 3:20

130 Q2

3 **True or false**?
Half past 6 is
_____

126 Q4

4 **True or false**?
It takes 35 minutes for the minute hand to move from the 12 to the 7. _____

128 Q1

5 Write the **time** as shown:
_____
_____

127 Q2 127 Q4

6 **Draw** the time 25 past 2 on the clock face.

128 Q4

7 Complete the **spaces**:
`10:56` _____ minutes to _____

129 Q2 129 Q4

8 If the time is quarter past eight, draw on the clock face what the **time** will be in 10 minutes.

128 Q4 130 Q4

9 How many minutes has passed **between** the two clocks?
_____

128 Q1 128 Q2

10 Use lines to join the **same** times together.
3:30   thirty minutes past five
5:30   half past eleven
11:30   three thirty

129 Q1 129 Q2 129 Q3 130 Q2 130 Q3

11 **Complete**:
`5:`   3 past _____

129 Q4 130 Q1 130 Q2 130 Q3

12 If it is 2:59, how many **minutes** before the TV program starts at 4:00? _____

130 Q4

Score = /12

---

1 How many **days** are there in July?
A 30   B 31   C 28   D 29

UNIT 132 Q1

2 What is the **time**?
A quarter to 3   B quarter past 3
C quarter to 4   D quarter past 2

131 Q2

3 **True or false**?
December always ends on a Sunday. _____

132 Q4

4 **True or false**? _____
`12:55` can be written as 5 minutes to 1.

131 Q4

5 If Tom caught the bus at 11:20 at Gol Gol, at what time would he **arrive** in Euston?

133 Q1

Bus timetable

Wentworth	9:00	11:00
Gol Gol	9:20	11:20
Euston	9:55	11:55 _____

6 Using the information from question 5, **how long** does it take to travel between Wentworth and Euston? _____

133 Q1

7 What is the **date** of the first Tuesday of the month?

132 Q4

October

S	M	T	W	T	F	S
30	31					1
2	3	4	5	6	7	8
9	10	11	12	13	14	15
16	17	18	19	20	21	22
23	24	25	26	27	28	29

8 Using the information from question 7, calculate the **number of days**, including the first and last days, from 14 to 24 October. _____

132 Q3

9 Here are the times in a TV guide.
6:00   news
6:30   current affairs
7:00   cartoons
7:25   lotto
7:30   movie
How long do the cartoons go for? _____

133 Q3

10 Using the information from question 9, Sally starts her homework at 7:00 and it takes her 45 minutes. Does she **finish** in time for the movie? _____

133 Q3

11 If today is Tuesday, what **day** of the week was it one week ago? _____

132 Q1 132 Q3

12 Show the **time** on the clock five minutes after half past three.

131 Q3

Score = /12

1 2 m 8 cm written in **cm** is:　　　　　　　**UNIT 136 Q3 138 Q2**
　A 208 cm　　　　　B 280 cm
　C 28 cm　　　　　　D 8 cm

2 45 mm written as **centimetres and millimetres** is:　　**137 Q3**
　A 40 cm 5 mm　　　　B 5 cm 4 mm
　C 450 cm　　　　　　D 4 cm 5 mm

3 **True or false**?　　　　　　　　　　　　**134 Q2**
The crayon is approximately 5 cm in length.

4 **True or false**?　　　　　　　　　　　　**135 Q4 136 Q3**
You would use metres to measure the length of a book. _____

5 Use a **ruler** to draw a line 59 mm long.　**134 Q4**

6 Use the **short form** to write:　　　　　**135 Q3**
3 metres 29 centimetres _____

7 Measure the **length** of the marked side to the nearest mm.　**135 Q1**

8 Use **decimal** form to write one metre and fifteen centimetres.　**138 Q2**
_____

9 What is the **best measure** of length of a car?　**135 Q4 136 Q3 136 Q4**
　A　4 kg　　　B　4 m　　　C　40 cm
　D　10 cm　　　E　20 mm

10 Is the **length** of your hand more or less than a metre? _____　**135 Q4 136 Q3 136 Q4**

11 Circle the **shortest piece** of ribbon.　**134 Q3 138 Q4**
　A　_____
　B　_____
　C　_____

12 The object Alex holds has a **length** of 3 cm. Which of the following could it be?　**136 Q4**
　A　　　　　B　　　　　C

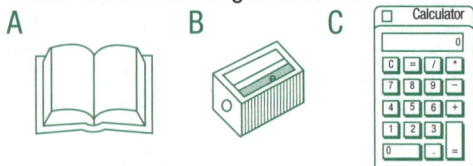

Score = **/12**

---

1 The **perimeter** is:　　　　　　　　**UNIT 140 Q1 140 Q2 140 Q3**
　A 8 cm　　　　　B 4 cm
　C 6 cm　　　　　D 3 cm

2 The **short form** of nineteen square metres is:　**142 Q3**
　A 90 m²　　B 19 cm²　　C 9 m²　　D 19 m²

3 **True or false**?　　　　　　　　　　**139 Q1**
An estimate of the perimeter of the triangle is 10 cm.
_____

4 **True or false**?　　　　　　　　　　**142 Q2**
The area of a piece of A4 paper is smaller than 1 square metre. _____

5 Draw a triangle with a **perimeter** of 9 cm.　**139 Q4**

6 Find the **perimeter** of: if all sides are of equal length. _____　**140 Q1 140 Q2 140 Q3**

7 Find the **area** of:　　　　　　　　　**141 Q1 141 Q2 142 Q1**
_____

8 Circle which would have the **larger** perimeter: a football field or a table?　**139 Q3 141 Q4**

9 Draw a rectangle that has an **area** of 10 square units.　**141 Q1 141 Q2 142 Q1**

10 Estimate the **area** of the triangle:　**141 Q1**
_____

11 How many squares fill this **area**?　**141 Q1 141 Q2 142 Q1**
_____

12 Which coin has the **smallest** perimeter?　**139 Q1 139 Q2 139 Q3 139 Q4 140 Q1 140 Q2 140 Q3**

Score = **/12**

REVIEW TESTS: Units 143 – 150

1 Fifty kilograms written in **short form** is: UNIT 144 Q4 145 Q1
A 15 kg   B 50 kg   C 50 g   D 15 g

2 110 g written in **long form** is: 144 Q2 145 Q1
A   one hundred and ten kilograms
B   eleven kilograms
C   eleven grams
D   one hundred and ten grams

3 **True or false**?   145 Q2
A brick is heavier than 10 grams. _____

4 **True or false**?   143 Q3
A loaf of bread has a mass greater than 1 kg.

_____

5 Complete: ■ 2 kg   143 Q2

The dog **weighs** _____ than 2 kg.

6 What is the **total** mass of the cheese and the   144 Q3 145 Q3
chocolate?

Milk chocolate 250 g   cheese 500 g   biscuits 200 g

_____

7 **Complete** by adding a unit of mass: 143 Q4

Rice

2 ____

8 Circle the items **heavier** than 10 kg: 143 Q1
car   skateboard   bus   rollerblades

9 What is the **mass** of the brick?   144 Q1

kg

_____

10 **How many** tins of spaghetti can be packed into   144 Q4
a bag that holds 2 kg?

Spaghetti 500 g

_____

11 Circle the **best** answer.   143 Q1 143 Q2 145 Q2
An average adult's mass is:
12 kg or 75 kg or 200 kg?

12 If one bottle has the same mass as 20 blocks,   144 Q3 145 Q3
then **two bottles** will have the same mass as
_____ blocks.

1 Which of the following items could hold **more**   UNIT 147 Q3
than 1 litre?
A a glass   B a pool
C a teaspoon   D a teacup

2 17 cubic centimetres written in **short form is**:   149 Q3 150 Q3
A 17 cm^2 B 17 cm   C 17 cm^3 D 17^3 cm

3 **True or false**?   146 Q4
There is 100 L of milk in the average fridge. ____

4 **True or false**?   149 Q1 149 Q2 149 Q4 150 Q1
_____ has a volume of 16 cm^3.

5 Which container, A or B,   147 Q2 147 Q4
has the **greater** capacity?
A 3 L   B 5 L

____

6 If a container has 400 mL of water, **how much**   148 Q3
water needs to be added to make 1 L? _____

7 Of the following, which container holds the **most**?   146 Q2

Container	No. cups to fill
A	🍵 🍵 🍵 🍵
B	🍵 🍵 🍵
C	🍵 🍵 🍵 🍵 🍵

____

8 Order the volume of the following containers from   147 Q2 147 Q4 148 Q3
least to most:

6 L   3 L   8 L   2 L

_____

9 Draw a **model** which has a length of 4, a width   149 Q1 149 Q2 149 Q4 150 Q1 150 Q4
of 2 and a height of 3 centimetres.

10 What is the **total capacity** of these containers?   147 Q2 147 Q4 148 Q3

4 L   4 L   2 L   2 L   2 L

_____

11 Circle the item that is **not** measured in **litres**.   146 Q4 147 Q3 148 Q4

Coffee   Milk   Orange juice   Soft drink

12 Each cup holds $\frac{1}{2}$ litre. Colour the number of   146 Q2 146 Q3
cups that will make 4 litres.

Score = ____ /12   Score = ____ /12

❶ Which of the following is not an **arrangement** of: △○□   `UNIT 151 Q1`

A ○△□   B □△○   C △△□   D △□○

❷ What is the **chance** of rolling a 2 on a six-sided die?   `152 Q3`

A $\frac{1}{2}$ B $\frac{1}{6}$ C 3   D 1

❸ **True or false**?   `153 Q2`
1 is the most likely number to be spun.

_____

❹ **True or false**?   `152 Q1`
It is almost certain I will eat today. _____

❺ Write an example of something that is **impossible**. _____   `152 Q2`

❻ **Colour** the spinner as follows: `153 Q3`
* green has 2 chances of being spun
* red has half of all the chances of being spun
* orange and blue have equal chances of being spun.

❼ Gina has 3 red cards, 4 blue cards and 1 yellow card. Which colour is the colour **least likely** to be selected? _____   `151 Q2` `151 Q3` `152 Q4`

❽ List all of the different **arrangements** of tossing two coins. _____   `152 Q3`

❾ There were: 4 hot lunches on the school menu.   `151 Q4`
3 cold lunches
4 drinks

If I had a hot pie and I wanted a different hot lunch, **how many** could I choose from? ____

❿ Joe had two 5 cent coins and three 10 cent coins in his pocket. If he selects a coin from his pocket, which coin is he **most likely** to select?   `151 Q2` `151 Q3` `151 Q4`

_____

⓫ **How many** different **arrangements** of ★ ◇ ○ $ are there in a row? _____   `151 Q1`

⓬ If I rolled 2 dice, write down the **different totals** (e.g. 1 + 1 = 2) that I could get.   `152 Q3`

_____

❶ What **number** of toy cars were sold on Wednesday?   `UNIT 154 Q2`

Mon.	✓✓✓
Tues.	✓✓✓
Wed.	✓✓✓

A 8   B 3   C 5   D 4

❷ The **tally** of ◇ is: `155 Q2` `155 Q4`
A 10   B 9   C 8   D 7

☆	ЖΙ ΙΙΙ
○	ЖΙ ЖΙ
◇	ЖΙ ΙΙΙΙ

❸ **True or false**? The total number of ○ and ☆ in question 2 is 18. _____   `156 Q4`

❹ **True or false**? _____   `158 Q3` `158 Q4`
The number of people who have a mobile is 8.

	Have a car	Don't have a car
Have a mobile	4	8
Don't have a mobile	3	2

❺ Pencils were collected and colours were noted: `155 Q3` `157 Q3`
Y G B R O Y G R B P
R G B Y O P G Y Y P
R O G G Y P P P Y R
Create a **tally sheet** of the numbers of different colours.

❻ Using the information about pencils in question 5, create a **column graph**.   `157 Q3`

❼ Information about students' pets was collected. How many pets were there in **total**? _____   `157 Q1`

No. of pets (graph: dog, cat, bird, sheep, fish) — Type of pet

❽ From the graph in question 7, what was the **most** popular pet? _____   `154 Q1` `154 Q3`

❾ From the tally of balls, create a **picture graph**.   `154 Q4`

tennis	ЖΙ ΙΙΙΙ
soccer	ΙΙΙΙ
football	ЖΙ ΙΙΙ
golf	ЖΙ ЖΙ ΙΙΙ
basketball	ЖΙ ЖΙ

❿ Create a **two-way table** from the information: `158 Q1` `158 Q2` `158 Q3` `158 Q4`
* 8 like ants; * 4 like spiders
* 5 like ants but not spiders
* 6 like neither ants nor spiders

⓫ In question 10, how many like ants and spiders? _____   `157 Q2` `157 Q3`

⓬ In question 1, what is the total number of cars sold in the 3 days? _____   `157 Q1` `157 Q2`

Score = ____ **/12**   Score = ____ **/12**

REVIEW TESTS: Units 159 – 166

1 5 **groups of** 0 is: **UNIT 161 Q1**
A 5   B 0   C 10   D 1

2 There were 6 cows in each of 4 paddocks. **160 Q3**
How many cows were there **altogether**?
A 44   B 30   C 28   D 24

3 **True or false**?   9
$\times$ 8
7 2   _____   **162 Q2**

4 **True or false**?   **160 Q3**
There were 50 chocolates to be divided
evenly among 10 people. Each person
received 6 chocolates. _____

5 Draw an **array** to   **161 Q4**
illustrate 5×6:

6 Complete the **boxes**:   1 3 5   **160 Q1**
$+$ ☐ 4 ☐
5 ☐ 2

7 There was the following money in mum's purse: **160 Q4**

How much was there **altogether**?

8 **Complete**: $\times$ | 9   **162 Q4**
6 |
5 |
7 |
10 |
9 |

9 The farmer finished baling hay. He had 9 rows **159 Q3**
of 10 bales and in the last row he had 14 bales.
How many bales of hay did he have **altogether**?
_____

10 Chris invited 10 people to his BBQ. He bought **159 Q3**
2 litres of drink and 3 pieces of food for each of **160 Q3**
his guests. **How much** drink did he buy?
_____

11 Share 16 straws among 3 children. How many **159 Q4**
straws are **left over**? _____   **160 Q3**

12 Complete the **spaces**:   **162 Q3**
nine $\times$ _____ = thirty-six = six $\times$ _____

1 $46 - 23 =$ **UNIT 164 Q1**
A 13   B 69   C 23   D 59

2 $81 \div 9 =$ **166 Q1**
A 8   B 9   C 10   D 7

3 **True or false**?   **165 Q3**
$5 \times 3 = 3 + 3 + 3 + 3$ _____

4 **True or false**?   **163 Q1**
$46 + 39 = 85$ _____

5 How many **groups of** 5 pens in 42? _____   **166 Q4**

6 **Complete**:   **163 Q2**
25
19
$+$ 32

7 Find the **difference** between 71 and 35.   **164 Q2**
164 Q4
_____

8 **Complete**: $10 \times 5 + 3 \times 2 =$ _____   **163 Q1**
163 Q2
163 Q3
163 Q4
165 Q1
165 Q2
165 Q3
165 Q4

9 **Complete**:   **166 Q3**
6)‾5‾4‾

10 Tammy had 52 buttons in a container and she **163 Q1**
added another 16. She then used 7. **How many** **163 Q2**
buttons were there now in the container?   **163 Q3**
163 Q4
164 Q1
_____   **164 Q2**
164 Q3
164 Q4

11 **Complete**:   **164 Q1**
164 Q3
164 Q4

	14	17	22	36
-6				

12 Find the **total** number of cards if there are **163 Q1**
3 groups of 9 cards plus another 6.   **165 Q2**
_____

Score = ☐ /12

Score = ☐ /12

General revision

1 3 tenths written as a **decimal is:**
UNIT 168 Q1

A $\frac{3}{10}$ B 0.3 C $\frac{30}{1000}$ D 0.03

2 63c rounded to the **nearest 10c** is:
169 Q3
A 60c B 65c C 70c D 55c

3 **True or false?**
167 Q1

$\frac{4}{5}$ is 5 parts out of 4 equal parts. _____

4 **True or false?**
169 Q4
An estimate of 5 × $3.95 is $20.00 _____

5 Show a **quarter past** 3 on the clock face.
170 Q2

6 Order the fractions from **smallest to largest**.
167 Q4

$\frac{3}{10}$ $\frac{8}{10}$ $\frac{4}{10}$ $\frac{9}{10}$ $\frac{10}{10}$

_____

7 **Add:**
168 Q3

$$\begin{array}{r} 1.59 \\ + 3.14 \\ \hline \end{array}$$

8 If I spend $3.07, $2.23 and $5.00, how much **change** would I receive from $20.00?
169 Q1
169 Q2

_____

9 Write **quarter to** six as a digital time.
170 Q1

_____

10 **Colour** $\frac{1}{4}$ of the group.
167 Q3

11 What is the **difference** between 3.27 and 5.62?
168 Q4

_____

12 Draw on the clock face the time **15 minutes after**
170 Q2
170 Q4
6:50 .

Score = ____ /12

1 The **largest** possible number that can be written with the digits 5, 3, 9, 8 is:
UNIT 14 Q2
A 8593 B 9583 C 9853 D 8953

2 The **total** number of 25 apples and 69 apples is:
20 Q4
A 95 apples B 94 apples
C 84 apples D 44 apples

3 **True or false?**
40 Q1
1286 rounded to the nearest hundred is 1300.
40 Q2

_____

4 **True or false?**
53 Q1
99 is a square number. _____
53 Q2
53 Q3
53 Q4

5 Complete the **boxes:**
36 Q2

H	T	U
☐	9	3
− 2	4	☐
5	☐	7

6 50 ÷ 6 = _____
63 Q4

7 Write a fraction in **words** to describe:
76 Q4

_____

8 Circle the **largest** number:
83 Q3

$\frac{5}{100}$, $\frac{50}{100}$, $\frac{15}{100}$

9 Find:
92 Q3

26.43 **subtract** 12.62 _____

10 Draw the **lines of symmetry** on:
101 Q2

11 Is △ a **trapezium?**
106 Q1
106 Q2
106 Q3

_____

12 Sketch a **pyramid** which has a square base.
118 Q1
118 Q2
118 Q3
118 Q4

Score = ____ /12

Excel Start Up Maths Year 3
☞ Answers on page 148

Unit 1 Page 13

1 a 142 b 469 c 821 d 205 e 326 f 767 **2** a 297 b 426 c 691 d 801 e 49 f 963 **3** a two hundred and twenty-six
b four hundred and sixteen c three hundred and twenty-five d fifty-six e nine hundred and eighty-nine f one hundred and two
4 a 162 b 821 c 399 d 86 e 513 f 902 **5** 415 **6** 983 **7** six hundred and twenty-one **8** 316 **9** two hundred and fifty

Unit 2 Page 13

1 a 123 b 406 c 693 d 552 e 313 f 921 **2** a 5 units b 5 hundreds c 5 tens d 5 units e 5 tens f 5 hundreds **3** a 306
b 914 c 272 d 753 e 690 f 111 **4** a 207 b 400 c 430 d 690 e 902 f 861 **5** 780 **6** 5 tens **7** 251 **8** 310 **9** 8 units

Unit 3 Page 14

1 a 1269 b 2618 c 9346 d 6204 e 3205 f 8982 **2** a 2 b 3 c 4 d 4 e 4 f 4 **3** a 5372 b 2680 c 8295 d 6706 e 2159
f 3425 **4** a six thousand, three hundred and eight b five thousand, two hundred and fifty-one c one thousand and six
d one thousand, three hundred and twenty-nine e nine thousand, nine hundred and nine f three thousand, two hundred and sixty-six
5 5021 **6** 4 **7** 3049 **8** two thousand, three hundred and forty-six **9**

Unit 4 Page 14

1 a 2 b 1 c 9 d 0 e 8 f 0 **2** a 410 b 231 c 890 d 370 e 301 f 900 **3** a 206, 210, 220, 236 b 245, 326, 589, 691
c 259, 295, 529, 952 d 678, 687, 786, 876 e 302, 503, 609, 805 f 976, 980, 989, 998 **4** a 603, 301, 205, 103 b 84, 64, 46, 44
c 132, 125, 119, 108 d 605, 506, 406, 305 e 972, 899, 876, 792 f 580, 536, 520, 511 **5** 0 **6** 690 **7** 198, 208, 298, 691
8 896, 696, 526, 325 **9** two hundred and ninety-one, three hundred and eleven, four hundred and twenty-nine, four hundred and
eighty-five, five hundred and six

Unit 5 Page 15

1 a 64 b 116 c 57 d 108 e 74 f 132 **2** a 40, 50, 60 b 130, 140, 150 c 100, 110, 120 d 280, 290, 300 e 33, 43, 53
f 382, 392, 402 **3** a 70, 60, 50 b 470, 460, 450 c 20, 10, 0 d 340, 330, 320 e 185, 175, 165 f 407, 397, 387 **4** a 102, 122
b 56, 86 c 423, 433 d 285, 255 e 340, 320 f 87, 77 **5** 59 **6** 86, 96, 106 **7** 92, 82, 72 **8** 104, 124 **9** 1630

Unit 6 Page 15

1 a 870 b 420 c 930 d 55 e 562 f 731 **2** a 70, 80, 90 b 105, 115, 125 c 63, 73, 83 d 38, 48, 58 e 186, 196, 206
f 397, 407, 417 **3** a 80, 70, 60 b 120, 110, 100 c 159, 149, 139 d 53, 43, 33 e 381, 371, 361 f 826, 816, 806
4 a 130, 150, 180 b 345, 355, 375, 385 c 846, 876, 886, 906 d 380, 370, 350 e 545, 525, 505, 495 f 926, 906, 886, 876
5 282 **6** 153, 163, 173 **7** 347, 337, 327 **8** 951, 921, 911 **9** a 1065, 1075, 1085, 1095, 1105
b 1432, 1422, 1412, 1402, 1392

Unit 7 Page 16

1

	100 less	Number	100 more
a	300	400	500
b	450	550	650
c	821	921	1021
d	663	763	863
e	1130	1230	1330
f	1469	1569	1669

2 a 400, 500, 600 b 398, 498, 598 c 751, 851, 951 d 1050, 1150, 1250 e 1570, 1670 f 3196, 3296
3 a 600, 500, 400 b 501, 401, 301 c 260, 160, 60 d 499, 399, 299 e 1545, 1445 f 2866, 2766 **4** a 217, 417, 617
b 240, 340, 540 c 405, 705, 805 d 632, 532, 332 e 416, 316, 116 f 725, 425, 325 **5**
6 1785, 1885 **7** 463, 363, 263 **8** 942, 1042
9 a 1999, 2099, 2199, 2299 b 2555, 2455, 2355, 2255

100 less	Number	100 more
765	865	965

Unit 8 Page 16

1 a 2, 6, 7, 14, 19 b 11, 18, 26, 32, 45 c 66, 73, 75, 86, 98 d 248, 325, 346, 486, 496 e 519, 527, 666, 752, 896 f 1005, 1027, 1156, 1170, 1279 **2** a 469 b 357 c 138 d 208 e 1359 f 1678 **3** a 632 b 864 c 910 d 221 e 6510 f 9863 **4** a true b false c false d true e true f false **5** 1186, 1269, 1286, 1372, 1437 **6** 406 **7** 9876 **8** true **9** <

Unit 9 Page 17

1 a 28 b 33 c 34 d 36 e 31 f 30 **2** a 34 b 30 c 32 d 28 e 36 f 19 **3** a 57 b 62 c 59 d 57 e 64 f 74 **4** a 80 b 77 c 84 d 82 e 90 f 96 **5** 43 **6** 18 **7** 40 **8** 62 **9** a 7 b 8

Unit 10 Page 17

1 a ▲■ b ▲▼ c ●◆● d e f

2 a 8, 10, 12 b 32, 40, 48 c 7, 9, 11 d 25, 30, 35 e 15, 18, 21 f 27, 29, 31 **3** a 2, 6, 10, 14, 18, 22 b 1, 4, 7, 10, 13, 16 c 3, 7, 11, 15, 19, 23 d 10, 13, 16, 19, 22, 25 e 20, 22, 24, 26, 28, 30 f 100, 105, 110, 115, 120, 125 **4** a add 4 b halving/divide by 2 c double/times by 2 d subtract 10 e halving/divide by 2 f add 7 **5** **6** 26, 28, 30 **7** 4, 9, 14, 19, 24, 29 **8** add 3 **9** 82, 127, 182 increasing by 5, 15, 25, 35 etc.

Unit 11 Page 18

1 a [2 H 2 T 6 U] b [4 H 0 T 9 U] c [6 H 7 T 0 U] d [1 H 1 T 1 U] e [H 8 T 0 U] f [8 H 0 T 2 U] **2** a 625 b 269 c 307 d 836 e 480 f 999 **3** a 800 + 20 + 6 b 200 + 70 c 400 + 2 d 900 + 80 + 9 e 700 + 20 + 5 f 500 + 10 + 9 **4** a 6 hundreds b 9 tens c 1 unit d 5 tens e 1 hundred f 0 units **5** [5 H 0 T 7 U] **6** 753 **7** 600 + 10 + 3 **8** 5 units **9** 339

Unit 12 Page 18

1 a 3746 b 9252 c 2033 d 1089 e 9207 f 3210 **2** a 1623 b 4387 c 2465 d 8042 e 5901 f 7938 **3** a 6000 + 200 + 40 + 1 b 7000 + 700 + 70 + 7 c 2000 + 40 + 9 d 1000 + 400 + 6 e 3000 + 200 + 20 f 9000 + 800 + 90 + 8 **4** a 2 thousands b 6 tens c 1 ten d 3 hundreds e 6 thousands f 8 hundreds **5** 6205 **6** 3762 **7** 5000 + 200 + 70 + 5 **8** 3 hundred **9** 3298, 3300

Unit 13 Page 19

1 a 4000 + 500 + 20 + 6 b 6000 + 800 + 40 + 9 c 8000 + 400 + 7 d 9000 + 200 + 60 e 3000 + 60 + 6 f 1000 + 200 + 90 + 9 **2** a 96, 98 b 8459, 8461 c 3425, 3427 d 367, 369 e 8876, 8878 f 648, 650 **3** a 2578, 7582, 8572, 8752 b 1999, 2500, 2870, 3420 c 249, 870, 972, 1672 d 1098, 1111, 2671, 4213 e 3264, 3999, 4086, 4628 f 9329, 9685, 9989, 9990 **4** a 9421 b 8763 c 8432 d 6642 e 9210 f 4321 **5** 2000 + 300 + 10 **6** 3098, 3100 **7** 909, 1021, 1051, 1161, 1211 **8** 9831 **9** 2345: two thousand, three hundred and forty-five

Unit 14 Page 19

1 a 95, 85, 72, 62, 36 b 135, 127, 115, 110, 102 c 563, 429, 333, 273, 121 d 926, 886, 852, 739, 608 e 1485, 1312, 1269, 1139, 1026 f 1995, 1990, 1852, 1789, 1763 **2** a 641 b 653 c 987 d 765 e 9771 f 5310 **3** a 239 b 467 c 255 d 123 e 1346 f 1349 **4** a 94 b 110 c 914 d 583 e 1935 f 1628 **5** 106, 94, 87, 32, 15 **6** 8731 **7** 789 **8** 1408 **9** 432, 342, 243, 423, 324, 234

Unit 15 Page 20

1 a, e **2** a, c, d, f **3** a 8, 10, 12 b 26, 28, 30 c 64, 66, 68 d 108, 110, 112 e 134, 136, 138 f 154, 156, 158

4 a b c d e f

5 No **6** Yes **7** 196, 198, 200 **8**
9 even, odd. Because all of the even numbers can be evenly divided by 2. All the odd numbers have remainders when divided by 2.

Unit 16   Page 20

1 a 12 b 15 c 18 d 14 e 13 f 15 **2** a 13 b 15 c 16 d 12 e 16 f 13 **3** a 23 b 27 c 22 d 29 e 23 f 28
4 a 16 b 17 c 12 d 12 e 19 f 15 **5** 17 **6** 19 **7** 26 **8** 18 **9** $3 + $7 + $4 = $14

Unit 17   Page 21

1 a 10 + 6 = 16 b 6 + 5 = 11 c 3 + 11 = 14 d 14 + 5 = 19 e 3 + 13 = 16 f 10 + 10 = 20 **2** a 19 b 12 c 15 d 17 e 16 f 13
3 a 6 + 5 = 11 b 13 + 6 = 19 c 3 + 7 = 10 d 9 + 4 = 13 e 5 + 12 = 17 f 7 + 2 = 9
4

a

+	3
4	7
5	8
6	9
7	10

b

+	8
7	15
8	16
9	17
10	18

c

+	11
2	13
3	14
4	15
5	16

d

+	5
1	6
6	11
9	14
14	19

e

+	15
2	17
1	16
4	19
3	18

f

+	7
3	10
5	12
11	18
8	15

5 12 + 5 = 17 **6** 18 **7** 14 + 3 = 17 **8**

+	4
8	12
6	10
12	16
15	19

9 19

Unit 18   Page 21

1 a 22 + 15 = 37 b 33 + 7 = 40 c 10 + 16 = 26 d 14 + 22 = 36 e 6 + 13 = 19 f 27 + 11 = 38 **2** a 27 b 38 c 48 d 49
e 39 f 38 **3** a 44 b 38 c 29 d 18 e 46 f 37 **4** a 15 b 2 c 21 d 23 e 24 f 11 **5** 12 + 23 = 35 **6** 37 **7** 46 **8** 14
9 16 + 12 = 28

Unit 19   Page 22

1 a 33 + 25 = 58 b 26 + 52 = 78 c 24 + 62 = 86 d 19 + 50 = 69 e 84 + 15 = 99 f 50 + 47 = 97 **2** a 58 b 98 c 99 d 96
e 88 f 89 **3** a 75 b 39 c 87 d 77 e 78 f 99 **4** a 56 b 87 c 78 d 75 e 74 f 93 **5** 35 + 23 = 58 **6** 88 **7** 87 **8** 79
9 e.g. 30 + 18 = 48 or 34 + 14 = 48

Unit 20   Page 22

1 a 7 tens + 8 units b 6 tens + 9 units c 9 tens + 4 units d 7 tens + 8 units e 9 tens + 8 units f 6 tens + 9 units
2 a 45 b 57 c 79 d 59 e 89 f 98 **3** a 45 b 69 c 98 d 97 e 93 f 89 **4** a 15 + 23, 38 apples b 23 + 71, 94 sweets
c 36 + 22, 58 buttons d 85 + 13, 98 paperclips e 32 + 47, 79 pencils f 63 + 14, 77 books **5** 9 tens + 4 units **6** 57 **7** 87
8 56 + 23, 79 mice **9** 14 + 13 + 1, 28 people

Unit 21   Page 23

1 a 37 + 21 = 58 b 55 + 13 = 68 c 25 + 40 = 65 d 33 + 65 = 98 e 76 + 22 = 98 f 12 + 80 = 92 **2** a 99 b 77 c 87 d 69
e 89 f 89 **3** a $79 b $88 c $78 d $67 e $68 f $98 **4**

a

```
  7 2
+ 1 4
  8 6
```

b

```
  2 2
+ 3 7
  5 9
```

c

```
  4 0
+ 2 8
  6 8
```

d

```
  1 2
+ 5 2
  6 4
```

e

```
  4 5
+ 3 3
  7 8
```

f

```
  5 5
+ 4 4
  9 9
```

5 41 + 27 = 68 **6** 97 **7** $76 **8**

```
  2 3
+ 5 6
  7 9
```

9

(wheel +12: inner numbers 72, 8, 66, 57, 41, 35, 23, 14 → outer 84, 20, 26, 35, 47, 53, 69, 78)

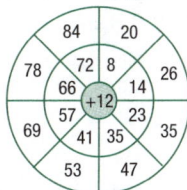

Unit 22   Page 23

1 a 23 + 28 = 51 b 35 + 27 = 62 c 45 + 39 = 84 d 27 + 19 = 46 e 46 + 36 = 82 f 23 + 38 = 61 **2** a 20 + 20 = 40
b 30 + 40 = 70 c 50 + 40 = 90 d 20 + 40 = 60 e 60 + 30 = 90 f 50 + 30 = 80 **3** a 57 b 73 c 6, 63 d 5, 63 e 20 + 4, 91
f 30 + 4, 92 **4** a 54 b 61 c 92 d 83 e 94 f 83 **5** 25 + 38 = 63 **6** 80 + 20 = 100 **7** 30 + 7, 93 **8** 91 **9** 35 + 28, 63c

Unit 23   Page 24

1 a 13 + 28 = 41 b 24 + 36 = 60 c 26 + 14 = 40 d 47 + 25 = 72 e 17 + 24 = 41 f 26 + 19 = 45 **2** a 83 b 82 c 86 d 64
e 72 f 71 **3** a 86 b 53 c 71 d 92 e 82 f 64 **4** a 93 b 64 c 93 d 60 e 82 f 71 **5** 26 + 16 = 42 **6** 83 **7** 53 **8** 72
9 35 + 27, 62 animals

Unit 24 Page 24

1 a 94 b 92 c 86 d 91 e 84 f 84 **2** a $64 b $96 c $80 d $72 e $76 f $81 **3** a 81 pencils b 61 hats
c 81 counters d 34 birds e 83 trees f 75 beads

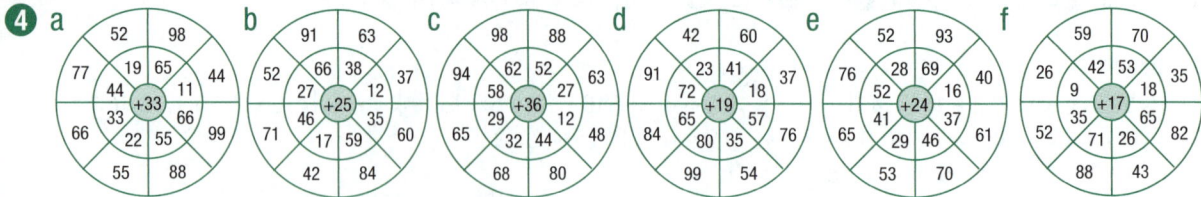

4 a (+33) b (+25) c (+36) d (+19) e (+24) f (+17)

5 92 **6** $75 **7** 66c **8** (+27) **9** e.g. 22 + 30 = 52, 20 + 32 = 52, 21 + 31 = 52, 17 + 35 = 52

Unit 25 Page 25

1 a 76 b 83 c 81 d 73 e 85 f 81 **2** a 90 b 78 c 54 d 93 e 70 f 54
3 a 81 eggs b 57 fish c 71 sweets d 87 bees e 63 L of water f 43 cars

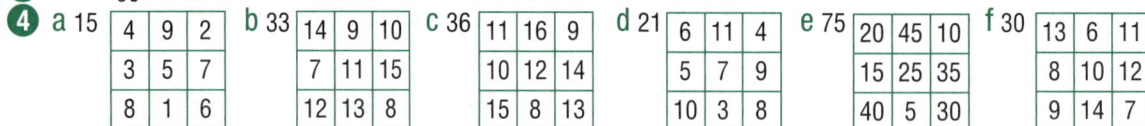

4 a 15

4	9	2
3	5	7
8	1	6

b 33

14	9	10
7	11	15
12	13	8

c 36

11	16	9
10	12	14
15	8	13

d 21

6	11	4
5	7	9
10	3	8

e 75

20	45	10
15	25	35
40	5	30

f 30

13	6	11
8	10	12
9	14	7

5 58 **6** 83 **7** $64 **8** 66

28	18	20
14	22	30
24	26	16

9 e.g. hat, game and book is $84; CD, calculator and book is $78

Unit 26 Page 25

1 a 373 b 738 c 869 d 799 e 929 f 895 **3** a 914 b 872 c 932 d 985 e 582 f 937 **3** a 631 b 873 c 431 d 636
e 636 f 262 **4** a 180 + 298, $478 b 155 + 265, $420 c 567 + 376, $943 d 376 + 298, $674 e 155 + 567, $722
f 180 + 265, $445 **5** 378 **6** 584 **7** 734 **8** 298 + 325, $623 **9** 176 marbles + 208 marbles = 384 marbles

Unit 27 Page 26

1 a 900 b 1100 c 1700 d 1100 e 1400 f 1400 **2** a 14 b 26 c 23 d 28 e 27 f 26 **3** a 43 b 36 c 51 d 43 e 36 f 71
4 a 73 b 69 c 67 d 94 e 39 f 49 **5** 900 **6** 28 **7** 35 **8** 54 **9** 52 + 23 = 75

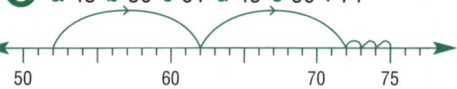

(number line: 50, 60, 70, 75)

Unit 28 Page 26

1 a 200 b 700 c 500 d 600 e 900 f 100 **2** a 200 b 300 c 500 d 200 e 500 f 400 **3** a 170 b 430 c 860 d 410 e 400 f 210
4 a true b false c true d false e true f true **5** 800 **6** 500 **7** 820 **8** true **9** 5400, rounded down

Unit 29 Page 27

1 a 4 b 12 c 10 d 2 e 11 f 2 **2** a 5 b 8 c 6 d 12 e 9 f 4 **3** a 6 – 2 = 4 b 10 – 4 = 6 c 12 – 5 = 7 d 12 – 7 = 5
e 11 – 5 = 6 f 6 – 6 = 0 **4** a 7 crayons b 7 books c 8 biscuits d 6 shirts e 11 sheets of paper f 3 mice **5** 10 **6** 6
7 16 – 6 = 10 **8** 5 chocolates **9** (17 –)

Unit 30 Page 27

1 a 5, 50, 500 b 7, 70, 700 c 4, 40, 400 d 2, 20, 200 e 3, 30, 300 f 2, 20, 200 **2** a 7, 2 b 5, 4 c 6, 5 d 6, 4 e 3, 9 f 8, 5
3 a 13 – 10 = 3 b 14 – 10 = 4 c 15 – 10 = 5 d 16 – 10 = 6 e 17 – 10 = 7 f 18 – 10 = 8 **4** a 3, 8 b 12, 8 c 14, 5 d 9, 6
e 6, 7 f 5, 11 **5** 2, 20, 200 **6** 11, 11, 4, 7 **7** 19 – 10 = 9 **8** 8, 7 **9** $8

Unit 31 Page 28

1 a 27 b 15 c 29 d 12 e 19 f 34 **2** a 18 b 13 c 10, 33 d 20, 25 e 20, 5, 14 f 20, 3, 13 **3** a 32 b 34 c 12 d 15
e 36 f 14 **4** a 15 b 42 c 11 d 22 e 22 f 16 **5** 18 **6** 20, 8, 21 **7** 32 **8** 22 **9** 46 – 13 = 33

Unit 32 Page 28

1 a 81 b 42 c 22 d 42 e 31 f 12 **2** a 6 b 7 c 2 d 7 e 55 f 62 **3** a 43 b 32 c 31 d 54 e 43 f 21 **4** a 31 birds b 41 candles c 22 flowers d 11 boxes e 25 girls f 25 cats **5** 61 **6** 52 **7** 12 **8** 26 apples **9** she added instead of subtracted, answer 31 marbles

Unit 33 Page 29

1 a 16 b 33 c 63 d 44 e 38 f 56 **2** a 58 b 28 c 15 d 58 e 44 f 15 **3** a answer 59 b correct c 45 – 38 = 7 not 3 d correct e correct f 7 not 17 **4** a 59 b 83 c 71, 85 d 17, 92 e 46, 75 f 18, 63 **5** 44 **6** 27 **7** correct **8** 27, 91 **9** $91 – $83 = $8

Unit 34 Page 29

1 a 34 b 51 c 67 d 82 e 76 f 43 **2** a 44 b 17 c 19 d 27 e 15 f 9 **3** a correct b incorrect, answer 9 c correct d incorrect, answer 17 e incorrect, answer 29 f correct **4** a 3 b 5 c 8, 1 d 4, 9 e 34 f 15 **5** 81 **6** 17 **7** correct **8** 4, 4 **9** a 36 b 33

Unit 35 Page 30

1 a 24 b 36 c 89 d 68 e 49 f 26 **2** a 25 b 55 c 19 d 25 e 58 f 9 **3** a $62 b $26 c $27 d $49 e $35 f $79 **4** a 44 children b 22 cars c 29 pens d 26 contestants e 17 birds f 8 loaves **5** 57 **6** 25 **7** $9 **8** 6 DVDs **9** example: 47 – 10 = 37

Unit 36 Page 30

1 a 865 b 345 c 314 d 222 e 354 f 115

2
a
H	T	U
9	3	5
−7	2	2
2	1	3

b
H	T	U
4	9	9
− 3	4	3
1	5	6

c
H	T	U
7	5	6
−5	4	5
2	1	1

d
H	T	U
8	9	6
− 6	4	3
2	5	3

e
H	T	U
7	7	8
− 2	6	3
5	1	5

f
H	T	U
9	4	7
− 5	1	1
4	3	6

3 a $184 b $50 c $344 d $12 e $134 f $262 **4** a $121 b $82 c $28 d $81 e $60 f $73 **5** 722 **6**
H	T	U
3	9	8
− 2	4	2
1	5	6

7 $154 **8** $176 **9** $22

Unit 37 Page 31

1 a 17 b 7 c 27 d 37 e 18 f 38 **2** a 65 b 75 c 85 d 55 e 77 f 67 **3** a 15c b 6 pins c 18 pencils d 8 baby pins e 16 nails f 17 matches **4** a 18, 28 b 7, 17, 6 c 6, 21, 5 d 5, 7, 32 e 5, 24, 25 f 7, 19, 36 **5** 23 **6** 66 **7** 9 nails **8** 8, 9, 37 **9** 20 – 11 = 9, 20 – 9 = 11

Unit 38 Page 31

1
a
$$\begin{array}{r} 24 \\ -13 \\ \hline 11 \end{array} \rightarrow \begin{array}{r} 11 \\ +13 \\ \hline 24 \end{array}$$
b
$$\begin{array}{r} 46 \\ -34 \\ \hline 12 \end{array} \rightarrow \begin{array}{r} 12 \\ +34 \\ \hline 46 \end{array}$$
c
$$\begin{array}{r} 39 \\ -17 \\ \hline 22 \end{array} \rightarrow \begin{array}{r} 22 \\ +17 \\ \hline 39 \end{array}$$
d
$$\begin{array}{r} 32 \\ -9 \\ \hline 23 \end{array} \rightarrow \begin{array}{r} 23 \\ +9 \\ \hline 32 \end{array}$$
e
$$\begin{array}{r} 42 \\ -16 \\ \hline 26 \end{array} \rightarrow \begin{array}{r} 26 \\ +16 \\ \hline 42 \end{array}$$
f
$$\begin{array}{r} 51 \\ -29 \\ \hline 22 \end{array} \rightarrow \begin{array}{r} 22 \\ +29 \\ \hline 51 \end{array}$$

2 a 23 b 23 c 62 d 9 e 27 f 28 **3** a 14 km – 5 km = 9 km, correct b 55 km – 14 km = 41 km, incorrect c 55 km – 22 km = 33 km, incorrect d 22 km – 5 km = 17 km, correct e 22 km – 14 km = 8 km, correct f 55 km – 5 km = 50 km, incorrect **4** a 25 – 17, 8 books b 47 – 28, 19 frogs c 93 – 48, $45 d 45 – 18, 27 cows e 25 – 19, 6 sweets f 42 – 26, 16 pens **5**
$$\begin{array}{r} 52 \\ -29 \\ \hline 23 \end{array} \rightarrow \begin{array}{r} 23 \\ +29 \\ \hline 52 \end{array}$$
6 24 **7** 42 km – 18 km = 24 km, correct **8** 31 – 17, 14 mice **9** 874

Unit 39 Page 32

1

	Question	Estimate
a	9 + 6 + 15 + 20	20 or (60) or 100
b	15 + 20 + 25 + 30	10 or 50 or (100)
c	10 + 11 + 12 + 13	20 or (40) or 60
d	21 + 35 + 14 + 2	50 or (70) or 90
e	8 + 2 + 6 + 5	(30) or 40 or 50
f	15 + 21 + 13 + 5	30 or (60) or 90

2

	Question	Estimate
a	30 + 60 + 50 + 21	130 or (160) or 190
b	90 + 100 + 20 + 40	150 or 200 or (250)
c	46 + 24 + 59 + 63	150 or (190) or 230
d	112 + 14 + 110 + 21	(250) or 290 or 330
e	92 + 56 + 108 + 29	250 or (290) or 340
f	121 + 205 + 36 + 50	(420) or 440 or 460

③

	Question	Estimate
a	14 + 14 + 14	(30) or 70 or 100
b	8 + 8 + 8 + 8 + 8	20 or (50) or 80
c	21 + 21 + 21 + 21	60 or (80) or 100
d	32 + 32 + 32 + 32	100 or (120) or 140
e	53 + 53 + 53	100 or (150) or 200
f	19 + 19 + 19 + 19 + 19	(100) or 110 or 120

④

	Question	Estimate
a	90 – 1 – 1 – 1 – 1	(90) or 70 or 50
b	140 – 8 – 8 – 8 – 8 – 8	(120) or 90 or 60
c	130 – 9 – 9 – 9 – 9	100 or (90) or 80
d	150 – 1 – 1 – 1 – 1 – 1	(150) or 120 or 100
e	200 – 9 – 9 – 9 – 9	220 or 190 or (160)
f	190 – 7 – 7 – 7 – 7 – 7	220 or 180 or (140)

⑤ 50 **⑥** 170 **⑦** 100 **⑧** 90 **⑨** a 30 × 5 = 150, 140 b 50 × 7 = 350, 336 c 70 × 9 = 630, 639 d 80 × 4 = 320, 328

Unit 40 — Page 32

① a 100 b 100 c 200 d 200 e 400 f 600 **②** a 1100 b 4700 c 6300 d 3600 e 5800 f 4000 **③** a 10 b 30 c 50 d 90 e 90 f 50 **④** a 120 b 170 c 210 d 500 e 260 f 340 **⑤** 600 **⑥** 4 000 **⑦** 100 **⑧** 330 **⑨** a 50 + 40, 90 seeds b 90 + 90 = 180 so less than 200

Unit 41 — Page 33

① a 1290 b 1350 c 1190 d 4830 e 3640 f 2010 **②** a 30 + 60 = 90 b 40 + 40 = 80 c 80 + 20 = 100 d 80 + 10 = 90 e 60 + 50 = 110 f 50 + 40 = 90 **③** a 60 – 20 = 40 b 90 – 30 = 60 c 70 – 30 = 40 d 70 – 20 = 50 e 80 – 40 = 40 f 90 – 60 = 30 **④** a 167, 3 b 438, 2 c 104, 6 d 19, 1 e 315, 5 f 46, 6 **⑤** 3 990 **⑥** 70 + 20 = 90 **⑦** 100 – 50 = 50 **⑧** 43, 3 **⑨** 30 + 20 + 30, 80 children

Unit 42 — Page 33

① a 12 b 10 c 3, 15 d 2, 14 e 3, 10, 30 f 1, 5, 5 **②** a 40 b 16 c 15 d 18 e 10 f 24 **③** a 28 hats b 18 fish c 40 pens d 20 girls e 42 boys f 32 nails **④** a yes b yes c yes d yes e yes f yes **⑤** 3, 6, 18 **⑥** 14 **⑦** 15 cups **⑧** yes **⑨** 1 × 12, 12 × 1, 2 × 6, 6 × 2, 3 × 4, 4 × 3

Unit 43 — Page 34

① a 12 b 28 c 36 d 2 e 1, 4 f 10, 40 **②** a 8 b 20 c 14 d 5 e 8 f 6 **③** a 6 b 20 c 14 d 24 e 20 f 32 **④** a 3 × 2 b 4 × 4 c 2 × 2 d 9 × 4 e 8 × 2 f 7 × 4 **⑤** 16 **⑥** 9 **⑦** 8 **⑧** 5 × 4 **⑨**

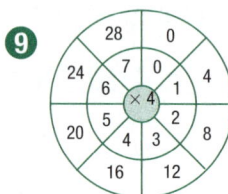

Unit 44 — Page 34

① a 60 b 90 c 40 d 70 e 20 f 100 **②** a 40 b 25 c 10 d 7 e 10 f 9 **③** a 5 × 3 b 10 × 8 c 5 × 10 d 10 × 7 e 5 × 4 f 10 × 3

4 a

×	1	2	3	4
5	5	10	15	20

b

×	1	2	3	4
10	10	20	30	40

c

×	9	10	7	4
5	45	50	35	20

d

×	5	6	7	8
10	50	60	70	80

e

×	5	6	7	8
5	25	30	35	40

f

×	9	10	5	3
10	90	100	50	30

5 50 **6** 9 **7** 6 × 10

8

×	3	4	5	6
5	15	20	25	30

9 Various

Unit 45   Page 35

1 a 6 b 0 c 9 d 0 e 20 f 16   **2** a 0 b 4 c 0 d 10 e 0 f 5

3 a

×	4	5	6	7
4	16	20	24	28

b

×	7	8	9	10
1	7	8	9	10

c

×	8	9	10	3
0	0	0	0	0

d

×	1	2	3	4
1	1	2	3	4

e

×	5	6	7	8
2	10	12	14	16

f

×	3	4	5	6
4	12	16	20	24

4 a 2 b 0 c 12 d 20 e 16 f 10   **5** 0   **6** 7   **7**

×	7	8	9	10
1	7	8	9	10

8 6   **9**

1	2	3	(4)	5	6	7	(8)	9	10
11	(12)	13	(14)	15	(16)	17	(18)	19	(20)
21	(22)	23	(24)	25	(26)	27	(28)	29	(30)
31	(32)	33	(34)	35	(36)	37	38	39	(40)

c every second 2 times is circled

Unit 46   Page 35

1 a 3 × 3 = 9 b 4 × 6 = 24 c 8 × 3 = 24 d 6 × 6 = 36 e 10 × 3 = 30 f 2 × 6 = 12   **2** a 6 b 60, 6 c 5, 30 d 9, 9 e 48, 6 f 18, 6   **3** a 3 b 12 c 24 d 6 e 21 f 30   **4** a 30 b 6 c 54 d 3 e 7 f 27   **5** 5 × 6 = 30   **6** 6, 18   **7** 15   **8** 6   **9** $48

Unit 47   Page 36

1 a 27 b 72 c 18 d 90 e 63 f 81   **2** a 1, 9 b 2, 18 c 3, 27 d 4, 36 e 5, 45 f 6, 54   **3** a 3 × 9 b 2 × 9 c 7 × 9 d 4 × 9 e 1 × 9 f 5 × 9   **4** a 3 b 9, 6 c 90, 10 d 1, 3 e 54, 6 f 7, 7   **5** 45   **6** 8, 72   **7** 6 × 9 = 54   **8** 3, 9
9 27 biscuits

Unit 48   Page 36

1 a 21 b 54 c 45 d 18 e 24 f 18   **2** a 12 b 48 c 72 d 30 e 42 f 63   **3** a 15 b 12 c 63 d 24 e 42 f 81   **4** a 6, 6 b 6, 4 c 8, 4 d 3, 9 e 4, 6 f 30, 10   **5** 12   **6** 54   **7** 27   **8** 9, 6   **9**

×	2	4	5	6	8	10
3	6	12	15	18	24	30
6	12	24	30	36	48	60

Unit 49   Page 37

1 a 80 b 48 c 56 d 72 e 24 f 40   **2** a 48 b 0 c 32 d 16 e 40 f 64   **3** a 8 b 4 c 7 d 8 e 8 f 8   **4** a 16 b 64 c 40 d 80 e 32 f 72   **5** 32   **6** 56   **7** 10   **8** 24   **9**

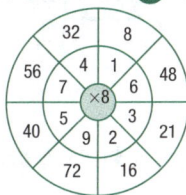

Unit 50   Page 37

1 a 14 b 28 c 24 d 12 e 20 f 48   **2** a 6 b 32 c 56 d 18 e 8 f 72

3 a

×	7	8	9	10
2	14	16	18	20

b

×	3	4	5	6
4	12	16	20	24

c

×	9	10	5	8
8	72	80	40	64

d

×	3	6	5	4
2	6	12	10	8

e

×	2	8	10	7
4	8	32	40	28

f

×	3	7	4	8
8	24	56	32	64

4 a 8 b 24, 3 c 8, 4 d 2, 5 e 2, 12 f 4, 24 **5** 20,10 **6** 36 **7**

×	1	3	5	7
4	4	12	20	28

8 4, 8 **9** $24

Unit 51   Page 38

1 a 21 b 7 c 42 d 28 e 56 f 35 **2** a 0 b 42 c 28 d 70 e 14 f 63 **3** a 49 b 5 c 63 d 3 e 8 f 0 **4** a 21 b 28 c 56
d 14 e 42 f 63 **5** 49 **6** 21 **7** 6 **8** 77 **9** Various

Unit 52   Page 38

1 a 24 b 8 c 48 d 25 e 24 f 63 **2** a 5 b 30 c 72 d 20 e 42 f 16

3 a   b   c   d   e   f

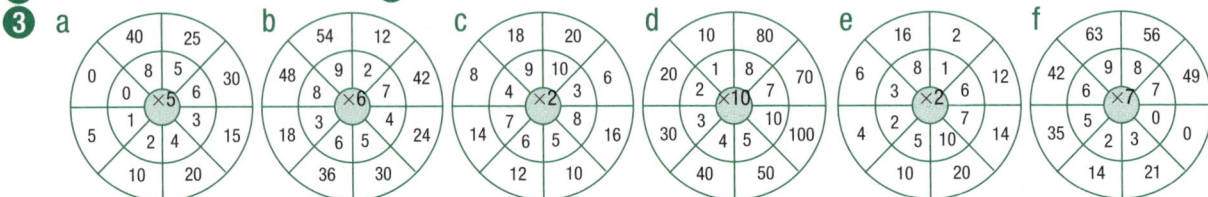

4 a 80 b 0 c 15 d 14 e 35 f 72 **5** 80 **6** 24 **7** **8** 63

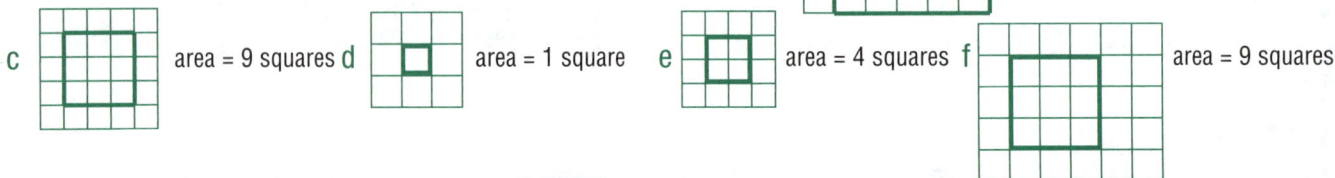

9 a 1, 12, 2, 6, 3, 4 b 1, 18, 2, 9, 3, 6 c 1, 20, 2, 10, 4, 5

Unit 53   Page 39

1 a 1 b 4 c 9 d 16 e 25 f 36 **2** a   area = 4 squares b   area = 25 squares

c   area = 9 squares d   area = 1 square   e   area = 4 squares f   area = 9 squares

3 a 3 × 3   = 9 b 2 × 2   = 4 c 4 × 4   = 16 d 1 × 1 = 1 e 5 × 5   = 25 f 6 × 6   = 36

4 a yes b yes c no d yes e no f yes **5** 49 **6**   area = 16 squares **7** 64 squares

8 no **9** 1, 4, 9, 16, 25, 36, 49, 64, 81, 100

Unit 54   Page 39

1

1	②	3	④	5	⑥	7	⊗	9	⑩
11	⑫	13	⑭	15	⊗	17	⑱	19	⑳
21	㉒	23	㉔	25	㉖	27	㉘	29	㉚
31	⊗	33	㉞	35	㊱	37	㊳	39	㊵
41	㊷	43	㊹	45	㊻	47	⊗	49	㊿

d 8 = 4 × 2 (yes) e yes f not a multiple of 8 **2** a 5 b 10 c 15 d 20 e 25 f 30

3 a 2, 4, 6, 8, 10, 12, 14, 16, 18, 20 b 3, 6, 9, 12, 15, 18, 21, 24, 27, 30 c 9, 18, 27, 36, 45, 54, 63, 72, 81, 90
d 5, 10, 15, 20, 25, 30, 35, 40, 45, 50 e 6, 12, 18, 24, 30, 36, 42, 48, 54, 60 f 7, 14, 21, 28, 35, 42, 49, 56, 63, 70

4 a (50) (5) (12) (b) (26) (24) (22) (c) (14) (22) (40) (d) (29) (62) (35) (e) (18) (96) (36) (f) (36) (28) (40)

(30) **5** (10) (3) **3** (9) (36) **4** (20) (48) **7** (70) (25) **9** (72) (46) **6** (33)

(22) (25) (18) (31) (12) (28) (32) (30) (18) (23) (51) (49) (63) (85) (90) (20) (18) (24)

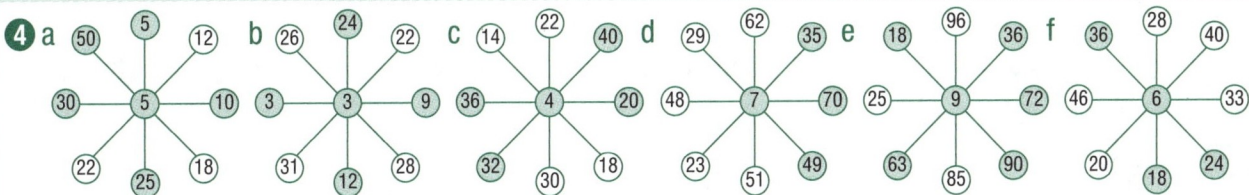

5 not a multiple of 4 **6** 45 **7** 10, 20, 30, 40, 50, 60, 70, 80, 90, 100 **8**

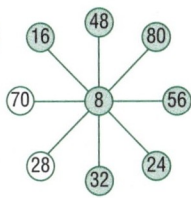

(16) (48) (80)

(70) **8** (56)

(28) (32) (24)

9 Liam $20, Joe $40, Lisa $80

Unit 55 Page 40

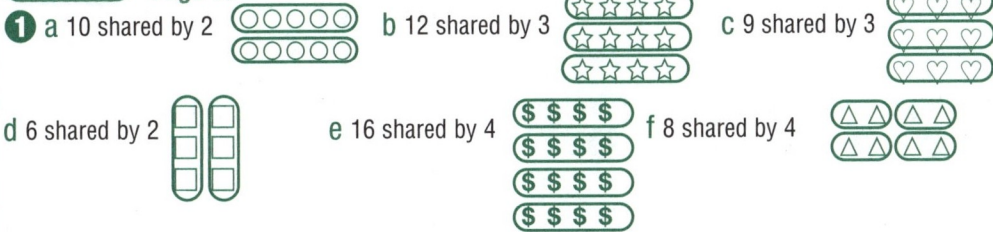

1 a 10 shared by 2 (○○○○○)(○○○○○) b 12 shared by 3 (☆☆☆☆)(☆☆☆☆)(☆☆☆☆) c 9 shared by 3 (♡♡♡)(♡♡♡)(♡♡♡)

d 6 shared by 2 ▯▯ e 16 shared by 4 ($ $ $ $)($ $ $ $)($ $ $ $)($ $ $ $) f 8 shared by 4 (△△)(△△)(△△)(△△)

2 a 7 b 2 c 2 d 4 e 5 f 1 **3** a 5 apples b 5 oranges c 4 stickers d 6 biscuits e 2 charts f 3 boxes
4 a 2 b 5 c 10 d 3, 1 e 2, 2 f 1, 4 **5** 12 shared by 6 (▽▽)(▽▽)(▽▽)(▽▽)(▽▽)(▽▽) **6** 5 **7** 5 cupcakes **8** 2, 1

9 48 − 6 − 6 − 6 − 6 − 6 − 6 − 6 − 6 = 0
i.e. 8 times,
therefore 8 pens each

Unit 56 Page 40

1 a 3, 3 b 3, 3 c 4, 4 d 6, 6 e 2, 2 f 7, 7 **2** a 20 ÷ 2 = 10 b 18 ÷ 6 = 3 c 9 ÷ 3 = 3 d 9 ÷ 9 = 1 e 8 ÷ 4 = 2 f 8 ÷ 1 = 8
3 a 4 b 4, 6 c 3, 8 d 8, 3 e 2, 12 f 12, 2 **4** a 5 b 4 c 9 d 7 e 10 f 8 **5** 1, 1 **6** 18 ÷ 3 = 6 **7** 1, 24
8 7 **9** 12 ÷ 1 = 12, 12 ÷ 2 = 6, 12 ÷ 3 = 4, 12 ÷ 4 = 3, 12 ÷ 6 = 2, 12 ÷ 12 = 1

Unit 57 Page 41

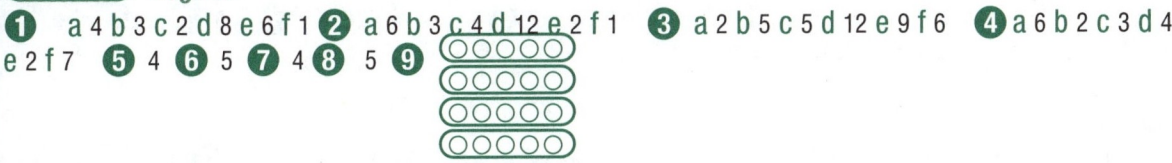

1 a 4 b 3 c 2 d 8 e 6 f 1 **2** a 6 b 3 c 4 d 12 e 2 f 1 **3** a 2 b 5 c 5 d 12 e 9 f 6 **4** a 6 b 2 c 3 d 4
e 2 f 7 **5** 4 **6** 5 **7** 4 **8** 5 **9** (○○○○○)(○○○○○)(○○○○○)(○○○○○)

Unit 58 Page 41

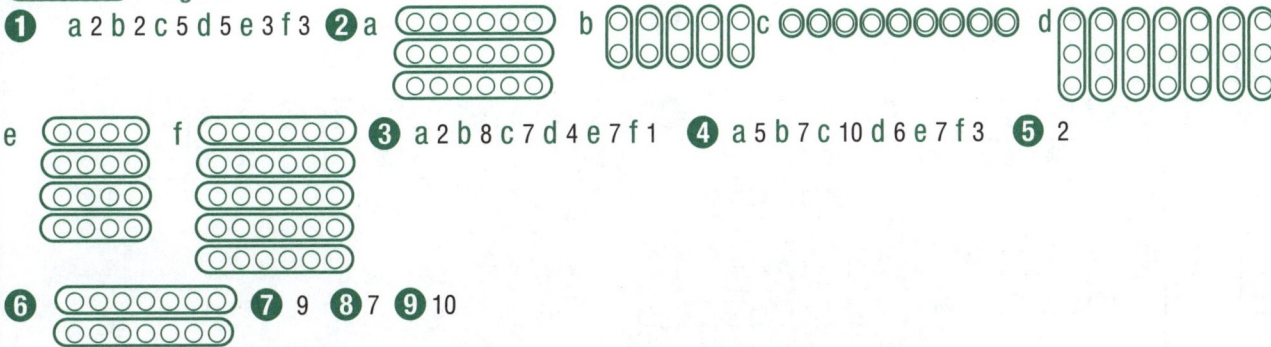

1 a 2 b 2 c 5 d 5 e 3 f 3 **2** a (○○○○○)(○○○○○)(○○○○○) b ▯▯▯▯▯ c ○○○○○○○○○ d ▯▯▯▯▯

e (○○○○)(○○○○)(○○○○)(○○○○) f (○○○○○)(○○○○○)(○○○○○)(○○○○○)(○○○○○) **3** a 2 b 8 c 7 d 4 e 7 f 1 **4** a 5 b 7 c 10 d 6 e 7 f 3 **5** 2

6 (○○○○○○○○)(○○○○○○○○) **7** 9 **8** 7 **9** 10

Unit 59 Page 42

1 a 2 b 3 c 4 d 6 e 4 f 3 **2** a 1 b 2 c 4 d 1 e 2 f 3 **3** a 1 b 2 c 3 d 4 e 5 f 4 **4** a 2 b 5 c 6 d 1 e 3 f 2 **5** 5
6 3 **7** 3 **8** 5 **9** 3, 9, 3

Unit 60 Page 42

1 a 5 b 8 c 7 d 9 e 9 f 7 **2** a 6 b 3 c 10 d 9 e 5 f 7 **3** a 5 b 9 c 4 d 6 e 8 f 10 **4** a 6 b 9 c 9 d 3 e 2 f 4 **5** 7
6 8 **7** 7 **8** 10 **9** 6 keys

Unit 61 Page 43

1 a 3, 1 b 5, 1 c 3, 3 d 2, 2 e 3, 1 f 1, 2 **2** a 3 b 6 c 2 d 3, 3 e 2, 4 f 4, 2 **3** a 5 b 2 c 10 d 6, 2 e 3, 2 f 2, 6
4 a 3, 1 b 3, 1 c 5, 1 d 6, 1 e 2, 1 f 4, 3 **5** 2, 1 **6** 2, 2 **7** 2, 2 **8** 5, 5 **9** 6 boxes full, 2 in an extra box

Unit 62 Page 43

1 a 7 b 5 c 3 r 5 d 8 r 3 e 5 r 5 f 4 r 3 **2** a 2 b 7 c 2 r 7 d 5 e 2 f 5 r 2 **3** a 2 r 4 b 4 r 2 c 1 r 4 d 2 r 2 e 7 r 2
f 4 r 4 **4** a 2 r 2 b 2 r 3 c 2 r 2 d 2 r 3 e 2 r 6 f 2 r 6 **5** 2 r 4 **6** 2 r 2 **7** 2 r 6 **8** 4 r 3 **9** 8 sets, 1 left over

Unit 63 Page 44

1 a 5 b 7 c 6 d 8 e 9 f 8 **2** a 4 b 8 c 5 d 7 e 9 f 7 **3** a 7 r 2 b 6 r 2 c 5 r 1 d 3 r 2 e 3 r 1 f 4 r 2 **4** a 2 r 1
b 2 r 3 c 2 r 4 d 3 r 3 e 2 r 4 f 5 r 1 **5** 9 **6** 2 **7** 3 r 2 **8** 3 r 2 **9** 6 sheep and 2 sheep left over

Unit 64 Page 44

1 a 6 b 5 c 2 d 5 e 4 f 3 **2** a 5, 3 b 6, 4 c 10, 9 d 8, 7 e 7, 9 f 9, 6 **3** a 4, 4 b 9, 9 c 6, 6 d 10, 10
e 3, 3 f 6, 6 **4** a $8 \div 2 = 4$, $8 \div 4 = 2$, $2 \times 4 = 8$, $4 \times 2 = 8$ b $15 \div 3 = 5$, $15 \div 5 = 3$, $5 \times 3 = 15$, $3 \times 5 = 15$
c $7 \div 1 = 7$, $7 \div 7 = 1$, $7 \times 1 = 7$, $1 \times 7 = 7$ d $12 \div 4 = 3$, $12 \div 3 = 4$, $4 \times 3 = 12$, $3 \times 4 = 12$
e $30 \div 5 = 6$, $30 \div 6 = 5$, $6 \times 5 = 30$, $5 \times 6 = 30$ f $9 \div 3 = 3$, $3 \times 3 = 9$ **5** 3 **6** 5, 7 **7** 7, 7
8 $10 \div 1 = 10$, $10 \div 10 = 1$, $10 \times 1 = 10$, $1 \times 10 = 10$ **9**

A	20	42	40	36
B	48	42	48	48
C	46	8	7	32

B wins

Unit 65 Page 45

1 a 51 b 59 c 53 d 60 e 52 f 55 **2** a 37 b 22 c 28 d 26 e 27 f 28 **3** a 15 b 24 c 28 d 27 e 30 f 14
4 a 4 b 2 c 3 d 4 e 6 f 9 **5** 93 **6** 78 **7** 24 **8** 7 **9** various, 40 + 10 = 50

Unit 66 Page 45

* Note: answers may vary for question numbers 1, 3, 5 and 7
1 a 6, 8 b 9, 15 c 7, 24 d 8, 17 e 5, 26 f 8, 35 **2** a 6, 14 b 8, 21 c 19, 25 d 17, 36 e 28, 37 f 6, 23 **3** a 7, 5 b 3, 9
c 9, 4 d 6, 8 e 9, 2 f 10, 3 **4** a 4, 16 b 7, 21 c 6, 18 d 4, 20 e 6, 42 f 5, 50 **5** 17, 29 **6** 16, 24 **7** 7, 8 **8** 9, 27
9 various, $5 + 5 = 10$, $20 - 10 = 10$, $2 \times 5 = 10$, $10 \div 1 = 10$

Unit 67 Page 46

1 a $6 + 4 + 7 = 17$ b $18 + 2 + 4 = 24$ c $17 + 3 + 6 = 26$ d $7 + 3 + 8 = 18$ e $5 + 15 + 8 = 28$ f $12 + 8 + 9 = 29$ **2** a 10, 10
b 22, 22 c 15, 15 d 13, 13 e 19, 19 f 25, 25 **3** a 18, 18 b 8, 8 c 42, 42 d 40, 40 e 90, 90 f 32, 32 **4** a 16, 9 b 18, 13
c 20, 11 d 42, 6 e 24, 8 f 80, 8 **5** $14 + 6 + 9 = 29$ **6** 21, 21 **7** 48, 48 **8** 40, 10 **9** had the same!

Unit 68 Page 46

1
17	4	6	16
3	8	14	2
10	15	7	14

2
5	12	8	4
7	10	4	1
3	11	7	9

3
6	16	15	4
10	14	9	8
7	18	12	20

4
10	4	1	8
12	9	5	6
1	16	7	7

5
10	8	5
6	1	7

6
8	6	3
2	1	9

7
5	8	16
7	12	10

8
4	2	1
7	3	6

9
	14		7		1		28
9		25		26		30	

	17		16		4		14
3		24		5		22	

	20		16		14		2
8		17		9		10	

Unit 69 Page 47

1 a 6 b 15 c 14 d 8 e 13 f 34 **2** a 4 b 5 c 4 d 3 e 10 f 8 **3** a 2 b 3 c 4 d 10 e 2 f 6 **4** a + b × c − d + e − f × **5** 22 **6** 7 **7** 10 **8** + **9** a × + b − + c × − d × +

Unit 70 Page 47

1 a 8, 10, 12 b 15, 18, 21 c 30, 36, 42 d 25, 30, 35 e 20, 24, 28 f 35, 42, 49 **2** a 70, 75, 80   add 5 b 90, 100, 110   add 10 c 58, 60, 62   add 2 d 54, 60, 66   add 6 e 72, 80, 88   add 8 f 55, 66, 77   add 11 **3** a 20 b 30 c 56 d 55 e 109 f 145

4 a

+	4	14	24	34	44
4	8	18	28	38	48

b

+	6	16	26	36	46
6	12	22	32	42	52

c

+	5	15	25	35	45
3	8	18	28	38	48

d

+	4	14	24	34	44
6	10	20	30	40	50

e

+	8	18	28	38	48
8	16	26	36	46	56

f

+	9	19	29	39	49
9	18	28	38	48	58

5 54, 63, 72 **6** 42, 45, 48   add 3 **7** 76 **8**

+	11	21	31	41	51
6	17	27	37	47	57

9 various, 100, 103, 106, 109

Unit 71 Page 48

1 a 40 b 66 c 12 d 35 e 31 f 46 **2** a 25, 30, 35, 40 b 100, 90, 80, 70 c 4, 8, 16, 32 d 20, 28, 36, 44 e 49, 42, 35, 28 f 1, 3, 9, 27 **3** a starting at 2 add 2 b starting at 20 subtract 3 c starting at 10 add 10 d starting at 10 add 6 e starting at 50 subtract 4 f starting at 4 multiply by 3 **4** a add 2 b add 3 c multiply by 2 d add 1 e subtract 2 f add 1 **5** 14 **6** 11, 17, 23, 29 **7** start at 5, multiply by 10 **8** + 2, + 3, + 4, … **9** various, start at 100, add 2

Unit 72 Page 48

1 a 54 − 4 = 50 b 35 − 5 = 30 c 91 − 1 = 90 d 180 + 7 = 187 e 230 + 6 = 236 f 720 + 6 = 726 **2** a 86 − 80 = 6 b 49 − 40 = 9 c 35 − 30 = 5 d 106 + 80 = 186 e 508 + 50 = 558 f 402 + 90 = 492 **3** a 427 − 400 = 27 b 960 − 900 = 60 c 829 − 800 = 29 d 73 + 400 = 473 e 20 + 100 = 120 f 14 + 200 = 214 **4** a 1426 − 1000 = 426 b 2385 − 2000 = 385 c 4520 − 4000 = 520 d 291 + 3000 = 3291 e 160 + 5000 = 5160 f 945 + 8000 = 8945 **5** 419 − 9 = 410 **6** 906 + 40 = 946 **7** 73 + 500 = 573 **8** 491 + 6000 = 6491 **9**

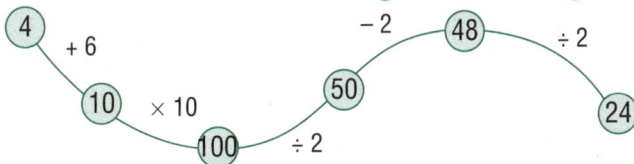

4 + 6 10 × 10 100 ÷ 2 50 − 2 48 ÷ 2 24

Unit 73 Page 49

1 a 717 b 1455 c 1308 d 2735 e 7217 f 8771 **2** a 90 b 26 c 476 d 375 e 762 f 656 **3** a 1207 b 128 c 4301 d 327 e 2263 f 568 **4** a 324 + 479, 803 items b 441 − 279, 162 nails c 872 + 584, 1456 $1 coins d 1424 − 956, 468 strawberries e 235 + 198, 433 jelly beans f 275 + 349, 624 pieces **5** 4388 **6** 3554 **7** 2477 **8** 945 − 489, 456 bricks **9** 1652 + 2476 = 4128

Unit 74 Page 49

1 a 297 b 144 c 440 d 1498 e 1195 f 2472 **2** a 102 b 34 c 99 d 34 e 60 f 35 **3** a 728 b 312 c 126 d 42 e 19 f 17 **4** a 12 × 15, 180 apples b 25 × 35, 875 matches c 5 × 155, 775 sheets of paper d 198 ÷ 6, 33 brochures e 136 ÷ 4, 34 nails f 612 ÷ 12, 51 oranges **5** 2884 **6** 39 **7** 106 **8** 9 × 25, 225 students **9** various, e.g. 200 × 5 = 1000

Unit 75 Page 50

1 a 2 b 1 c 3 d 4, 10 e 6, 8 f 3, 5 **2** a $\frac{2}{5}$ b $\frac{7}{8}$ c $\frac{4}{6}$ d $\frac{3}{10}$ e $\frac{1}{3}$ f $\frac{3}{4}$

3 a one half b four fifths c two sixths d three eighths e two thirds f seven tenths
4 various e.g. a b c d e f

5 5, 8 **6** $\frac{2}{10}$ **7** one sixth **8** sample answer: **9** a three sixths or half b six eighths or three quarters

Unit 76 Page 50

1 a 1, 2 b 1, 4 c 3, 4 d 2, 3 e 4, 6 f 5, 8 **2** a 3 b 5 c $\frac{1}{2}$ d 4 e 10 f $\frac{2}{5}$ **3** a $\frac{1}{4}$ b $\frac{4}{6}$ c $\frac{2}{3}$ d $\frac{7}{10}$ e $\frac{4}{5}$ f $\frac{5}{8}$

4 a $\frac{3}{6}$ (= $\frac{1}{2}$) b $\frac{3}{8}$ c $\frac{1}{3}$ d $\frac{1}{5}$ e $\frac{5}{10}$ (= $\frac{1}{2}$) f $\frac{7}{8}$ **5** 2, 6 **6** $\frac{3}{4}$ **7** $\frac{1}{3}$ **8** $\frac{2}{5}$ **9** yes

Unit 77 Page 51

1 a $\frac{1}{4}$ b $\frac{2}{6}$ c $\frac{4}{6}$ d $\frac{7}{10}$ e $\frac{5}{8}$ f $\frac{1}{3}$ **2** a $\frac{1}{2}$ b $\frac{2}{3}$ c $\frac{3}{4}$ d $\frac{5}{6}$ e $\frac{3}{8}$ f $\frac{4}{5}$

3 a $\frac{6}{7}$ b $\frac{1}{10}$ c $\frac{1}{6}$ d $\frac{5}{8}$ e $\frac{1}{3}$ f $\frac{3}{4}$

4 a $\frac{2}{5}$ of the boxes b $\frac{1}{2}$ of the circle c $\frac{1}{8}$ of the square d $\frac{1}{10}$ of the triangles e $\frac{3}{4}$ of the group f $\frac{5}{8}$ of the block **5** $\frac{3}{6}$

6 **7** **8** **9**

Unit 78 Page 51

1 a $\frac{1}{4}$ b $\frac{3}{8}$ c $\frac{2}{3}$ d $\frac{4}{8}$ e $\frac{4}{6}$ f $\frac{5}{6}$ **2** a b c d e f

3 a $\frac{1}{2}$ b 1 c $\frac{1}{4}$ d $\frac{1}{2}$ e $\frac{1}{3}$ f $\frac{3}{5}$ **4** a b c d e f

5 $\frac{1}{4}$ **6** **7** 1 **8** **9** $\frac{6}{8}$

Unit 79 Page 52

1 a b c d e f

$\frac{1}{4}$ or $\frac{2}{4}$ $\frac{4}{6}$ or $\frac{5}{6}$ $\frac{2}{3}$ or $\frac{1}{3}$ $\frac{4}{8}$ or $\frac{2}{8}$ $\frac{3}{4}$ or $\frac{2}{4}$ $\frac{2}{5}$ or $\frac{3}{5}$

2 a b c d e f

$\frac{1}{4}$ or $\frac{2}{4}$ $\frac{4}{6}$ or $\frac{5}{6}$ $\frac{4}{8}$ or $\frac{2}{8}$ $\frac{2}{3}$ or $\frac{1}{3}$ $\frac{3}{4}$ or $\frac{2}{4}$ $\frac{2}{5}$ or $\frac{3}{5}$

3 a $\frac{1}{4}, \frac{2}{4}, \frac{3}{4}, \frac{4}{4}$ b $\frac{1}{5}, \frac{2}{5}, \frac{3}{5}, \frac{4}{5}$ c $\frac{1}{8}, \frac{2}{8}, \frac{3}{8}, \frac{4}{8}$ d $\frac{2}{6}, \frac{3}{6}, \frac{4}{6}, \frac{6}{6}$ e $\frac{3}{10}, \frac{5}{10}, \frac{7}{10}, \frac{9}{10}$ f $\frac{3}{8}, \frac{5}{8}, \frac{6}{8}, \frac{8}{8}$

4 a $\frac{2}{10}$ or $\frac{9}{10}$ b $\frac{3}{4}$ or $\frac{1}{4}$ c $\frac{4}{5}$ or $\frac{2}{5}$ d $\frac{3}{3}$ or $\frac{1}{3}$ e $\frac{3}{8}$ or $\frac{5}{8}$ f $\frac{4}{6}$ or $\frac{2}{6}$ **5** $\frac{1}{3}$ or $\frac{2}{3}$

6 $\frac{4}{5}$ or $\frac{2}{5}$ **7** $\frac{1}{5}, \frac{3}{5}, \frac{4}{5}, \frac{5}{5}$ **8** $\frac{3}{4}$ or $\frac{1}{4}$ **9** various e.g. $\frac{1}{8}$

Unit 80 Page 52

1 a 3 apples b 2 cakes c 2 plums d 3 pears e 1 egg f 2 berries

2 a b c d e f

3 a 4 triangles b 5 squares c 2 circles d 1 trapezium e 2 rectangles f 4 ovals
4 a 5 points b 6 points c 5 points d 5 points e 10 points f 5 points **5** 3 oranges **6** ⬭⬭⬭⬭⬭⬭⬭ **7** 4 diamonds
8 2 points **9** 15 biscuits left

Unit 81   Page 53

1 a $\frac{1}{2}$ ▦ b $\frac{1}{2}$ ▦ c $\frac{1}{2}$ ⊘ d $\frac{1}{4}$ ▦ e $\frac{1}{4}$ ▦ f $\frac{1}{4}$ ⊘

2 a $\frac{4}{10}$ or $\boxed{\frac{5}{10}}$ b $\frac{1}{4}$ or $\boxed{\frac{3}{4}}$ c $\boxed{\frac{4}{5}}$ or $\frac{2}{5}$ d $\frac{1}{3}$ or $\boxed{\frac{2}{3}}$ e $\boxed{\frac{5}{8}}$ or $\frac{3}{8}$ f $\boxed{\frac{9}{10}}$ or $\frac{7}{10}$ **3** a $\frac{2}{8}$ — $\frac{2}{10}$

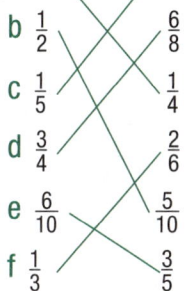

b $\frac{1}{2}$ — $\frac{6}{8}$

c $\frac{1}{5}$ — $\frac{1}{4}$

4 a false b true c false d true e true f false   d $\frac{3}{4}$ — $\frac{2}{6}$

e $\frac{6}{10}$ — $\frac{5}{10}$

5 ▦ **6** $\boxed{\frac{9}{10}}$ or $\frac{3}{10}$ **7** a $\frac{1}{4}$ b $\frac{2}{10}$ c $\frac{2}{3}$ f $\frac{1}{3}$ — $\frac{3}{5}$

$\frac{4}{6}$ $\frac{2}{8}$ $\frac{1}{5}$

8 false **9** a $\frac{3}{5}, \frac{4}{5}, \frac{5}{5}$ b $\frac{3}{8}, \frac{4}{8}, \frac{5}{8}$ c $\frac{7}{10}, \frac{8}{10}, \frac{9}{10}$

Unit 82   Page 53

1 a 15 b 42 c 25 d 69 e 83 f 95 **2** a $\frac{6}{100}$ b $\frac{31}{100}$ c $\frac{48}{100}$ d $\frac{52}{100}$ e $\frac{77}{100}$ f $\frac{90}{100}$

3 a 12 out of 100 b 36 out of 100 c 23 out of 100 d 57 out of 100 e 94 out of 100 f 72 out of 100

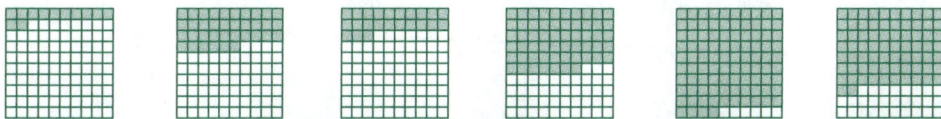

4 a $\frac{5}{100}$ b $\frac{45}{100}$ c $\frac{51}{100}$ d $\frac{63}{100}$ e $\frac{80}{100}$ f $\frac{100}{100}$

5 10 **6** $\frac{70}{100}$ **7** **8** **9** $\frac{32}{100}, \frac{40}{100}, \frac{14}{100}, \frac{3}{100}$ ordering $\frac{3}{100}, \frac{14}{100}, \frac{32}{100}, \frac{40}{100}$

Unit 83   Page 54

1 a $\frac{18}{100}$ b $\frac{44}{100}$ c $\frac{50}{100}$ d $\frac{65}{100}$ e $\frac{88}{100}$ f $\frac{74}{100}$

2 a $\frac{58}{100}$ b $\frac{98}{100}$ c $\frac{62}{100}$ d $\frac{85}{100}$ e $\frac{27}{100}$ f $\frac{35}{100}$

3 a $\frac{17}{100}$ b $\frac{39}{100}$ c $\frac{97}{100}$ d $\frac{60}{100}$ e $\frac{82}{100}$ f $\frac{53}{100}$

4 a

$\frac{10}{100}$	$\frac{11}{100}$	$\frac{12}{100}$	$\frac{13}{100}$	$\frac{14}{100}$	$\frac{15}{100}$	$\frac{16}{100}$	$\frac{17}{100}$

b

$\frac{52}{100}$	$\frac{53}{100}$	$\frac{54}{100}$	$\frac{55}{100}$	$\frac{56}{100}$	$\frac{57}{100}$	$\frac{58}{100}$	$\frac{59}{100}$

c

$\frac{20}{100}$	$\frac{21}{100}$	$\frac{22}{100}$	$\frac{23}{100}$	$\frac{24}{100}$	$\frac{25}{100}$	$\frac{26}{100}$	$\frac{27}{100}$

d

$\frac{81}{100}$	$\frac{82}{100}$	$\frac{83}{100}$	$\frac{84}{100}$	$\frac{85}{100}$	$\frac{86}{100}$	$\frac{87}{100}$	$\frac{88}{100}$

e

$\frac{70}{100}$	$\frac{71}{100}$	$\frac{72}{100}$	$\frac{73}{100}$	$\frac{74}{100}$	$\frac{75}{100}$	$\frac{76}{100}$	$\frac{77}{100}$

f

$\frac{40}{100}$	$\frac{41}{100}$	$\frac{42}{100}$	$\frac{43}{100}$	$\frac{44}{100}$	$\frac{45}{100}$	$\frac{46}{100}$	$\frac{47}{100}$

5 $\frac{78}{100}$ **6** **7** $\frac{91}{100}$ **8**

$\frac{90}{100}$	$\frac{91}{100}$	$\frac{92}{100}$	$\frac{93}{100}$	$\frac{94}{100}$	$\frac{95}{100}$	$\frac{96}{100}$	$\frac{97}{100}$

9 $\frac{13}{100}, \frac{44}{100}$

Unit 84   Page 54

1 a 1 tenth b 3 tenths c 9 tenths d 4 tenths e 7 tenths f 6 tenths
2 a $\frac{2}{10}$ b $\frac{5}{10}$ c $\frac{6}{10}$ d $\frac{8}{10}$ e $\frac{4}{10}$ f $\frac{1}{10}$

3 a 0.3 b 0.7 c 0.9 d 0.4 e 0.6 f 0.2   **4** a 0.1 b 0.5 c 0.8 d 0.3 e 0.9 f 0.4   **5**   **6** $\frac{7}{10}$ **7** 0.5   **8** 0.7

9

Unit 85   Page 55

1 a 0.5 b 0.9 c 0.2 d 0.7 e 0.3 f 0.6   **2** a 0.1 b 0.4 c 0.8 d 0.3 e 0.6 f 0.9

3 a b c d e f

4 a $\frac{6}{10}$ b $\frac{3}{10}$ c $\frac{8}{10}$ d $1\frac{5}{10}$ e $1\frac{2}{10}$ f $2\frac{4}{10}$ **5** 0.4   **6** 1.7   **7** **8** $\frac{7}{10}$

9 a 0.8, 1.0, 1.2 b $\frac{44}{100}, \frac{48}{100}, \frac{52}{100}$ c $\frac{80}{100}, \frac{85}{100}, \frac{90}{100}$

Unit 86   Page 55

1 a 0.6 b 0.7 c 0.9 d 1.0 e 1.2 f 1.5   **2** a 0.8 b 0.7 c 0.5 d 0.1 e 0.4 f 0   **3** a 0.6 b 0.4 c 0.1 d 0 e 0.6 f 1.1
4 a 1.1 b 1.8 c 1.6 d 1.5 e 1.1 f 2.0   **5** 0.9   **6** 0.2   **7** 0.6, 0.3   **8** 1.0, 1.4   **9** a 0.7 b 0.8

Unit 87   Page 56

1 a 0.02 b 0.41 c 0.96 d 0.24 e 0.75 f 0.68
2 a 0.93 b 0.16 c 0.48 d 0.89 e 0.67 f 0.08

3 a 0.73

7	tenths	3	hundredths

b 0.11

1	tenths	1	hundredths

c 0.86

8	tenths	6	hundredths

d 0.43

4	tenths	3	hundredths

e 0.22

2	tenths	2	hundredths

f 0.38

3	tenths	8	hundredths

4 a 0.62 b 0.29 c 0.15 d 0.75 e 0.41 f 0.36   **5** 0.28   **6**   **7**

8	tenths	4	hundredths

8 0.83

9 various, e.g.

1 a 0.4 b 0.6 c 0.8 d 0.37 e 0.61 f 0.87 **2** a 1.1 b 2.1 c 3.3 d 2.71 e 1.33 f 1.54 **3** a 0.2 b 0.5 c 0.9 d 0.21 e 0.59 f 0.84

4 a $\frac{4}{10}$, $\frac{6}{10}$, $\frac{9}{10}$ — 0.6, 0.9, 0.4 (crossed) b $\frac{3}{10}$, $\frac{2}{10}$, $\frac{8}{10}$ — 0.8, 0.3, 0.2 (crossed) c $\frac{61}{100}$, $\frac{99}{100}$, $\frac{55}{100}$ — 0.99, 0.55, 0.61 (crossed) d $\frac{92}{100}$, $\frac{30}{100}$, $\frac{81}{100}$ — 0.30, 0.92, 0.81 e $1\frac{9}{100}$, $2\frac{28}{100}$, $2\frac{66}{100}$ — 2.66, 1.09, 2.28 f $1\frac{70}{100}$, $1\frac{43}{100}$, $1\frac{97}{100}$ — 1.97, 1.70, 1.43

5 0.85 **6** 1.34 **7** 0.51 **8** $\frac{93}{100}$, $\frac{26}{100}$, $1\frac{76}{100}$ — 0.26, 1.76, 0.93 (crossed)

9 0.7, 0.3, 0.5, 0.2, 0.9 ordering: 0.2, 0.3, 0.5, 0.7, 0.9 or $\frac{2}{10}$, $\frac{3}{10}$, $\frac{5}{10}$, $\frac{7}{10}$, $\frac{9}{10}$

1 a $\frac{6}{10}$ b $\frac{9}{10}$ c $\frac{2}{10}$ d $\frac{8}{10}$ e $\frac{1}{10}$ f $\frac{5}{10}$ **2** a $\frac{81}{100}$ b $\frac{69}{100}$ c $\frac{14}{100}$ d $\frac{48}{100}$ e $\frac{72}{100}$ f $\frac{57}{100}$ **3** a 0.3 b 0.4 c 0.7 d 0.23 e 0.74

0.62 **4** a 0.2, 0.3, 0.4 b 0.6, 0.8, 0.9 c 0.3, 0.4, 0.5 d 0.1, 0.3, 0.9 e 1.2, 1.6, 1.7 f 1.5, 1.9, 2.2 **5** $\frac{7}{10}$

6 $\frac{58}{100}$ **7** 0.89 **8** 1.6, 1.9, 2.7 **9** a D b 0.11, 0.19, 0.5, 1.9

1 a true b false c false d true e false f true **2** a < b > c > d > e < f > **3** a 3 b 7 c 6 d 4 e 8 f 1

4 a < b > c > d < e < f < **5** false **6** > **7** 3 **8** > **9**

0 — $\frac{1}{10}$ — $\frac{1}{5}$ — $\frac{3}{10}$ — $\frac{2}{5}$ — $\frac{1}{2}$ — $\frac{3}{5}$ — $\frac{7}{10}$ — 1

1 a 0.5 b 0.8 c 0.3 d 0.8 e 0.9 f 0.9 **2** a 1.9 b 4.7 c 3.8 d 3.75 e 5.83 f 4.95 **3** a 2.73 b 0.68 c 3.19 d 7.88 e 3.98 f 5.88

4 a 3.67 b 3.97 c 9.49 d 3.99 e 9.28 f 9.89 **5** 0.8 **6** 4.69 **7** 3.99 **8** 3.79 **9** 1.55 + 1.80 + 0.80 = 4.15, $4.15

1 a 0.4 b 0.2 c 0.1 d 0.3 e 0.4 f 0.5 **2** a 1.3 b 1.7 c 6.2 d 8.13 e 4.21 f 2.22 **3** a 0.61 b 0.13 c 2.13 d 3.21 e 3.33 f 1.42

4 a 1.35 b 1.13 c 3.12 d 11.21 e 2.74 f 0.34 **5** 0.1 **6** 3.61 **7** 2.13 **8** 6.43 **9** $5.75 + $1.20 = $6.95, change is $3.05

1 a 7.5 b 8.1 c 7.4 d 8.84 e 8.42 f 4.33 **2** a 2.8 b 2.9 c 5.4 d 5.18 e 2.86 f 4.29 **3** a 5.91 b 2.16 c 9.52 d 0.63

6.08 f 1.26 **4** a 3.90 m b 0.26 m c 4.04 L d $1.50 e 7.58 km f 1.27 m **5** 8.36 **6** 5.18 **7** 6.08 **8** 0.54 L

9 e.g. Add 1 and 0.06; 9.54 from 10.6

1 a B b E c A d D e more f 100% **2** a 10% b 25% c 12% d 95% e 20% f 30% **3** a fifty percent b seventy-five percent

c seventeen percent d two percent e ninety-eight percent f sixty percent **4** a < b > c < d > e > f < **5** A **6** 45%

7 thirty-five percent **8** > **9** various

1 a 2 b 4 c 10 d 20 e 40 f 1 **2** a $1, 20c, 20c, 5c b $1, 20c, 5c c $1, 50c, 20c, 20c, 5c d $2, 20c, 5c e $1, 50c

$1, 50c, 20c, 10c, 5c **3** a 20c, 50c b 10c, 50c, $2 c 5c, 10c, 50c d 5c, $2 e 5c, $1 f 5c, 50c

4 e.g.

		$2	$1	50c	20c	10c	5c
a	Jane	2	1		1		1
b	William	1	3		1		1
c	Yana	2	1			2	1
d	Violet		5		1		1
e	Trent		5			2	1
f	Jay				10	1	1

5 5 **6** $2, 50c, 20c, 20c, 5c **7** 5c, 20c, $1

8 e.g.

		$2	$1	50c	20c	10c	5c
a	Peter	1		1	2		1
b	Robert		2		4	1	1

9 $5.25 + $2.45 + $0.40 = $8.10 need $5, $2, $1, 10c

Unit 96   Page 60

1 a 20 b 5 c 50 d 10 e 100 f 2 **2** a $50, $20, $5 b $50, $20, $20, $2, $1 c $20, $10, $5, $2 d $100, $5, $2, $1
e $100, $50, $10, $5, $2, $2 f $100, $50, $20, $20, $5, $2, $2 **3** a $1, $2 b $2, $5, $10 c $2, $20, $50 d $1, $2, $5, $50
e $5, $20, $20 f $2, $2, $10, $20 **4** a $95 b $20 c $77 d $54 e $128 f $9 **5** 10 **6** $100, $20, $20, $5, $1
7 $2, $10, $50 **8** $121 **9** e.g. $20 + $20 + $20 or $50 + $10 or $50 + $5 + $5

Unit 97   Page 61

1 a $3.80 b $5.35 c $8.09 d $5.18 e $5.45 f $3.19 **2** a $4.13 b $3.28 c $4.41 d $3.15 e $5.35 f $1.50 **3** a $1.95
b $4.15 c $4.15 d $3.15 e $4.50 f $3.75 **4** a $2.00 b 40c c $1.70 d $4.05 e $1.80 f $2.40 **5** $3.80 **6** $2.53
7 $5.25 **8** $1.35 **9** $24.95 + $21.65 − $30.00 = $16.60 (to pay)

Unit 98   Page 61

1 a $10.00 b $3.00 c $6.00 d 15c e $20.00 f 80c **2** a $2.00 b $2.00 c 10c d 10c e $2.00 f 30c **3** a 60c b $2.00
c 50c d $6.00 e 80c f 60c **4** a 2 b 5 c 10 d 2 e 1 f 10 **5** $15.00 **6** $2.00 **7** $6.00 **8** 5 oranges
9 $30 × 5 is approximately $150, actual is $149.75

Unit 99   Page 62

1 a $1.95 is closest to $1.00 or ($2.00) or $19.00? b $5.25 is closest to ($5.00) or $6.00 or $25.00?
c $10.85 is closest to $2.00 or $9.00 or ($11.00?) d $11.95 is closest to $10.00 or $11.00 or ($12.00?)
e $8.15 is closest to ($8.00) or $9.00 or $15.00? f $19.10 is closest to $18.00 or ($19.00) or $20.00?
2 a $6.00 b $6.00 c $10.00 d $3.00 e $11.00 f $19.00 **3** a 90c b 60c c 30c d 40c e 90c f 60c
4 a $9.00 b $12.00 c $12.00 d $17.00 e $20.00 f $16.00
5 $3.45 is closest to ($3.00) or $4.00 or $5.00? **6** $9.00 **7** 80c **8** $14.00 **9** $11.79, $11.80

Unit 100   Page 62

1 a $6.00 b 4, $24.00 c 3, $9.00 d $6.00, $30.00 e $3.00, $27.00 f $4.00, $16.00 **2** a $9.00 b $10.00 c $12.00 d $12.00
e $7.00 f $20.00 **3** a $2.00 b $10.00, $4.00 c $4.00, $1.00 d $2.00, $3.00 e $20.00, $3.00 f $11.00, $9.00 **4** a $12.00
b $9.00 c $16.00 d $16.00 e $9.00 f $5.00 **5** $2.00, $8.00 **6** $12.00 **7** $6.00, $4.00 **8** $20.00
9 $35.00 + $7.00 + $4.00 + $2.00 is approximately $48.00

Unit 101   Page 63

1 a b c d e f **2** a b c d e f

3 c, e **4** a b c d e f

5 **6** **7** no **8** **9**

Unit 102   Page 63

1 a square b triangle c circle d rhombus e hexagon f rectangle **2** various: e.g. a b c d e f

3 a 2 opposite sides parallel b 4 equal angles (or 2 sets of equal sides) c 4 equal sides
d curved, at equal distance from the centre e 3 sides with 2 equal f 8 equal sides

4 a 2 blocks   b 4 blocks   c 5 blocks

d 3 blocks   e 4 blocks   f 3 blocks

5 square **6** **7** 3 equal sides **8** 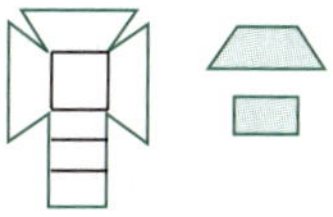 **9** various

Unit 103 Page 64

1 a b c d e f **2** a C, F b A, B, D, E, J c A, C, G, H, I, K d H e K f G

3 a 4 b 4 c 3 d 6 e 4 f 4

4 various, e.g. a b c d e f **5** 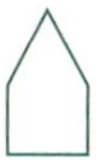 **6** A, B and D **7** 4 **8** **9** 3

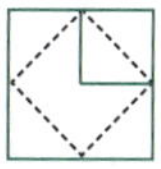

Unit 104 Page 64

1 a D b C c B d F e H f E **2** 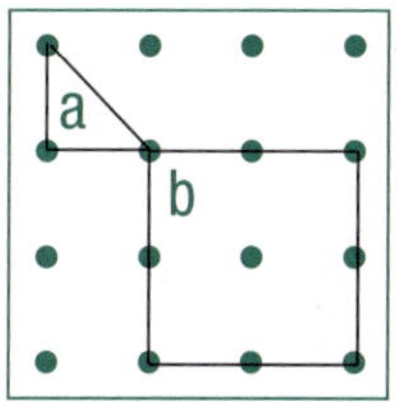 b 3 c 3 e 4 f 4 **3** various e.g. a b c
d e f

4 a triangle b pentagon c circle d square e semicircle f rectangle **5** A **6** 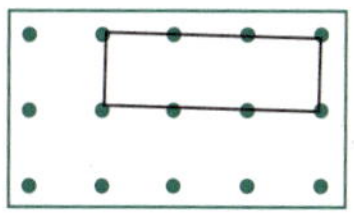
7 sample: **8** hexagon **9** various e.g. a shape with 4 equal sides

Unit 105 Page 65

1 a 4, 4 b 5, 5 c 6, 6 d 3, 3 e 5, 5 f 8, 8 **2** a C, J b E, H c D, I d F, G e A, L f B, K
3 a irregular pentagon b square c triangle d octagon e regular hexagon f regular pentagon
4 a 10 b 24 c 26 d 35 e 80 f 33 **5** 8, 8 **6** A, E **7** 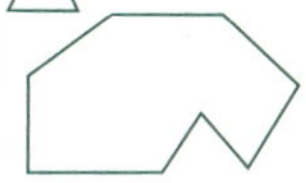 **8** 34 **9** 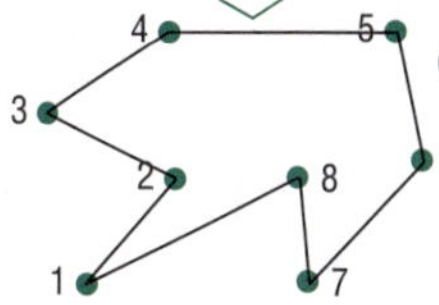 octagon

Unit 106 Page 65

1 a oval b trapezium c hexagon d triangle e rectangle f parallelogram **2** a 4 b 8 c 3 d 4 e 5 f 4 **3** b, e **4** a 8 b 20
c 20 d 21 e 13 f 24 **5** parallelogram **6** 6 **7** B, C **8** 24 **9** e.g.

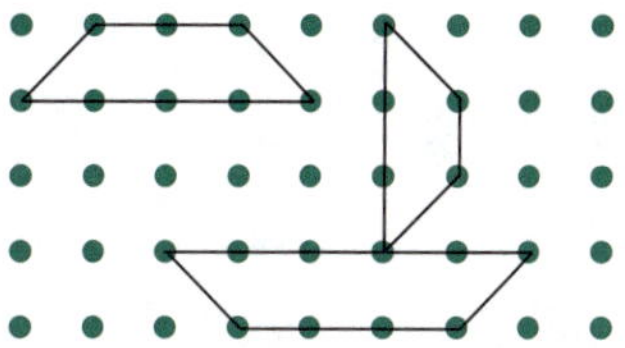

Unit 107 Page 66

1 a triangle b square c rectangle d triangle e hexagon f pentagon **2** a yes b no c no d yes e no f no **3** a triangle
b triangle c triangle d triangle e triangle f triangle **4** a b c d e f

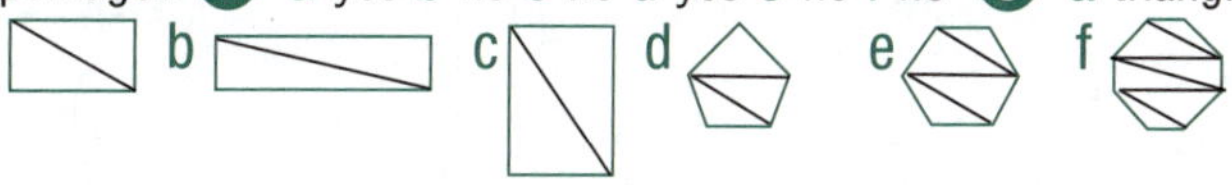

5 rectangle **6** no **7** triangle **8** 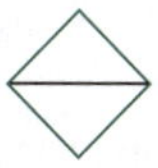 **9** various

Unit 108 Page 66

1 a irregular b irregular c irregular d regular e irregular f regular

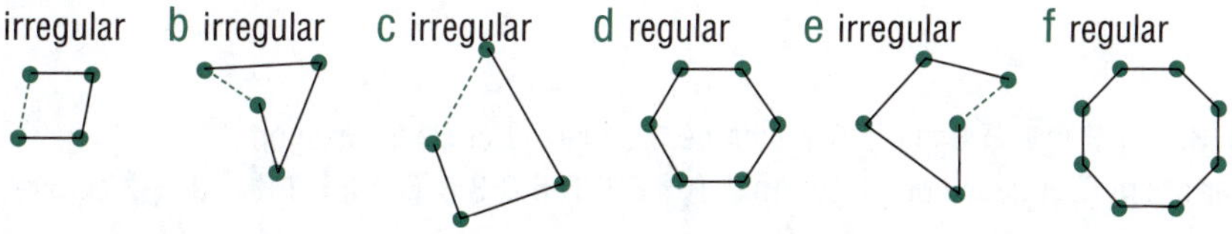

2 a triangle b square c pentagon d octagon e hexagon f square **3** a triangle b quadrilateral c pentagon d hexagon
e quadrilateral f octagon **4** a ⬚ b ⬡ c ⬡ d ⬡ e △ f ⬟ **5** ▱ irregular

6 triangle **7** pentagon **8** ⬠ **9** various

Unit 109 Page 67
1 a D b C c B d no e no f larger **2** a smaller b larger c smaller d larger e smaller f larger **3** a B b C c D d no e yes f A
4 a D b B c A and C d 15 e 25 f 30 **5** C and E **6** smaller **7** B **8** B **9** smallest – largest: D, A, B, E, C

Unit 110 Page 67
1 a 12 b 16 c 8 d 16 e 4 f 12 **2** a smaller b larger c smaller d larger e larger f smaller **3** a smaller b larger c smaller
d larger e larger f smaller **4** a 5 b 3 c 2 d 1 e 6 f 4 **5** 20 **6** larger **7** smaller **8** 2, 3, 1 **9** various

Unit 111 Page 68
1 b, d, f **2** c, d, e **3** a, f **4** For some parts of this question different answers would be acceptable. a A, B. C, D b A and B
c C and E d D and K e F and G f M and N **5** no **6** yes **7** no **8** A and D **9** various

Unit 112 Page 68
1 a 0 b 1 c 3 d 1 e 1 f 0 **2** b, d

3 a K b E c A d Z e H f M

4 a ⬜ b △ c ⬡ d ◠ e ▱ f ▱

5 3 **6** yes **7** ⬚ **8** ⬠ no **9** ▱

Unit 113 Page 69
1 a 2 b 1 c 3 d 1 e 0 f 1
2 a b c d e f

3 a △ b ▭ c trapezoid d ◠ e △ f ◇

4 a b Z c || d 5 e 6 f 3

5 1 **6** no **7** no **8** F **9** Perpendicular lines meet at right angles, these two lines do not.

Unit 114 Page 69
1 a A, I b B c G d A, H, I, J e C, F, G f A, B, H, I, J **2** a triangle b rectangle c square d circle e hexagon
f triangle **3** a sphere b cylinder c triangular prism d cube e cone f pyramid **4** a 6 b 6 c 3 d 6 e 5 f 2 **5** J **6** square
7 cylinder **8** 7 **9** cone or hemisphere

Unit 115 Page 70

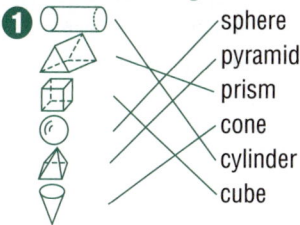

1 sphere / pyramid / prism / cone / cylinder / cube

2 a hemisphere and cone b pyramid and cube c 2 triangular prisms d cylinder and cone e 2 cylinders and rectangular prism f 2 triangular prisms

3 a □ b □ c □ d △ e △ f ○

4 a 2 b 1 c 3 d 0 e 0 f 3 **5** rectangular prism / triangular prism

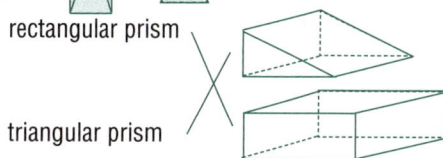

6 cylinder and cone **7** □ **8** 0 **9** various

Unit 116 Page 70

1 a rectangle and square b triangle and rectangle c square d square and triangle e triangle f hexagon and rectangle

2 a B b B c D d C A d B e D f E **3** a square b circle c circle d triangle e rectangle f circle

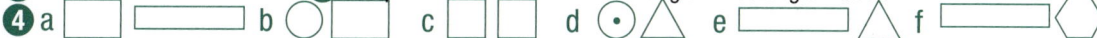

4 a □ b ○ □ c □ □ d · △ e □ △ f □ ○

5 rectangle **6** C, cylinder **7** hexagon **8** □ ⬠ **9** top / front / side

Unit 117 Page 71

1 a triangle and rectangle b squares c pentagon and rectangle d square and rectangle e rectangle f octagon and rectangle

2 a prism b neither c prism d cylinder e neither f prism **3** a 6 b 6 c 6 d 7 e 5 f 6 **4** a 12 b 24 c 2 d 9 e 12 f 12

5 rectangle **6** neither **7** 8 **8** 15 **9**

Prism	Shape of each face				
△	△	△	□	□	□

Unit 118 Page 71

1 b, d, and e **2** a 6 b 5 c 4 d 7 e 5 f 4 **3** a △ □ b □ △ c △ d □ △ e ◇ △ f ⬡ △

4 a 6 b 10 c 8 d 16 e 8 f 12 **5** no **6** 5 **7** △ **8** 8 **9** square base meeting at a point, has 5 faces and 8 edges

Unit 119 Page 72

1 a 6 b 6 c 5 d 3 e 2 f 6 **2** a and c **3** a 4 b 8 c 6 d 3 e 12 f 4

4 a □ □ b □ □ c ○ □ d ○ ▽ e □ □ f □ □

5 7 **6** yes **7** 6 **8** □ □ **9** various: it would be similar to that for a cube:

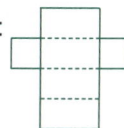

Unit 120 Page 72

1 a reflection b rotation c translation d rotation e reflection f translation

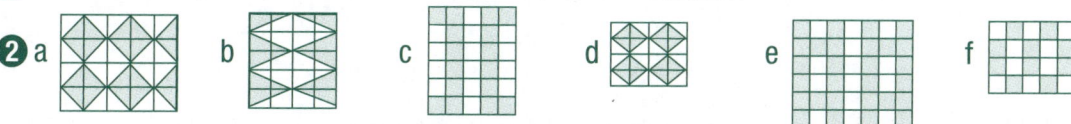

2 a b c d e f

3 a yes b yes c yes d yes e no f yes

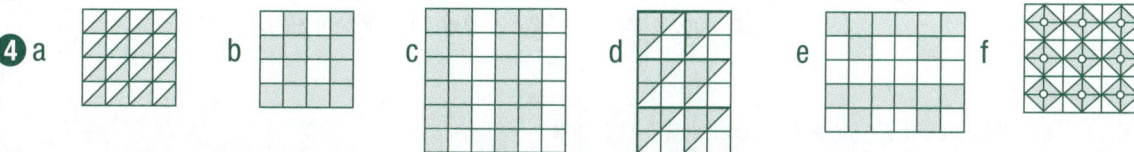

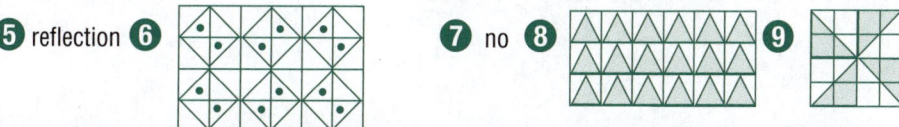

4 a b c d e f

5 reflection **6** **7** no **8** **9**

Unit 121   Page 73

1 a Eddy b Morgan c Veronica d top row left e bottom row in the middle f middle row, middle position **2** sample of answers:
a up from A to F, turn right at G, past C, turn left into B b up from C, turn right, continue to G, turn right c E turn right to G turn right
to F d right from F to G, turn right, past C, turn left into B e up from C, turn right, past G, turn left into E f D through G to F
3 a J b L c D d move 1 to right and 1 back e move 1 forward, 1 to left, 1 diagonally forward to the left f move 2 to left, 2 back
4 e.g.

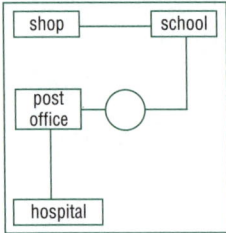

```
shop          school
post
office    ◯
hospital
```

5 Arthur   **6** up, turn right, through G, turn left into E   **7** move 2 to the right, 1 diagonally backwards to right, 1 to the right
8 see 4.   **9** various, e.g. front door, past bedroom 3 and 2, turn right, through laundry and kitchen to back door

Unit 122   Page 73

1 a 🍦 b 🧁 c 🎂 d bottom left e middle left f top centre **2** a top cupboard second from left b bottom far right
c bottom far left d trays e cups f bottles **3** a cards b train c drum d dolls e ball f truck **4** a bottom row right
b middle row second from the left c middle row right d top row middle e bottom row left f middle row left **5** top right
6 top row far left **7** teddy **8** top row right **9** various

Unit 123   Page 74

1 a north b west c south d snake e cat f lion **2** a Northern Territory b Tasmania c Western Australia d Queensland
e South Australia or Northern Territory f Victoria or New South Wales **3** a Diary Mountain b Pencil Point c Calculator Cove
d north e west f west **4** a east b west c north d north e west f south **5** south **6** Victoria
7 Ruler Pier **8** north **9**

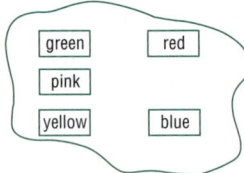

```
green      red
pink
yellow     blue
```

Unit 124   Page 74

1 a 5 b 3 c 2 d 2 e 2 f 3 **2** [grid] **3** a Adam b Jo c Bob d Tia e corner of House Rd and Book Rd
f Bob or Jo **4** a Beach Town b Seagull River c train d no e train
f yes **5** 1 **6** see Q 2 **7** Bike Lane **8** by road
9 [graph with points on A–D axis and 1–4 axis]

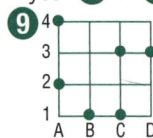

Unit 125   Page 75

1 a C b E c C d D e D f B **2** various for example: a 1 up, 3 right, 4 up b 4 up, 3 right, 1 up c 4 up, 2 left, 1 up d 1 left, 5 up
e 3 up, 3 left, 2 up f 2 up, 2 right, 3 up **3** a △ b 🌳 c • d # e D f ☺ **4** a C2 b F2 c F4 d C3 e B1 f E5 **5** E
6 3 up, 2 left, 2 up **7** @ **8** A4 **9** sample: B1 → B2 → F2 → F5

Unit 126   Page 75

1 a 5 o'clock b 9 o'clock c 1 o'clock d 7 o'clock e 11 o'clock f 12 o'clock
2 a 2 o'clock   b 10 o'clock   c 4 o'clock   d 8 o'clock   e 6 o'clock   f 3 o'clock

[six clock faces]

3 a half past 10 b half past 6 c half past 2 d half past 9 e half past 4 f half past 7

4 a half past 2   b half past 3   c half past 8   d half past 5   e half past 1   f half past 12

5 6 o'clock   **6**   **7** half past 11   **8**   **9** 60 minutes

Unit 127   Page 76

1 a quarter past 6 b quarter to 5 c quarter past 3 d quarter to 10 e quarter past 7 f quarter to 1

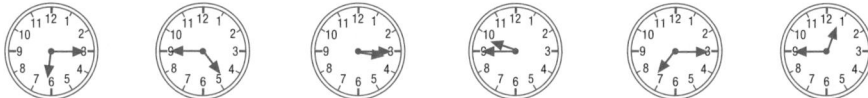

2 a quarter to 12 b quarter past 4 c quarter to 2 d quarter past 9 e quarter to 7 f quarter past 1

3 a quarter to 4   b 5 o'clock   c quarter past 2 d half past 9   e quarter to 11 f quarter past 10

4 a 3 o'clock b quarter past 5 c half past 12 d quarter to 8 e half past 6 f 2 o'clock

5   **6** quarter past 8 **7**   **8** half past 11 **9** $1\frac{3}{4}$ hours

Unit 128   Page 76

1 a 5 minutes b 25 minutes c 45 minutes d 55 minutes e 30 minutes f 50 minutes **2** a 10 minutes b 20 minutes c 10 minutes d 20 minutes e 10 minutes f 40 minutes **3** a 10, 4 b 20, 2 c 25, 9 d 5, 7 e 20, 8 f 10, 1

4 a 5 past 7   b 25 past 4   c 10 past 2   d 5 past 3   e 20 past 8   f 10 past 12

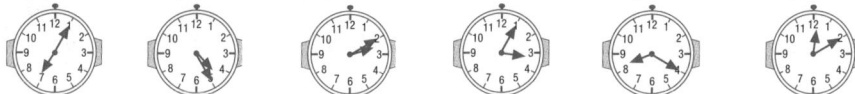

5 15 minutes **6** 20 minutes **7** 5, 6 **8**   **9** 40, 3   50, 7
20, 4   10, 8

Unit 129   Page 77

1 a 6:16 b 9:22 c 10:55 d 2:35 e 4:03 f 12:45 **2** a 7:36 b 12:03 c 4:00 d 11:14 e 8:42 f 9:25
3 a eighteen minutes past six b twenty-one minutes past three c one minute to nine d thirty-two past one e six minutes past five f quarter to one **4** a 5, 8 b 9, 3 c 4, 2 d 5, 5 e 1, 10 f 7, 12 **5** 8:43 **6** 5:29 **7** forty-nine minutes past eleven **8** 7, 6
9 maths, art, science, reading

Unit 130   Page 77

1 a 36 b 21 c 15 d 30 e 6 f 55 **2** a 3:36 b 5:42 c 7:56 d 8:27 e 11:13 f 12:06 **3** a forty-nine minutes past two b fifty-eight minutes past nine c twenty-three minutes past four d ten sixteen e six minutes past seven f thirty-four minutes past eleven **4** a 1:18 b 3:28 c 5:40 d 6:56 e 8:09 f 12:51 **5** 29 **6** 1:19 **7** thirty-two minutes past six **8** 9:31 **9** 8 + 15 = 23, 23 minutes

Unit 131   Page 78

1 a 2:10 b 5:25 c 12:05 d 8:20 e 10:15 f 4:40 **2** a 35, 9:35 b 55, 7:55 c 5, 1:05 d 40, 11:40 e 40, 3:40 f 50, 6:50
3 a half past 11   b quarter to 5   c quarter past 3 d 10 minutes past 10 e 7 o'clock   f 20 minutes past 1

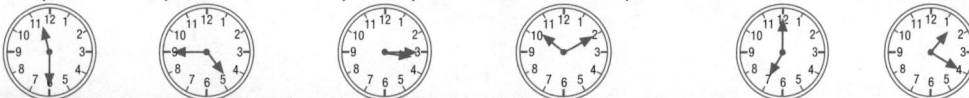

4 a forty-five minutes past eleven b thirty minutes past nine c two o'clock d thirty-six minutes past eight e nine minutes past six f fifty-five minutes past four **5** 6:20 **6** 25, 11:25 **7** **8** six o'clock **9** 45 minutes

Unit 132   Page 78

1 a 7 days b 14 days c 31 days d 30 days e 31 days f 30 days **2** a Monday b Saturday c Thursday d Tuesday e Sunday f Friday
3 a 6 days b 5 days c 4 days d 6 days e 3 days f 8 days **4** a 31 days b Thursday c Sunday d 4th e 29th f 4 **5** 30 days
6 Thursday **7** 9 days **8** Saturday **9** Monday

Unit 133   Page 79

1 a 9:30 b 10:00 c 10:30 d 30 minutes e 18 minutes f 15 minutes
2

3 a 7:15 b 5 minutes c 30 minutes d yes e 30 minutes f 7:00

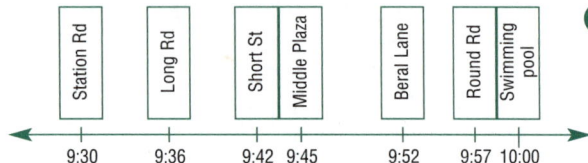

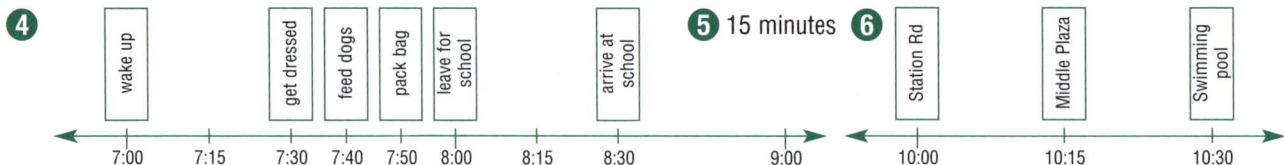

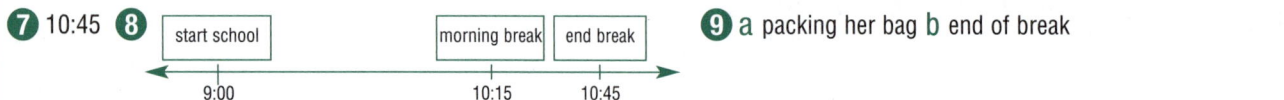

4

5 15 minutes **6**

7 10:45 **8**

9 a packing her bag b end of break

Unit 134   Page 79

1 a 2 b 8 c 5 d 7 e 1 f 4 **2** a 3 cm b 6 cm c 1 cm d 8 cm e 7 cm f 4 cm **3** a 3 cm b 6 cm c 1 cm d 8 cm e 7 cm f 4 cm
4 a 2 cm _____ b 5 cm _____
c 7 cm _____ d 3 cm _____

e 6 cm _____ f 4 cm _____ **5** 3 cm **6** 4 cm **7** 4 cm
8 1 cm _____ **9** 5 cm, 5 cm, 1 cm, 1 cm

Unit 135   Page 80

1 a 2 cm, 2 cm, 2 cm, 2 cm b 3 cm, 3 cm, 2 cm, 2 cm c 2 cm, 2 cm, 2 cm d 2 cm, 2 cm, 3 cm, 3 cm
e 2 cm, 2 cm, 2 cm, 2 cm f 1 cm, 2 cm, 2 cm
2 a 5 cm
b 6 cm
c 3 cm
d 1 cm
e 7 cm
f 4 cm

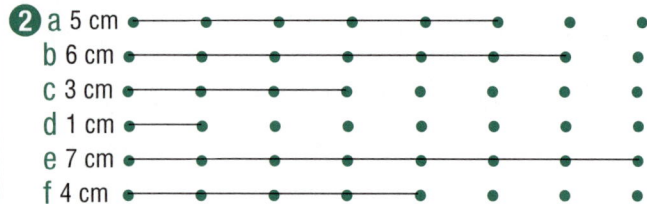

3 a 1 m 15 cm b 7 m 2 cm c 15 m 50 cm d 2 m 30 cm e 5 m 89 cm f 10 m 90 cm
4 a centimetres b centimetres c metres d centimetres e centimetres f metres **5** 1 cm, 1 cm, 1 cm, 1 cm, 1 cm, 1 cm
6 _____ **7** 3 m 29 cm **8** centimetres **9** e.g. pencil, cake, purse

Unit 136   Page 80

1 a 115 cm b 182 cm c 250 cm d 395 cm e 211 cm f 107 cm **2** a 1 m 35 cm b 2 m 90 cm c 3 m 5 cm d 2 m 36 cm
e 1 m 42 cm f 3 m 36 cm **3** a metres b centimetres c centimetres d centimetres e metres f centimetres **4** a scissors
b die, thumb tack, counter c 6 cm d pen e 2 cm f 7 cm **5** 219 cm **6** 1 m 72 cm **7** centimetres **8** die, thumb tack, counter
9 with a piece of string

Unit 137 Page 81

1 a 9 mm b 6 mm c 13 mm d 33 mm e 21 mm f 25 mm **2** a 12 mm b 28 mm c 35 mm d 83 mm e 39 mm f 47 mm
3 a 1 cm 4 mm b 2 cm 6 mm c 3 cm 9 mm d 1 cm 9 mm e 4 cm 2 mm f 5 cm 1 mm **4** **5** 17 mm **6** 23 mm
7 5 cm 2 mm **8** •——•——•——• • • • • **9** a 10 b 100

Unit 138 Page 81

1 a 1 m 23 cm b 1 m 69 cm c 3 m 72 cm d 1 m 78 cm e 2 m 56 cm f 3 m 14 cm **2** a 2.06 m b 3.42 m c 6.72 m d 1.58 m
e 2.97 m f 3.25 m **3** a 2.7 cm b 240 cm c 4.9 cm d 125 cm e 8.5 cm f 375 cm **4** a 5.6 cm b 2.4 cm c 1.8 cm d 3.3 cm
e 1.2 cm f 4.6 cm **5** 1 m 6 cm **6** 3.75 m **7** 119 cm **8** 6.8 cm **9** a m b mm c cm

Unit 139 Page 82

1 a 4 cm b 6 cm c 6 cm d 8 cm e 8 cm f 10 cm **2** a 4 cm b 6 cm c 6 cm d 8 cm e 8 cm f 10 cm
3 a 4 cm b 8 cm c 6 cm d 10 cm e 6 cm f 5 cm
4 a b c d e f

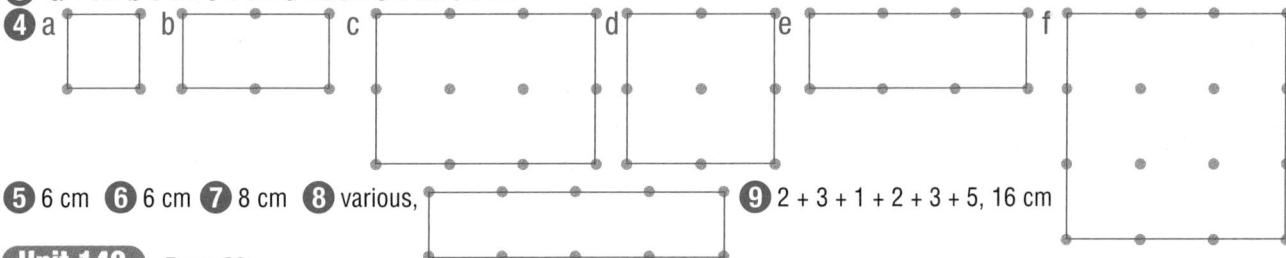

5 6 cm **6** 6 cm **7** 8 cm **8** various, **9** 2 + 3 + 1 + 2 + 3 + 5, 16 cm

Unit 140 Page 82

1 a 3 b 6 c 6 d 5 e 8 f 6 **2** a 16 b 3.5 c 16 d 12 e 8 f 12 **3** a 20 cm b 8 cm c 13 cm d 6 cm e 8 cm f 7 cm
4 a b c d e f

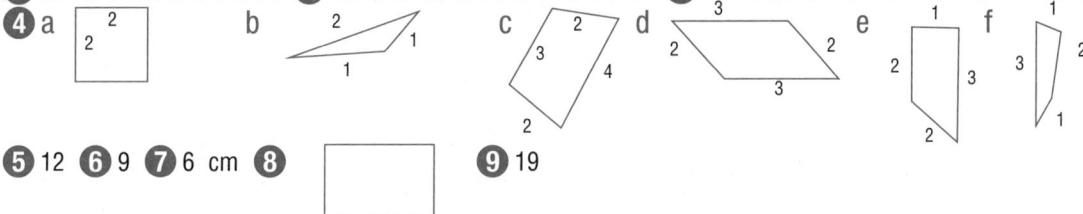

5 12 **6** 9 **7** 6 cm **8** **9** 19

Unit 141 Page 83

1 a 4 b 2 c 4 d 6 e 5 f 7 **2** a 4 b 2 c 4 d 6 e 5 f 7 **3** a B b F c A and C d smaller e smaller f 2
4 a book or crayon b football field or table c T-shirt or tent d pizza or doughnut e 5c coin or 50c coin f poster or credit card
5 7 **6** 10 **7** smaller **8** a pillowcase or a blanket **9** various

Unit 142 Page 83

1 a 4 squares b 3 squares c 4 squares d 5 squares e 6 squares f 6 squares
2 a calculator b sports oval c school yard d basketball court e a pancake f a mobile phone **3** a 3 m² b 5 m² c 9 m² d 16 m²
e 100 m² f 50 m² **4** a m² b cm² c m² d cm² e cm² f m² **5** 6 squares **6** yes **7** 20 m² **8** m² **9** various

Unit 143 Page 84

1 a lighter b heavier c lighter d heavier e lighter f heavier **2** a more b less c more d less e less f more
3 a a pair of scissors b a chair c a car tyre d a mushroom e a bag of potatoes f a dog
4 a b c d e f **5** lighter **6** more **7** yes **8** yes **9** various

Unit 144 Page 84

1 a 5 kg b 1 kg c 8 kg d 3 kg e 4 kg f 1 kg **2** a 5 kg b 9 kg c 16 kg d 2 kg e 18 kg f 10 kg **3** a 16 kg b 3 kg c 17 kg
d 22 kg e 12 kg f 2 kg **4** a 1 b 4 c 3 d 2 e 12 f 1 **5** 5 kg **6** 13 kg **7** 11 kg **8** 4 **9** 36 kg

Unit 145 Page 85

1 a 60 g b 45 g c 300 g d 150 g e 10 g f 200 g **2** a a feather b a bird c a grain of rice d a truck e a basketball
f a ball of cotton wool **3** a 600 g b 70 g c 500 g d 520 g e 350 g f 300 g **4** a 50 g, 100 g, 200 g b 200 g, 500 g, 750 g
c 300 g, 600 g, 750 g d 50 g, 200 g, 2 kg e 2 kg, 5 kg, 10 kg f 300 g, 400 g, 450 g **5** 25 g **6** yes **7** 400 g **8** 500 g, 1 kg, 3 kg
9 1050 g or 1.05 kg

Unit 146 Page 85

1 a B b B b A c B d C e B f B **2** a D b A c 5 d C and E e F f A **3** a bigger b 1 c D d Tom's e D f A **4** a false b false
c true d true e false f true **5** B **6** yes **7** A **8** false **9** e.g. petrol, milk

Unit 147 Page 86

1 a 3 L b 10 L c 15 L d 24 L e 8 L f 13 L **2** a B b A c D d C D B e E A f 5 L **3** a a bucket b medicine container c sink
d teaspoon e pool f small teacup **4** a 5 L b 2 L c A d 3 L e B f 7 L **5** 3 L **6** A **7** yes **8** 2 L **9** e.g. tea cup, egg cup

Unit 148 Page 86

1 a 6 L b 11 L c 19 L d 250 mL e 400 mL f 700 mL **2** a 1000 mL b 2000 mL c 3000 mL d 5000 mL e 7000 mL
f 4000 mL **3** a 800 mL b 300 mL c 200 mL d 100 mL e 200 mL f 800 mL **4** a an eggcup b a swimming pool
c a small jam jar d a bath e a medicine cup f a water tank **5** 80 mL **6** 9000 mL **7** 450 mL **8** no **9** 50 L + 36 L = 86 L

Unit 149 Page 87

1 a 4 b 2 c 5 d 3 e 6 f 5 **2** a 1, 7 b 2, 2 c 1, 4 d 2, 5 e 3, 9 f 4, 2 **3** a 3 cm³ b 25 cm³ c 13 cm³ d 40 cm³ e 7 cm³ f 1 cm³
4 a 6 cm³ b 6 cm³ c 5 cm³ d 10 cm³ e 10 cm³ f 10 cm³ **5** 16 **6** 1, 4 **7** 17 cm³ **8** 4 cm³ **9** e.g.

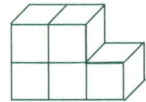

Unit 150 Page 87

1 a 6 cm³ b 4 cm³ c 8 cm³ d 6 cm³ e 5 cm³ f 2 cm³ **2** a c b f c a and d d e e c f f **3** a 4 cm³ b 10 cm³ c 1 cm³ d 3
cm³ e 7 cm³ f 9 cm³ **4** **5** 6 cm³ **6** b **7** 12 cm³
8 10 cm³ **9**

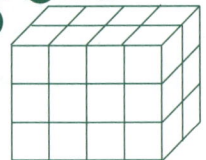

	Length (cm)	Breadth (cm)	Height (cm)	Volume (cm³)
a	4	1	1	4
b	3	1	2	6
c	2	2	2	8
d	3	2	3	18
e	3	3	3	27
f	5	1	2	10

Unit 151 Page 88

1 a 6 b 2 c 3 d 12 e 6 f 6 **2** a pink b brown c pink d yes e yes f no **3** a green b yes c yes d yes e yes f no
4 a 4 b 3 c 3 d 4 e 3 f 2 **5** 6 **6** triangle **7** peppermint **8** 2 **9** various

Unit 152 Page 88

1 a unlikely b impossible c certain d likely e certain f unlikely **2** various **3** a 6 b 1 – 6 c $\frac{1}{6}$ d $\frac{1}{6}$ e no f yes

4 a 3 b 4 c 5 d 8 e purple f red **5** certain **6** various **7** $\frac{1}{6}$ **8** no **9** 6: RG, RB, RY, GB, GY, BY

Unit 153 Page 89

1 a 4 b no c plain d spots e yes f plain **2** a false b true c true d false e false f true **3** **4**

f dots = stripes + triangles **or** dots + stripes + triangles = stars + green **5** yes **6** true **7** **8** **9** various

Unit 154 Page 89

1 a sheep b horses c 5 d 7 e 4 f 7 + 11 + 5 + 3 = 26 **2** a 3 b Friday c Thursday d 14 e 2 f 6 **3** a apples b pears
c 5 d 1 e 1 f 12 **4**

5 10 **6** 9 **7** 20 **8** brown

9 e.g. How many students have 3 children in their family?

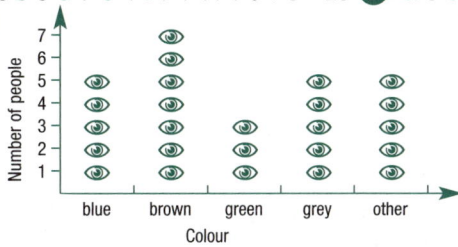

Unit 155 Page 90

1 a water b milk c 7 d 5 e 1 f 13 **2** a violin b flute c 20 d 4 e 6 f 4 **3**
4 a 2 b 0 c 4 d 19 e 7 f 1 and 4 **5** 25 **6** 12 **7** 1 **8** 30
9

Shape	Tally
△	卌 l
☐	卌 l
○	卌 lll

	Tally	Number
Heads	a 卌 lll	b 8
Tails	c 卌 llll	d 9
Total	e 17	f 17

Unit 156 Page 90

1 a brown b red c brown d 19 e red, blue, green, black f 9 **2** a 29 b 16 c 45 d 19 e 25 f 27 **3** a October b May c January
d Fred e Mike f Jack **4**

Insects	Tally	Total
ants	a 卌 卌	e 10
bees	b 卌 lll	8
flies	c 卌 llll	f 9
butterflies	d 卌 l	6

5 54 **6** 51 **7** Gerri **8** 33 **9**

Shape	Tally	Number
☐	lll	3
○	卌	5
△	llll	4

Unit 157 Page 91

1 a Chinese and Japanese b 2 c 4 d 14 e 8 f 2 **2**

Colour	Tally
a white	卌 llll
b red	卌 lll
c yellow	卌
d green	lll
e blue	llll
f pink	l

3

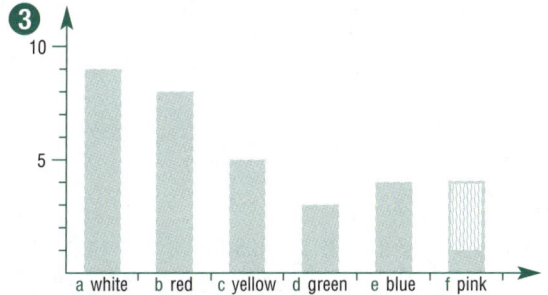

4 a white b pink c green d 3 e 9 f 2 **5** 24
6 new tally is 4 for pink **7** see different shading in Q3 **8** 7 **9**

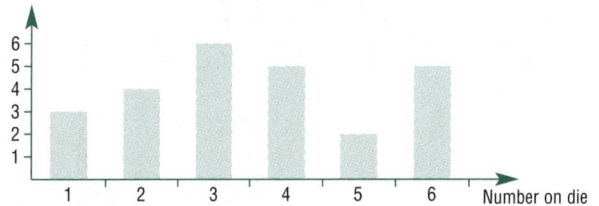

Unit 158 Page 91

1 a 8 b 1 c 2 d 2 e 3 f 3 **2** a 7 b 5 c 4 d 2 e 11 f 12 **3** a 6 b 5 c 3 d 7 e 13 f 8 **4** a 6 b 5 c 3 d 4 e 6 f 7
5 4 **6** 7 **7** 21 **8** 2 **9**

	Like burgers	Don't like burgers
Like pizza	6	5
Don't like pizza	4	3

Unit 159 Page 92

1 a total number of birds b 25 c 49 d addition e 25 + 49 f 74 birds **2** a the amount of apples b 85 c 17 + 25 + 14 d 56
e 85 – 56 f 29 apples **3** a total number of plants b 8 c 7 d multiplication e 56 f 56 + 6, 62 flowers **4** a number of blocks in a
row b 48 c 6 d division e 48 ÷ 6 f 8 rows **5** addition **6** subtraction **7** multiplication **8** division **9** various

Unit 160 Page 92

1 a 16 b 53 c 5 d 5 e $\begin{array}{r} 215 \\ + 546 \\ \hline 761 \end{array}$ f $\begin{array}{r} 243 \\ - 116 \\ \hline 127 \end{array}$ **2** a 26 big cats b 44 birds c 71 taps d 35 frogs e 7 chicks f 55 butterflies

3 a 30 cows b 28 sheep c 32 pigs d 5 chickens e 6 ducks f 9 horses **4** a $35.55 b $92 c $37 d $5.00 e $2.25
f $2.10 **5** 9 **6** 93 employees **7** 20 emus **8** $1.10 **9** various

Unit 161 Page 93

1 a 18 b 56 c 40 d 10 e 18 f 35 **2** a 6 b 54 c 28 d 100 e 72 f 0 **3** a 5 b 4 c 6 d 8 e 3 f 3 **4** a 30 b 21 c 18 d 28
e 32 f 81 **5** 54 **6** 15 **7** 10 **8** 30 **9** $6 \times 2 \times 3 = 36$, 36 chocolates

Unit 162 Page 93

1 a 35 b 12 c 56 d 90 e 4 f 0 **2** a 49 b 27 c 63 d 30 e 63 f 20 **3** a 6, 2 b 40, 10 c 4, 6 d 4, 10 e 6, 9 f 6, 3

4 a

×	6	7	8	9
3	18	21	24	27

b

×	9	10	8	7
9	81	90	72	63

c

×	8	9	10	7
5	40	45	50	35

d

×	9	10	8	7
8	72	80	64	56

e

×	4	6	8	9
4	16	24	32	36

f

×	2	4	6	9
7	14	28	42	63

5 42 **6** 54 **7** 4, 8 **8**

×	4	7	8	9
6	24	42	48	54

9 $1 + $0.40 + $12 + $25 = $38.40

Unit 163 Page 94

1 a 56 b 71 c 97 d 82 e 91 f 95 **2** a $\begin{array}{r} 28 \\ + 49 \\ \hline 77 \end{array}$ b $\begin{array}{r} 54 \\ + 28 \\ \hline 82 \end{array}$ c $\begin{array}{r} 26 \\ + 19 \\ \hline 45 \end{array}$ d $\begin{array}{r} 36 \\ 25 \\ + 17 \\ \hline 78 \end{array}$ e $\begin{array}{r} 636 \\ + 123 \\ \hline 759 \end{array}$ f $\begin{array}{r} 735 \\ + 128 \\ \hline 863 \end{array}$

3 a 56 + 29 = 85 b 83 + 9 = 92 c 57 + 38 = 95 d 27 + 50 = 77 e 18 + 25 + 32 = 75 f 17 + 34 + 11 = 62 **4** a 63 animals
b 101 items c 62 bricks d 47 insects e 169 pieces of paper f 80 eggs **5** 82 **6** $\begin{array}{r} 26 \\ 13 \\ + 45 \\ \hline 84 \end{array}$ **7** 15 + 16 + 17 = 48
8 51 biscuits **9**

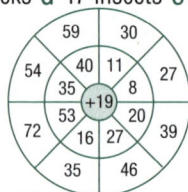

Unit 164 Page 94

1 a 4 b 12 c 44 d 12 e 25 f 33 **2** a 14 b 32 c 20 d 9 e 21 f 42

3 a
T	U
2	9
− 1	8
1	1

b
T	U
5	6
− 3	0
2	6

c
T	U
6	6
− 2	5
4	1

d
T	U
9	6
− 6	4
3	2

e
H	T	U
5	9	9
− 3	4	2
2	5	7

f
H	T	U
8	5	6
− 3	2	1
5	3	5

4 a
T	U
4	5
− 3	8
	7

b
T	U
5	5
− 3	6
1	9

c
T	U
7	3
− 4	5
2	8

d
T	U
9	4
− 6	6
2	8

e
T	U
9	1
− 4	6
4	5

f
T	U
6	0
− 3	4
2	6

5 23 **6** 22 **7**
H	T	U
4	8	9
− 2	6	1
2	2	8

8
T	U
7	2
− 3	8
3	4

9 792

Unit 165 Page 95

1 a 15 b 45 c 54 d 12 e 80 f 35 **2** a 30 fish b 18 eggs c 56 children d 7 monkeys e 56 days f 90 pencils **3** a true
b true c true d false e false f true **4** a 90 b 81 c 48 d 32 e 56 f 42 **5** 28 **6** 72 insects **7** true **8** 45 **9** no

Unit 166 Page 95

1 a 5 b 3 c 4 d 9 e 1 f 6 **2** a 10 b 7 c 9 d 10 e 9 f 7 **3** a 9 b 8 c 5 d 6 e 8 f 4 **4** a 2 r 4 b 2 r 2 c 8 r 1
d 6 r 2 e 7 r 2 f 6 r 4 **5** 3 **6** 10 **7** 9 **8** 4 r 3 **9** a 8 boxes b 8 pears

Unit 167 Page 96

1 a 1, 3 b 3, 4 c 2, 5 d 7, 10 e 3, 8 f 2, 2 **2** a $\frac{2}{4} = \frac{1}{2}$ b $\frac{3}{4}$ c $\frac{1}{3}$ d $\frac{4}{5}$ e $\frac{9}{10}$ f $\frac{5}{8}$

3 a $\frac{1}{3}$ ☆☆☆ b $\frac{1}{2}$ △△△△△△ c $\frac{3}{10}$ d $\frac{7}{8}$ e $\frac{1}{4}$ f $\frac{3}{5}$

4 a $\frac{1}{4}, \frac{2}{4}, \frac{3}{4}, \frac{4}{4}$ b $\frac{1}{5}, \frac{2}{5}, \frac{3}{5}, \frac{4}{5}$ c $\frac{1}{7}, \frac{3}{7}, \frac{4}{7}, \frac{6}{7}$ d $\frac{2}{6}, \frac{3}{6}, \frac{4}{6}, \frac{5}{6}$ e $\frac{2}{8}, \frac{3}{8}, \frac{4}{8}, \frac{5}{8}$ f $\frac{3}{9}, \frac{5}{9}, \frac{7}{9}, \frac{8}{9}$ **5** 4, 10

6 $\frac{4}{8} = \frac{1}{2}$ **7** $\frac{2}{5}$ ○○○○●● **8** $\frac{2}{10}, \frac{4}{10}, \frac{5}{10}, \frac{7}{10}$ **9** $\frac{1}{3}$ is larger than $\frac{1}{4}$

Unit 168 Page 96

1 a 0.4 b 0.7 c 0.1 d 0.36 e 0.89 f 0.12 **2** a 0.9 b 0.3 c 0.49 d 0.72 e 1.6 f 2.93 **3** a 0.7 b 5.9 c 3.8 d 4.17 e 9.99 f 5.18 **4** a 0.2 b 1.3 c 4.3 d 1.43 e 1.61 f 1.17 **5** 0.25 **6** 1.2 **7** 7.68 **8** 2.23 **9** 6.49 + 2.36 = 8.85

Unit 169 Page 97

1 a $3.95 b $4.50 c $4.35 d $3.99 e $6.25 f $5.48 **2** a $2.40 b $1.90 c $2.10 d 40c e 20c f 80c **3** a 40c b 40c c 80c d 50c e 60c f 80c **4** a 3 × $2.00 = $6.00 b 4 × $2.00 = $8.00 c 8 × $5.00 = $40.00 d 6 × $1.00 = $6.00 e 5 × $5.00 = $25.00 f 7 × $4.00 = $28.00 **5** $10.18 **6** $1.05 **7** 20c **8** 2 × $9.00 = $18.00 **9** estimate is $4.00 + $3.00 + $3.00 + $5.00 + $3.00 = $18.00

Unit 170 Page 97

1 a 6:25 b 3:15 c 1:08 d 9:52 e 5:30 f 10:47

2 a 11 o'clock b half past 2 c quarter to 6 d quarter past 4 e 25 past 3 f 5 past 1

3 a 12 past 8 | 8:12 | b 59 past 6 | 6:59 | c 33 past 2 | 2:33 |
d 27 past 7 | 7:27 | e 10 past 10 | 10:10 | f 41 past 11 | 11:41 |

4 a 45 past 9; 9:45 b 50 past 8; 8:50 c 10 past 1; 1:10 d 5 past 12; 12:05 e 5 past 7; 7:05 f 20 past 4; 4:20

5 11:43 **6** **7** 6 past 4 | 4:06 | **8** 35 past 5 5:35 **9** 11:35

Review Tests Units 1 – 4   Page 98

1 C **2** B **3** false **4** true **5** 4 **6** 491 **7** 2065 **8** 128, 129, 130 **9** 156, 203, 425, 815
10 4 tens **11** four hundreds **12** 1943, 1933, 1930, 1923, 1913, 1903, 1893

Review Tests Units 5 – 10   Page 98

1 C **2** A **3** false **4** true **5** 21, 31, 51, 81, 101, 121 **6** △ ▱ ○ **7** 26, 32, 38, 44, 50, 56
8 560, 550, 540, counting backwards by 10 **9**

100 less	100 less	Number	100 more	100 more	100 more
692	792	892	992	1092	1192

10 815, 615 counting backwards by 100

11 579, 569, 539 **12**

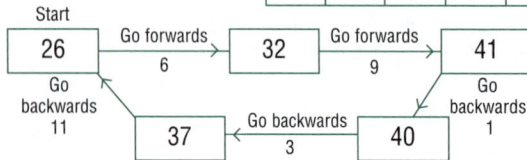

Start
26 — Go forwards 6 → 32 — Go forwards 9 → 41
Go backwards 11 ↙ 37 ← Go backwards 3 — 40 ← Go backwards 1

Review Tests Units 11 – 15   Page 99

1 B **2** D **3** false **4** false **5** 9000 + 100 + 50 + 2 **6** 84, 86, 88 **7** | 4 | Th | 0 | H | 2 | T | 7 | U |

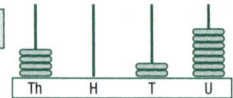

8 six hundred and eighteen, six hundred and twenty **9** 1026, 1062 **10** 481, 841, 491, (852) **11** 45, 89, 107
12 a 369, 482, 495, 582, 691 **b** 691, 582, 495, 482, 369 **c** reverse order of each other

Review Tests Units 16 – 21   Page 99

1 D **2** B **3** true **4** false **5** 59 **6** 37 + 42 = 79 **7** 67 **8** $79 **9** 53 **10**

+	14
6	20
12	26
35	49
43	57

11 $7 + $9 + $3 = $19 **12**

$$\begin{array}{r} 31 \\ + 26 \\ \hline 57 \end{array}$$

Review Tests Units 22 – 27   Page 100

1 B **2** C **3** true **4** false **5** 965 **6**

8	8	11
12	9	6
7	10	10

7 66 + 16 = 60 + 10 + 6 = 82

8 66 + 29 = 95 **9** 814 **10** 62 **11** 100 **12** 28 + 13 + 6 = 47 insects

Review Tests Units 28 – 32   Page 100

1 D **2** B **3** true **4** false **5** 31 **6** 12 − 5 = 7 **7** 87 − 36 = 51 **8** 512 → 510 **9** 19 − 12 = 7

10 7, 90, 200 **11** 32, 32, 8, 24 **12**

−	16	24	39	48	53
13	3	11	26	35	40

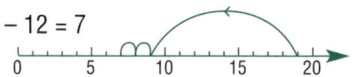

Review Tests Units 33 – 38   Page 101

1 A **2** C **3** false **4** true **5** 16 **6** 4, 8, 32, 34 **7**

$$\begin{array}{r} \$17 \\ + \$65 \\ \hline \$82 \end{array}$$

8 Use the equation $\begin{array}{r} 42 \\ + 39 \\ \hline 81 \end{array}$ to complete $\begin{array}{r} 81 \\ - 39 \\ \hline 42 \end{array}$

9 74 − 59 = 15 **10** $325 - $159 = $166 **11** 28 counters **12** | 926 | − 6 | 920 | − 20 | 900 | −155 | 745 |

Review Tests Units 39 – 42   Page 101

1 A **2** D **3** true **4** false **5** 160 **6** 2, 4, 8 **7** 100 **8** 1100 **9** 61 + 48 ≈ 60 + 50 ≈ 110, 110 pieces of fruit
10 40 players **11** 100 − 70 = 30 yes! **12** 4 m

Review Tests Units 43 – 47   Page 102

1 B **2** D **3** false **4** true **5** 10, 8 **6** 3, 30 **7** 6 × 9 = 54 **8** increasing by 9 **9** sample: ○○○○○○○○○○ ○○○○○○○○○

10 $10 \times 4 = 40$, $5 \times 8 = 40$ **11**

×	5
3	15
4	20
7	35
9	45

12 $5 \times 4 \times 2 = 40$ apples

Review Tests Units 48 – 52   Page 102

1 D **2** C **3** false **4** true **5** 40 legs **6** 4, 5 **7** $6 \times 3 = 18$

8 six **9**

×	2	5	9	7
5	10	25	45	35

10 12 weeks **11** $5 \times 9 = 45$ buns **12**

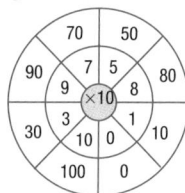

Review Tests Units 53 – 56   Page 103

1 B **2** D **3** false **4** true **5** Area = 16 squares **6** 4, 8, 12, 16, 20, 24, 28, 32, 36, 40 **7** 4, 4, 16

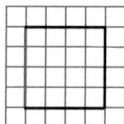

8

| 1 | 2 | 3 | 4 | ⑤ | 6 | 7 | 8 | 9 | ⑩ |
| 11 | 12 | 13 | 14 | ⑮ | 16 | 17 | 18 | 19 | ⑳ |

9 various, 6 groups with 2 remainder **10** yes **11** $30 \div 10 = 3$

12

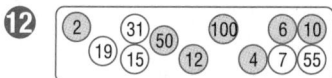

Review Tests Units 57 – 60   Page 103

1 A **2** A **3** false **4** true **5** 3 **6** 4 **7** 8 stickers **8** $36 \div 4 = 9$

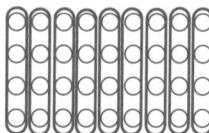

9 9 $27 \div 3 = 9$ **10** 6 **11**

Divide by 4

40	32	8	16	24	4
10	8	2	4	6	1

12 10c each stamp

Review Tests Units 61 – 64   Page 104

1 D **2** B **3** true **4** false **5** 12, 4 **6** 5 r 1 **7** 3 r 3 **8** 3 frogs in each bucket and 4 frogs left over **9** 8, 8, 8, 9

10 3 each with 3 remainder **11** 7 sweets **12** $5 \times 4 = 20$ $4 \times 5 = 20$ $20 \div 4 = 5$ $20 \div 5 = 4$

Review Tests Units 65 – 71   Page 104

1 B **2** D **3** false **4** false **5** add 11 **6** $27 \div 3 = 9$ **7** 61 **8** 20, 29, 38, 47, 56, 65 **9**

−	101	91	81	71	61
7	94	84	74	64	54

10 $5 \times 4 = 20$ **11** 54, 6
54, 54
9, 9, 9

12

A   B   C

C is the winner.

Review Tests Units 72 – 74   Page 105

1 A **2** C **3** true **4** false **5** $325 + 6000 = 6325$ **6** $569 + 325 = 894$ **7** $365 + 272 + 299 = 936$, 936 sweets

8 should be 1000 not 100 **9** $908 - 380 = 528$ **10** $21 \times 16 = 336$ **11** $238 \div 7 = 34$ **12** $20 \times 40 = 800$

Review Tests Units 75 – 77   Page 105

1 C **2** B **3** true **4** false **5** $\frac{5}{8}$ **6** 1, 5 **7** $\frac{1}{6}$ **8** **9** $\frac{3}{5}$ **10** $\frac{4}{9}$

11 **12** both!

Review Tests Units 78 – 81 Page 106

1 B **2** A **3** false **4** false **5** $\frac{3}{5}$ △△△△△ △△△△△ **6** **larger** fraction $\boxed{\frac{5}{8}}$ or $\frac{4}{8}$ ◇◇◇◇ ◇◇◇◇ **7** 3 slices of bread **8** 5 cakes

9 $\frac{1}{10}$, $\frac{2}{10}$, $\frac{4}{10}$, $\frac{5}{10}$, $\frac{7}{10}$, $\frac{8}{10}$ **10** three fifths or (one fifth) **11** 15 bears **12** a $\frac{30}{50} = \frac{3}{5}$ b $\frac{10}{50} = \frac{1}{5}$

Review Tests Units 82 – 85 Page 106

1 D **2** A **3** true **4** true **5** $\frac{75}{100} = \frac{3}{4}$ **6** 0.3 **7** $\frac{9}{100}$ **8** | 0.1 | 0.2 | 0.3 | 0.4 | 0.5 | 0.6 | 0.7 | 0.8 | **9** $\frac{20}{100}$

10 0.8 **11** five tenths **12**

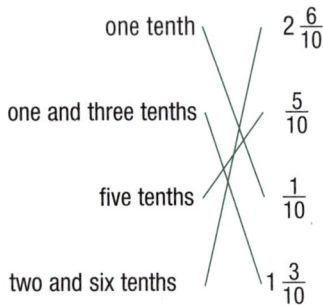

one tenth $2\frac{6}{10}$

one and three tenths $\frac{5}{10}$

five tenths $\frac{1}{10}$

two and six tenths $1\frac{3}{10}$

Review Tests Units 86 – 90 Page 107

1 A **2** C **3** true **4** false **5** 0.7, 0.5 **6** 0.52 **7** $\frac{91}{100}$ **8** 0.1, 0.7, 0.8 **9** >

10 **11** thirty-one hundredths **12**

In words	Decimal	Fraction
five tenths	0.5	$\frac{1}{2}$
nine tenths	0.9	$\frac{9}{10}$
sixty-one hundredths	0.61	$\frac{61}{100}$
thirty-four hundredths	0.34	$\frac{34}{100}$
three hundredths	0.03	$\frac{3}{100}$

Review Tests Units 91 – 94 Page 107

1 C **2** B **3** true **4** false **5** 8.17 **6** 90% **7** 1.62 + 3.59 = 5.21 **8** 1.97 − 1.65 = 0.32 m (32 cm) **9** 1.17 **10** $2.67
11 20% or (sixty percent) or $\frac{40}{100}$ **12** 8.19

Review Tests Units 95 – 100 Page 108

1 D **2** B **3** false **4** true **5** 5c, 10c, 50c, $2.00 **6** $50, $20, $10, $5, $2, 50c **7** $6.10 **8** $10.00 − $8.35 = $1.65
9 $8.00 **10** 2 × $5.00 = $10.00 **11** 2 × $25 = $50, change is $20 (approximately)
12 $20.00 − $12.98 = $7.02, change is $7.00

Review Tests Units 101 – 104 Page 108

1 D **2** A **3** true **4** true **5** yes **6** **7** (A)(B)(C)(D)(E) F G **8** e.g. **9** □ ○ △ □ ▷
10 rectangle and triangle **11** 4 **12**

Review Tests Units 105 – 108 Page 109

1 B **2** A **3** false **4** true **5** ⬠ **6** **7**

8 4 **9** sample **10** 5 + 4 + 4 = 13 **11** regular shape has all sides of equal length and all angles equal **12**

Shape	Picture	No. of sides	No. of angles
triangle	△	3	3
quadrilateral	□	4	4
pentagon	⬠	5	5
hexagon	⬡	6	6
octagon	⬡	8	8

Review Tests Units 109 – 113   Page 109

1 C **2** B **3** true **4** false **5** **6** A **7** **8** a right angle **9** smaller **10**

11 A **12**

Review Tests Units 114 – 119   Page 110

1 B **2** C **3** false **4** true **5** **6** 27 **7** **8** **9**

10 **11** chocolate **12**
a   pyramid   6 rectangles
b   rectangular prism   6 squares
c   cube   4 triangles, 1 square

Review Tests Units 120 – 125   Page 110

1 D **2** A **3** false **4** true **5** **6** J **7** example: 2 up, 3 left, 1 up **8** **9**

10 4 forward to K, 2 right to L **11** **12** a C4 b B1 c A2 d ○ e c f □

Review Tests Units 126 – 130   Page 111

1 C **2** B **3** false **4** true **5** 8:15 (quarter past 8) **6** **7** 4, 11 **8** **9** 15 minutes

10
3:30   thirty minutes past five
5:30   half past eleven
11:30   three thirty
11 5:03, 3 past 5 **12** 61 minutes

Review Tests Units 131 – 133   Page 111

1 B **2** A **3** false **4** true **5** 11:55 **6** 55 minutes **7** 4th October **8** 11 days **9** 25 minutes **10** no

11 Tuesday **12**

Review Tests Units 134 – 138   Page 112

1 A **2** D **3** true **4** false **5** 59 mm _____ **6** 3 m 29 cm or 3.29 m **7** 29 mm

8 1.5 m **9** B **10** less **11** B **12** B

Review Tests Units 139 – 142   Page 112

1 C **2** D **3** true **4** true **5** **6** 6 cm **7** 7 square units **8** a football field or a table?

9 **10** 4$\frac{1}{2}$ square units **11** 6 **12** 5 cents

Review Tests Units 143 – 145   Page 113

1 B **2** D **3** true **4** false **5** more **6** 750 grams **7** kg **8** car skateboard bus rollerblades

9 1$\frac{1}{2}$ kg **10** 4 tins **11** 12 kg or 75 kg or 200 kg **12** 40 blocks

Review Tests Units 146 – 150   Page 113

1 B **2** C **3** false **4** true **5** B **6** 600 mL **7** C **8** 2 L, 3 L, 6 L, 8 L **9**

10 14 L **11**   **12**

Review Tests Units 151 – 153   Page 114

1 C **2** B **3** false **4** true **5** various **6**   **7** yellow **8** HH, HT, TT, TH **9** 3 **10** 10 cents **11** 24 combinations

12 2, 3, 4, 5, 6, 7, 8, 9, 10, 11, 12

Review Tests Units 154 – 158   Page 114

1 D **2** B **3** true **4** false **5** e.g.

Colour	Tally
yellow	HHT II
green	HHT I
blue	III
red	HHT
orange	III
pink	HHT I

6

Colours of pencils

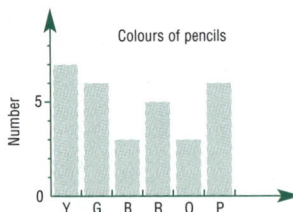

7 6 + 8 + 5 + 2 + 7 = 28 pets **8** cat **9** various **10**

	Like spiders	Don't like spiders
Like ants	3	5
Don't like ants	1	6

11 3 **12** 11

Review Tests Units 159 – 162   Page 115

1 B **2** D **3** true **4** false **5**   **6**
$$\begin{array}{r} 135 \\ +\ 447 \\ \hline 582 \end{array}$$
7 $153.85 **8**

×	9
6	54
5	45
7	63
10	90
9	81

9 90 + 14, 106 bales **10** 20 L **11** 1 straw left over **12** four, six

Review Tests Units 163 – 166   Page 115

1 C **2** B **3** false **4** true **5** 8 r 2 **6** 76 **7** 36 **8** 50 + 6 = 56 **9** 9 **10** 52 + 16 = 68, 68 − 7 = 61, 61 buttons

11

	14	17	22	36
− 6	8	11	16	30

12 3 × 9 + 6 = 33, 33 cards

Review Tests Units 167 – 170   Page 116

1 B **2** A **3** false **4** true **5**   **6** $\frac{3}{10}, \frac{4}{10}, \frac{8}{10}, \frac{9}{10}, \frac{10}{10}$ **7** 4.73 **8** $3.07 + $2.23 + $5.00 = $10.30,

$20 − $10.30 = $9.70 **9** 5:45 **10**   **11** 2.35 **12**

General revision   Page 116

1 C **2** B **3** true **4** false **5**
$$\begin{array}{c|c|c} H & T & U \\ 7 & 9 & 3 \\ -\ 2 & 4 & 6 \\ \hline 5 & 4 & 7 \end{array}$$
6 8 r 2 **7** seven tenths **8** $\frac{5}{10}, \boxed{\frac{50}{100}}, \frac{15}{100}$ **9** 13.81

10   **11** no **12**